MICROCOMPUTERS AND CHILDREN IN THE PRIMARY SCHOOL

MICROCOMPUTERS AND CHILDREN IN THE PRIMARY SCHOOL

Edited
by Roy Garland
University
of Exeter

The Falmer Press

(A member of the Taylor & Francis Group)

LB
1028.5
.M49
1982

© This selection and editorial matter copyright Roy Garland 1982. All rights reserved. No part of this publication may be reproduced, stored in a retrieval system, or transmitted, in any form or by any means, electronic, mechanical, photocopying, recording or otherwise, without the prior permission in writing from the Publisher.

First published 1982

ISBN 0 905273 32 X paper
     0 905273 33 8 cased

Jacket design by Leonard Williams

Printed and bound by Taylor and Francis (Printers) Ltd
Basingstoke
for
The Falmer Press
(*A member of the Taylor & Francis Group*)
Falmer House
Barcombe, Lewes
Sussex BN8 5DL
England

Contents

Introduction Roy Garland	1
Tools for the Job Michael Thorne	11
Microcomputers and Marlcliffe Primary School David Ellingham	33
Managing the Micro Ronald Jones	47
A Role for the Microprocessor in Infant Education Marjorie Holloway	57
The Primary Curriculum/Micro Interface: Implications for In-Service Education and Resource Provision Peter Davies	71
Using Microcomputers across the Curriculum in a Primary School John Dodridge	111
Shall We Have a Microcomputer in our Primary School? Donald Walton	129
Microcomputers, Schools and the Initial Training of Teachers: A Case Study Roy Garland and Bernard Lane	135
Some Observations on Children's Attitudes to, and the Role of, Microcomputers in Primary Schools Tony Mullan	149
The Spanish Main: An Exploration of an Educational Role for Computer Simulation Barry Holmes	169
Teachers and the New Technology: Servant or Master? John Lane	181
Thoughts for the Future Derrick Daines	193
Microcomputers and the Primary Curriculum Michael Golby	205
The Contributors	217
Index	221

The Child is father of the Man;
And I could wish my days to be
Bound each to each by natural piety.

William Wordsworth, *Intimations of Immortality
from Recollections of
Early Childhood*

Introduction
Roy Garland

In the words of one of the contributors Derrick Daines: primary school computing is filled with youthful enthusiasm and joyous adventure. This volume has been compiled to assist the many schools and teachers who are contemplating using a microcomputer in their teaching. The authors are a group of teachers, advisers and academics who in their own ways have been very much involved in the young yet rapidly growing adventure into the uses of microcomputers in primary education.

The growth of interest in the possibilities of using microcomputers in primary schools has seemingly expanded exponentially during the past couple of years. A national survey in 1980 conducted by Ron Jones, another of the contributors, only discovered some thirty odd schools using machines. The number in 1981, judging by accounts appearing in the professional press and by attendance at courses and conferences, must be very many hundreds with every likelihood of further expansion as the availability of relatively inexpensive and reliable micro-technology increases. This rapid growth has been inspired and developed by enthusiasm, energy and enterprise at grass roots level: it sprang to life, as do many new endeavours in human affairs, more or less simultaneously in a number of different schools and education authorities. It meant, at first, that individuals had to work in isolation, struggling without the benefit of past experience or advice and support from fellow professionals. A result, however, of a movement that is still very much in its infancy has been the start of a creative and imaginative appraisal of ways in which we might teach our younger children using the wide but as yet only lightly explored possibilities of micro-technology.

Education is filled with the traces and the ghosts of ideas and ideals that blazed into prominence like some super-nova and then burnt themselves out, leaving only a wisp of their previous glory. It could be that the same will happen in the case of using microcomputers in our teaching with primary-aged children: there will be a wave of enthusiasm that will subside into ripples of discontent and disillusionment as the problems that the new technology brings are realized by a wider and less committed audience than the innovators who write in these pages. Personally, I do not think that this will be the case. Whatever schools might do about the microchip and its associated technology, it is not going to disappear from the larger society that sustains and funds our schools; our children are growing up in a world where the products of micro-technology will be as familiar as the motor car and the television set are to their teachers.

It is reasonable to assume that, increasingly, primary schools will wish to explore and assess for themselves the possibilities of the microcomputer. There is sometimes disparaging talk in education of the re-invention of the wheel but, just as we would wish our children to explore and recreate experience for themselves, so there is a sense in which we have to recreate, as individuals, professional practice. There is no need, however, to go through this process with its pitfalls and trial and error learning without charts. The authors of the articles all have experiences, reflections and guidelines that will enable readers to be alert to possibilities as well as being mindful of hazards.

The book came about as the result of a series of fortunate coincidences: the work of the pioneers, and the inevitable informal networks that developed, led, in 1981, to a small conference at Homerton College, Cambridge and, shortly afterwards, to a larger national conference at the University of Exeter School of Education. Chapters have been written by those who attended these conferences and in many cases presented papers and gave accounts of their work and their thinking. From this material the book has emerged but contributors have been encouraged to develop ideas that they consider to be important. The result is a survey of central issues from a variety of differing viewpoints. But there is no duplication: there is no orthodox path to follow on issues. What does give a degree of unity, however, is a sense of professional optimism merged with practical reality regarding the use of the machines, combined with the belief that we are at the beginning of something that is important for primary education. Present is a desire to encourage teachers who have not yet started to experiment and to take the first steps, while suggesting to those who have begun and who are looking for ideas that there is an enormous number of possibilities that deserve to be developed and tried out. The contributors do not write with their heads in clouds of enthusiasm that hide and obscure the professional landscape: there is acknowledgement and identification of the very real problems of curriculum, classroom and school management that arise.

Although the authors were encouraged to develop their own ideas, various important and practical issues recur and are examined in depth but in a way that is designed to assist and stimulate those who look for guidance and ideas. For any teacher, or indeed school, that wishes to begin there is a bewildering choice of machines available: which one would suit our particular purposes? What snags are there to be avoided? Dr Michael Thorne is a computer scientist by profession but one who has knowledge of and sympathy with the ways of working in primary education. He gives plain advice to schools that wish to buy, paying full attention to the educational considerations that are at stake. At a time when many primary schools are considering buying, his words deserve wide attention as, in a non-technical manner, he points to some of the pitfalls that should be avoided. He goes further, however, than talking about the machines themselves – or to use the jargon the 'hardware'. He discusses the principles that should guide the 'software' – or the programs that the machines use – and identifies the characteristics of what could be judged to be good educational software.

Once a school has a machine, how is it to be used? Perhaps it was bought because of the keenness of one member of staff or the generosity and interest of a parent–teacher association. Where do we go from here? David Ellingham, headteacher of a Sheffield middle school, explores these questions but, quite rightly, he starts at the beginning: a micro is expensive in terms of the capitation allowances available to schools so how do we justify in educational terms its purchase? And, having obtained it because we are convinced of its educational potential, how do we start to use it? How can members of staff who are perhaps both apprehensive and sceptical of its use be given opportunities to make their own informed judgements? These complicated but important issues are reviewed in the form of a case study, based on David Ellingham's school, in a manner that locates and identifies the underlying principles. In doing so a broad yet undogmatic set of guidelines is provided that schools in general will find helpful.

Ron Jones continues the theme started by David Ellingham by exploring the problem of management. This might seem to be an esoteric topic to introduce into primary school considerations but it is not: it deals with real and important and thoroughly down-to-earth decisions that every primary school teacher will recognize. Ron Jones writes from practical experience as a headteacher who is determined that the micro will be used to the best advantage in ways that meet the requests of his colleagues. He also writes with a belief that the questions he raises will be facing the majority of our primary schools within the next five years. He draws our attention to the sophistication of the technology: probably the most complicated piece of gadgetry that has ever found its way into our schools, although fortunately, and perhaps surprisingly, one of the most reliable. He does not underestimate, neither does he exaggerate the problems. He examines in a logical fashion the various facets of a school's life that will have to be considered when installing a machine: those that are associated with the school and its environment; those that are a consequence of the micro-system itself; and those concerning the management of the use of the machine on a day-to-day basis.

One of the characteristics of the movement to use microcomputers with our primary school children has been a lack of reverence for established dogma. For example, the argument, based on assertion rather than investigation, that we should only introduce older children to the microcomputer so consequently only those of secondary school age would be eligible. Anyone who both owns a microcomputer and has young children will soon give the lie to that particular piece of dogma, but Marjorie Holloway, headmistress of an infant school, reminds us all that when we think of the computer in primary education we are spanning the age range from 5 to 11 years. She makes a strong case for the use of the machines in infant education and examines their possible roles within the established traditions and patterns of work of this sector of the education service. More than this, however, in an imaginative and original fashion, she identifies a number of what she calls pre-computer skills: just as there are pre-reading skills and particular activities which are necessary to acquire them so the same imperatives exist in the case of the microcomputer. Marjorie Holloway explains how these skills and activities can be placed within the work of the normal infant classroom. She finishes her exploratory chapter by a consideration of the possible wider curricular uses of these adaptable machines. Another of the features of the current work in using microcomputers is the enormous and exciting possibilities it provides for teachers of children of all ages and abilities to engage in professionally rewarding and exploratory work.

Peter Davies has taught in primary schools: he was formerly the warden of a teachers' centre and has become very interested in microcomputers both at a professional and a personal, hobbyist level. He illustrates another, and I suspect unnoticed, aspect of the ground swell of interest that microcomputers have raised: the emergence of what it might be as yet premature to describe as a discipline – educational computing. The study of interfaces – or boundaries – is fascinating, whether it be the seashore or plate tectonics, for it produces the novel and the unexpected with new ways of regarding the familiar. Exciting possibilities and new and sometimes uncomfortable ways of thinking also emerge at interfaces between streams of thought that represent differing traditions. The meeting of computing and education may be one such creative interface! Peter Davies' article is wide ranging: it contains many suggestions regarding curricular possibilities and it is particularly helpful for a beginner who is not familiar with the jargon or, indeed, is wondering exactly what a microcomputer is. Although there is much of practical help and guidance, the concerns of the article are broader: the author's worries and reservations come through and he draws on his own experience in in-service education to look at some of the wider issues of the continuing education of teachers.

A powerful, widely held and totally false view of microcomputers, or indeed of computers in general, is that their only use is in the field of mathematics. This is indeed unfortunate, for many highly intelligent and sensitive people will not wish to have anything to do with the machines, such is the influence of 'mathophobia' that Michael Thorne talks about. It is a pity that the historical accident that they were used in their early days for a particular type of operation has resulted in a name that only gives a small glimpse of their full potential. The article by John Dodridge is important on two counts: with brevity that does not forsake detail, he maps the ubiquitous uses of the microcomputer across the curriculum, continuing the task started by Peter Davies and giving actual examples of program listings. Secondly, although he is a mathematician, he demonstrates that mathematics as a subject does not have proprietary rights over the machines. Primary schools have the potential for adding considerably to our knowledge of the ways in which microcomputers may be used across the whole curriculum. It is most unlikely that they will be used for only one or two subjects, as could be the case in secondary education. For an educational computer beginner, the article gives a glimpse of the vast range of possibilities that the microcomputer offers and the idea that it can only be used for drill and practice type activities should be quickly dispelled; for those who can program or who are already using machines there is a large number of ideas that could be developed with both educational interest and profit. The task may seem formidable, even impossible, for the individual teacher, given the demands on his or her time simply to keep the normal daily demands of teaching within bounds, but there are ideas here that deserve to be taken up by study groups of teachers with possible programming assistance from local computer clubs, the many enthusiastic adolescents that are around or local institutes of further or higher education. The article ends with some helpful suggestions on the organization of computer materials at a classroom level.

There is not a strong tradition, in education, of teachers writing about their work. The theory of education abounds with analysis of relationships between schools and the wider social and cultural fabric but there is not an abundance of reflective accounts of work with children in what might be described as normal classroom conditions. The reasons may be perfectly straightforward; teachers are too busy teaching and preparing to engage in activities that are not seen as central to their daily work. Nevertheless, this is a pity on at least two counts: first, it means that others can suggest to teachers what their priorities and what their approaches should be and, secondly, as teachers tend to record their work in forms not necessarily suitable for a wider audience, there is not a cumulative range of case studies available that would enable future developments to build on past classroom experience and practice. It is important therefore to obtain accounts of work with children and micros and to consider the experiences and the judgements of those who have engaged in such activities. Don Walton is the deputy headteacher of a primary school but he is also a full-time practising classteacher. As such, his article is permeated with a strong sense of the pressing realities of classroom teaching, as well as a justifiable note of scepticism regarding the uses of the new technology. He is committed professionally to the use and to the educational value of microcomputers but he is under no illusions as to the problems that will beset anyone who decides to use them. He does not shy away from the problems, however, but identifies those of particular concern to the practitioner and makes positive suggestions regarding ways in which they might be tackled.

Both Bernard Lane and myself accept the particular importance, at this stage in the development of the use of microcomputers with our younger children, of providing reflective accounts of classroom work. In our article we chronicle the efforts of a group of student-teachers, a number of children of primary school age and ourselves, jointly engaged, in an investigation into the possible educational uses of a microcomputer. The machine that was available for our use had a disk system. Disks are admirable for the storage and retrieval of large amounts of data and it was this particular aspect that we decided to explore. Of course the work is not typical of that in a 'normal' classroom but we would not wish our efforts to be discounted entirely on that score. We have investigated, at a practical level, our own ideas on using databases and we have also raised the issue of computer literacy. Not only do we wish to use the microcomputer to enhance and extend normal classroom work but we wish to ask: 'What should our children know about computers?'. If we teach them about Norman castles is there not also a case that they sould learn something about the rapid advance in technology that we are experiencing?

In our delight or our bewilderment or our frustration with the new technology it is easy to forget that our pupils also have attitudes and views about it. At the risk of discovering the apparent, a major reason why it is suggested that the machines should be introduced into schools is that children will learn something! Yet this learning is going to be very much influenced by the attitudes that the children have towards computers. What do they know about them? Do they have favourable attitudes? I would suggest that any reader who wishes to have a revealing hour discusses these points with children. I did this myself with a class of mixed-ability ten-year-olds and was surprised how knowledgeable the children were when I asked what computers could and could not do. They certainly did not regard them as humans and one answer has lingered in my memory: computers can't pick flowers.

Tony Mullan has taken up the point of children's attitudes in a more systematic fashion. He acknowledges that the group that he was working with was very small and in no way can be considered typical, yet points emerge from his article that concern us all. Granted that we would wish our children to have informed but favourable attitudes towards the micros they will meet in the classroom, how are these attitudes formed? How might we use computers in ways that are likely to result in favourable attitudes? The article explores these and associated points by looking at different ways in which we might use a micro in the classroom. The author writes as a primary school headteacher with a great deal of experience of using the machines with children and also as an experienced educational programmer. One point that comes through in this, and I believe every, article is that the micro is not a dead lump of metal: they are not value neutral in the sense that the ways in which we use them and the manner in which it is urged that we should use them are very similar to statements regarding what is considered right and desirable within our wider educational practice.

This theme is considered important by Barry Holmes. In his article he briefly summarizes points that he has developed more fully elsewhere: that the claims of education are essentially moral in nature. He argues that the programs that we use in our teaching must therefore respect children as persons with ability to reason, to understand and to make, within limits, informed decisions. He is highly critical of programs that are based on stimulus-response or operant conditioning in that they fail to meet the criteria of what counts as education. From this position the article goes on to examine ways in which thinking about education and an appreciation of the computer's capabilities might be brought together. The result is an extraordinary, interesting and stimulating account of the emergence of ideas for simulation material.

The ensuing discussion illustrates admirably two points made earlier: creative and original thinking can occur when ideas from different disciplines rub shoulders; that it is important for practising teachers to make their thinking and their professional enterprises available to a wider audience. And one might also add that it demonstrates the significance of practising teachers deciding what the content and the style of presentation of material will be. The article chronicles the development of a simulation – the Spanish Main – from its broad conception in terms of the educational criteria that it should meet to its more detailed shaping. This is relevant reading for anyone who wishes to go beyond the routine and practice-type exercises which do not justify the purchase of a microcomputer to a wider more exciting vista which, although more exacting, is based on an essentially educational justification.

In a profession where success depends to a large degree on manipulating and mastering the immediate, thought of the future has, understandably, had little currency. Yet the microcomputer is already bringing to our classrooms a technology that, it is claimed, will qualitatively change our ways of teaching and possibly challenge the manner in which we think about schools. Perhaps it is easy to exaggerate: the micro, in spite of its decrease in cost in real terms, is still an expensive item and we are not yet at the point where there is one for every child. But it is also easy to be complacent: to think that this, like the majority of changes within our own professional lifetime, will be absorbed automatically into the old and trusted and tried ways of doing things. It has been observed that initially the new is defined and conceptualized in terms of the past: the first railway carriages resembled horseless coaches. It is not unreasonable or over-critical of teachers to suggest that this pattern will occur in education. A number of the authors have speculated, with varying degrees of optimism or foreboding, regarding the effects that the rapid development of new micro-technologies will have on our schools – those practices that we value and those human relationships that are at the heart of our educational encounters. They have queried how the microcomputer might facilitate or change what we do and the priorities that we give to our work. Three, however, John Lane, Derrick Daines and Michael Golby have explored this ground in more detail from differing but complementary view-points that bring real and pressing points from the future to our immediate concern.

John Lane has taken the challenge that is posed to primary education as the major starting point for his article. Can we say with any degree of certainty what the future holds for our schools? Perhaps answers to this kind of question are fraught with the dangers of leaping into the dark but it does seem reasonable to assume that things are not going to stay as they are: that problems, but also unexpected opportunities, are going to be created. It also seems sensible to suggest that it is imprudent to do nothing; burying our heads in the sand until we think that the storm has calmed. A number of possibilities are taken up in the article and examined. They represent a positive and measured response to the issues:

they illuminate that which is valued educationally and should be safe-guarded but there is also an agenda of the attainable for our consideration. There will be a need for re-training but what should be the thrust of the work? There will need to be a personal commitment on the part of teachers to try out new ideas and this, in itself, will mean innovation at a classroom level. It is no use hoping that problems can be solved by anonymous others or that solutions may be resourced into existence: an individual effort is going to be necessary.

The need for consultation between a variety of participants in this professional drama, of which we are all a part, is argued and there is a look at relationships between teacher and teacher, and teacher and taught. And, finally, questions of theory are raised. There is a deep rooted distrust of theory in English culture and in education this feeling resides nearer the surface than possibly in many other institutions, yet many questions regarding the uses of the machines are only going to yield their answers to systematic research within the social sciences.

Derrick Daines also considers future possibilities if we are willing to explore and exploit the potentiality of the microcomputer. There is a timely warning against dogmatism. The use of microcomputers in our schools is still very new: answers will needed to be found from work with children and not necessarily from a past experience that did not include the silicon chip. If we are willing to explore, a whole range of possibilities becomes available with options such as word processing, data processing, simulation and control. But these possibilities are not independent of questions regarding the purposes of schools.

Schools are not separate and distinct from the world outside. Their work is private in the sense that the public do not normally see teachers teaching or listen to the internal debates that shape policy. They are, nevertheless, accountable to the wider society that has established them. Primary schools educate younger children who have not reached the sophistications of adulthood but it is both illogical and simplistic, therefore, to regard these establishments as tranquil, gentle and uncomplicated replicas of childhood. Primary schools are heirs to traditions: the teachers who staff them are conscious of tensions within their work – a deep concern for the well-being and progress of the individual yet the operational need to keep the class under control and working, a desire to let children follow their own interests yet always the pressing uncertainties of progress in the skills of literacy and numeracy.

Michael Golby places the current concern to introduce microcomputers in our primary schools within an educational and historical perspective. He considers what it is to be educated; he analyzes the nature of the host curriculum where the computer will have to be nurtured and contemplates the likelihood of its adoption. But there are possible dangers and hazards associated with this adoption. The technology provides an opportunity for control previously unavailable not only in the curriculum but in society. For these reasons, he argues, children must be taught about the new technology; they must be alerted to its possibilities and its pitfalls in a new social science.

There are tremendous opportunities provided by microcomputers for imaginative and worthwhile work, as the authors of this volume have indicated, and there is a chance indeed of joyous adventure. There are also possibilities for the celebration of the mundane and the irrelevant. As Michael Golby argues, the micro can provide effective means to unconsidered ends. A crucial factor in successful adoption, or unfulfilled and frustrated rejection, will be the attitudes, priorities and values of the teachers. Making decisions about the purchase and use of a microcomputer within a school requires professional judgement. Such judgement, however, needs to be informed by knowledge of facts and implications. This volume will have achieved its aims if it provides assistance in this process.

Tools for the Job
Michael Thorne

As the title implies, this chapter concerns the tools necessary for the educational use of computers: the computers themselves ('hardware') and the programs to run on the computers ('software'). It is an attempt to combine practical advice with a critical look at both hardware and software in current use.

Since I am often asked what is *the* best microcomputer for educational use it seemed a good idea to try and explain why there cannot be a single best piece of hardware (or software for that matter). Making a choice between the contenders involves knowing the educational objectives the hardware is to be used to attain and a complex set of other factors concerned with the new and rapidly developing micro-electronic technology.

With regard to software I am not concerned here with arbitrating on whether fifteen IF statements and a single FOR loop in a BASIC program are better than nine GOTO statements, three GOSUBs and only two IFs. Neither am I here able to consider questions about the suitability or otherwise of the language BASIC for education or about the relevance of other languages, except as they relate to the issues I do take up. There are entire books on how to program; I have just a few thousand words. Consequently I shall concern myself here with the different styles which can be adopted by educational programs and their relationship to the hardware configuration a program is to be run on and the crucial issues of transportability, maintainability and adaptability. Readers interested in the avenues not to be explored may like to consult Thorne (1981a).

Choosing Hardware

Ever since the advent of the epidiascope and slide-projector, teachers have had to cope with an ever increasing range of gadgetry. In my recent experience a generous PTA bought a primary school a spirit duplicator but the teachers were not able to use it until the manufacturers of the duplicator were persuaded to send someone out to give a demonstration. And this is not a bad reflection upon the teachers concerned, but rather an indictment of the manufacturers who constantly refuse to make educational equipment easy to use for someone who just hasn't got a whole morning to spend familiarizing himself or herself with every new piece of hardware (and its attendant incomprehensible manuals) that comes through the door.

You don't have to be very clever to see where the manufacturers go wrong: buttons on overhead projectors which say 'OFF' but when you press them don't turn the thing off; hieroglyphics above tape recorder buttons with a perfectly obvious interpretation – to the manufacturer that is; computers where, in order to get something to go *up*, you have to press the 'D' key; computers where the 'reset' button is placed next to the button meaning 'end of message'; documentation that seems to have been written by randomly photographing someone's scrabble set.

Now, whilst this is a cry from the soul to manufacturers to make their equipment easy to use for the non-technically minded, it should not be taken as an indication that the microcomputers currently available to schools are very hard to use. Nor is it an indication that, if you're one of those people who manage to get smoke out of anything with a 3-pin 13 amp plug on the end of it, computers are not for you. The computer which comes to your school (as one will, sooner or later) will have its faults. If you realize these faults are the computer's and not yours then you will feel able to moan about them to the manufacturer who, eventually, will get so fed up with being complained at that the faults will be corrected. At the moment teachers blame themselves as Thorne and Wharry (1982) describe.

Regretfully, the number of faults of this kind which a particular make of computer has in practice rarely influences a decision whether or not to buy that machine. But for many schools there is no effective choice to be made other than how much to spend. This is because their LEA (or its advisers) has said that the authority will only 'support' machine 'X' for £600 or machine 'Y' for £2000. In effect what this means is that if you don't buy machine 'X' or 'Y' you are on your own: if technical problems arise the advisers won't help (in theory at any rate); if you get a bad deal it's your own fault.

Underlying this autocratic philosophy are four main principles. First, it makes more sense for all the decisions that have to be made (see below) regarding the purchase of computer equipment to be made centrally and once and for all. Second, by fixing on one or two machines it may be possible to negotiate particularly advantageous discounts. Third, and possibly most important, a maintenance contract for all the machines of a certain type in that particular authority can be taken out – or technicians employed and repair equipment purchased – so that maintenance is locally available. Local maintenance is both faster than sending equipment away for repair and cheaper, since transportation costs are non-trivial, often involving tens of pounds. Fourth, a lot of schools in the authority will thereby have a pool of experience with a given computer and so help will be available locally from colleagues. Moreover, software written locally will be entirely compatible between schools.

After all this what could possibly persuade anyone to go it alone and buy a non-standard machine? Lack of a standard in a given authority would be one reason, since many authorities have not yet decided on a machine they consider appropriate for primary school use. (This is a good thing in my view. Too much standardization at an early stage means too little experimentation with different machines and configurations.) Another reason for DIY selection may be that a school feels it has a better machine in mind than the LEA standard (and the PTA is putting up most of the cash!). Perhaps there is a member of staff with considerable experience of computing. But even a school fortunate enough to have such a person must beware of the maintenance costs of the non-standard machine which are often around fifteen per cent of the purchase price, per annum.

Enhancement

Many schools *will* go it alone when it comes to upgrading or purchasing enhancements for the basic machine. A gift from a generous PTA or parent can mean that the larger memory, which you've now realized is necessary for a lot of the programs you want to run, can be purchased. Provided, that is, the make of machine in the school has an *upgrade path*. If the only way of upgrading is to throw the old machine away and buy a new, larger or fancier one then the money spent on the initial purchase has been wasted. There is a particular danger of this with machines costing less than £400.

When such a product comes out, a full range of expansion options is promised 'in a few months time'. A few months later, a new version of the original machine is issued costing a few pounds less, incompatible with the earlier model and still the promise of the add-ons 'in a few months time'. To cut a long story short, the expansion hardware never materializes: the manufacturer is just too occupied with innovation on the basic product.

Beware also 'paper hardware'. It is currently the fashion to advertise a computer or computer hardware in the glossy magazines *before* manufacturing the product. If sufficient orders come in to warrant production, it goes ahead – if not, too bad. Thus, one can spend a year awaiting delivery of that which will never arrive. The moral is, find somebody who has already got one before ordering and never send cash with the order.

Another danger of this kind is that the manufacturer of your computer may go bust. This has happened with at least two machines which had started to gain popularity in secondary schools and could occur again. The whole microcomputer industry walks on a knife edge because of its rapid expansion and consequent cash–flow problems. Also, rumours circulate from time to time about various foreign companies which have just a few dealers in this country and which are intending to cease operations in the UK. In either case the net result is the same – you are left with a computer which no-one will maintain because parts cannot be obtained (due to bankruptcy proceedings) or which is very expensive and difficult to maintain because parts have to be obtained from abroad specially for you. If the manufacturer is bankrupt and a buyer can't be found, all possibility of upgrading and purchasing enhancements evaporates. To some, all this will be yet another reason for buying British. Others should beware of (foreign) machines which have few users in the education world, as there's some safety in numbers.

Purchasing Considerations

The phrase 'a microcomputer' is misleading since a given manufacturer may or may not take it to include the necessary keyboard and monitor. Even the connection cables may or may not be included. Since ready made cables can cost up to £10 each (and keyboards and monitors much more) it is crucial to be sure exactly what is supplied under a given heading. Going it alone, one is often dependent on finding a good dealer who has experience in supplying schools. To check this out, ask the dealer to nominate someone you can ring up who bought similar equipment from him for use in a similar environment. Don't expect a completely unbiased report from the dealer's nominee and *do* ask how long the dealer took to rectify any faults and if delivery was on time.

Before deciding on a particular make of machine or dealer you must decide as precisely as possible to what use the microcomputer (and its associated bits and pieces) is to be put. This is probably the most difficult part of the purchasing job, particularly at this early and experimental stage in our use of computers in schools.

Will you definitely need high resolution graphics or would they be just icing on the cake if they could be obtained for the cash available? How important is the availability of lower case print on the screen? Do you require the ability to display text and graphics simultaneously? Will you need noise creating devices like a beeper, or even music?

Gadgets

For a rather more detailed guide the reader may care to consult the CET USPEC (32) (1980) *A Guide to the Selection of Microcomputers* but note that this document pays little attention to the various gadgets currently available for microcomputers (such as games paddles, joysticks, light pens, graphics tablets and voice boxes). The popular view of these gadgets is exemplified by the Durham Microcomputer Project Report (Sledge, 1980) which says:

> The problem with some of these more exotic features is that the talent and effort required to use them to advantage is ... likely to be preoccupied with more urgent and less involved programming tasks.

I disagree with this point of view in two respects. First, that the level of difficulty which arises is no more than that associated with using graphics currently (both could be simplified considerably, given a disk system). Reading the current setting of a games paddle is a one-line instruction; some primary school teachers with no previous experience of graphics tablets or light pens – or computing, for that matter – have been using them with considerable success. Second, I believe that using these gadgets is one of *the* urgent tasks for educational computing. Games paddles and joysticks provide an analogue interface to a digital machine. The square on the right of a screen can be enlarged or contracted until it has the same area as the square (or rectangle, or triangle, or circle) on the left; a line can be moved until it seems to be the line of best fit for a set of points, a cursor can be moved up and down the screen by turning a dial until it is opposite the correct answer. Making a voice box 'speak' a foreign language or recite poems *might* help children learn about the phonetics of that language or about rhythm in poetry. Analogue controls could release a machine user from having to guess if a directory of files is obtained by the command CAT or DIR or DIRECTOR or LISTDIR or ... ? A good maxim for producing educational software would be: use the keyboard only as a very last resort.

Keyboards

Whilst on the subject of keyboards, it is important not to get infatuated by the current design – which was intended to *slow down* people using old fashioned mechanical typewriters which could not cope with rapid typing speeds. Microcomputers still have typewriter keyboards with a few extra symbols. But current keyboards are for data processing, not for our children. It seems reasonable to expect that a good keyboard arrangement for educational use might be a little different from a good layout for data processing. One possible change would be to insert a matrix LED display in every key which could then be programmed to display an A if pressing that key would deliver an A and so on. Reprogramming would then cause the key whose depression gave A to give Q or whatever. This would not be expensive to provide, relative to the total cost of the system.

Already there is considerable danger that the present 'standard' keyboard will be accepted as though it were a God-given immutable parameter of a computer system. Richard Horton (1980) suggests that 'keyboard literacy should be part of the curriculum for all'. Perhaps a CSE examination course would be appropriate, or even GCE O-level if we threw in 'tape recorder operating', '16 mm projector use' and 'basic oscilloscope use'.

Fortunately several people are challenging what Papert (1980) calls the QWERTY syndrome. An exciting keyboard development being pioneered in Birmingham is the 'Concept keyboard', a touch-sensitive A4-sized pad. The keys can be relabelled merely by positioning a new perspex overlay on the keyboard. The Walsall Educational Computing Centre has also come up with a new variety of keyboard along similar lines. In Bradford, Professor Tom Stonier has invented an attractive, colourful keyboard for children which uses an educationally motivated layout of the keys.

Printers

None of the USPEC(32) systems insists on a printer. If you don't want to write your own programs and your pupils do not want a written record of their work and you can devise a system to keep a record of their progress when working with a computer then a printer isn't really necessary. In the (hopefully) likely event that you now think you do need a printer beware of those that print 120 columns in one inch in pale pink ink on a dark blue background. Also remember that thermal printers – which require special paper – are cheap to buy but expensive to run. Connecting the printer may be troublesome. Here may be a chance to put your friendly dealer to the test. If he fails, some publishers are bringing out books to help with this sort of thing.

Disks

If the basic computer system (with a cassette reader) is going to cost you over £1000, there is no doubt in my mind that a disk drive should be purchased as well. A reasonably priced disk drive costs around £300 and the benefits are in no proportion to the extra cost. (I say this after watching over a hundred teachers using cassette systems in the classroom situation.)

With disks, a program takes a few seconds to load and the lesson may proceed without interruption. Loading a program from tape often involves several minutes rather than seconds. If in the course of using a program the teacher or a pupil crashes the system so that the program must be reloaded, this takes so long with tape based systems that the lesson suffers. Moreover, if it was his or her doing, the pupil can't help feeling bad about it – even if it was the fault of the program's design – and consequently gets distracted from the main task of learning.

Where the difference really counts is in the kind of facilities the manufacturer and the programmer can provide with a disk-based system over and above those practical for cassette-based ones. For example, a program can be written which requires more memory than your machine has but it can still be made to run on that machine given a disk system and a technique known as overlaying. Graphics are a case in point.

Graphics

The high resolution graphics facilities should include utilities to assist in the creation and storage of shapes and to allow shapes to be moved about the screen either from within a BASIC program or otherwise. In particular you should not need to understand hexadecimal to draw a map on the screen and store it away. PET graphics are particularly weak. Only low resolution is available, and, as far as we know, no utilities exist which enable shape manipulation from within a BASIC program though PETSOFT have a set of graphics utilities for the PET allowing shapes to be created and saved. One of these utilities contains the invitation 'hit the RETURN key twenty-one times' in order to save a shape on tape. This nonsense is a direct result of not being able to store things on a disk. On the other hand, the rash of sophisticated Shape Managers to emerge recently shows what is possible if disks are available.

Indeed, much of the generally poor quality of current graphics systems seems to stem from the manufacturer's insistence on producing tape-compatible systems. For schools, cassette-tape systems limit the uses to which the microcomputer can be put so much that they are not to be recommended. Time is limited in the school environment and teachers must be able to produce their own software quickly. This, in turn, means that they must have either a good graphics system in memory (where there is limited space) or in external storage, which necessitates disks since there will have to be several routines whose *total* storage requirement will quite probably exceed that available in *RAM*. Moreover, if a school has a disk system, outside software producers (commercial software houses and area computing services alike) are then able to provide programs which make the microcomputer into a very flexible educational tool without space inhibitions. It is my belief, then, that no school system should have less than a quarter-megabyte of disk storage. Cassettes are literally a waste of time, not to mention the attendant frustration of getting the volume right on some systems. Unfortunately many schools have already bought tape-based systems on the grounds that they can always expand later. Experiences described in the Durham Microcomputer Project Report (Sledge, 1980) demonstrate that this is not as easy as one's first thoughts might suggest.

Roy Atherton (1979) observes: 'When the hardware catches up to make software usable with little more than the touch of a button ... conditions might then favour a more encouraging response [to CAL] from our hard-pressed secondary school teachers and in due course from the junior schools as well'. Atherton's conclusion is right, but it is not only the hardware that must change. Hardware for 'touch-of-button' systems exists and is relatively cheap, but needs a considerable amount of software to drive it. With at most 64K of store available in an 8-bit micro (and often less!) this necessitates a disk system. A minimum requirement for the disk operating system would be the possibility of operating the entire machine in turnkey mode. In this way the ordinary teacher, who really does not want to know that after the machine says *QBLOSKDOS1371 you type SYS65327, can switch on and be in the system she wants to use.

Several schools have purchased machines for which the cassette-system price is about £600 and a disk drive unit costs £700 because you must buy two drives at a time. Consequently I have heard it suggested that such a school should buy a second cassette-system rather than disks for the first. Since the originators of this argument are clearly not interested that software can be developed much more quickly using disk systems, what I need to do is to convince them that the *educational* benefits of a disk system are greater than those derived from having two machines among twenty-five children .instead of one. Since currently available educational software is not allowed to assume disk systems (on the whole) this is going to be tough. Catch twenty-two in fact.

This is a highly appropriate point at which to turn our attention to software. Indeed it may be that the benefits to be derived from the use of computers in education can be enhanced by allowing a more subtle interplay between hardware and software than the separation of the two in this chapter might suggest. This is one of the themes of the next section which also argues that a lot of the currently available educational programs might be distracting us from the best way forward.

Software

Not all teachers write books, not all teachers prepare their own work cards. Similarly, not all teachers will want to write programs for distribution to others just as some teachers will not want to do any programming at all. If a teacher wants to do some programming in connection with a particular teaching point and is prepared to give the not inconsiderable amount of his or her time that will be necessary for the task, then why not? The problems only arise when the resulting program is particularly good, for then other teachers, not necessarily with the same variety of computer, want a copy of it. Unless the program was written with an eye to transporting it to other machines this may prove difficult. Even if it was, preparing a version for a different computer will not be trivial.

To see why this is the case, consider the instructions for clearing the screen on two popular microcomputers. For one it is the command HOME and the other PRINT '♣'. The graphics on one machine are also unlikely to be compatible with those of another. Even the number of points on the screen may differ.

Various people have come up with good ideas which, if followed, will make programs more easily transportable. Charles Sweeten (1980) was the first to publish a scheme under the banner 'The MUSE Software Standards' (MUSE stands for Microcomputer Users in Education). More recently Chelsea College, London, has come up with a similar scheme. Unfortunately there are certain kinds of program which are not really amenable to either of these two approaches in practice. Summarizing, my answer to the question 'should teachers program' is 'yes, if they want to', but teachers should be aware that if a program is eventually to run on several machines, there are techniques not described in ordinary programming manuals which, if incorporated at the writing stage, will assist matters considerably.

Often at the back of people's minds when they ask about teachers programming is the fear that their programs will be technically poor. What they should remember is that the most important qualities recognized in a program nowadays are those of readability and maintainability. That is, a good program from a computer scientist's point of view is one which is easily followed and easily altered.

These days, technical wizardry in the form of doing the whole program in three fantastically complicated and obscure lines of code is frowned upon. Computer time is comparatively cheap (to human time) so we don't mind if we waste a bit of that in reducing the time humans need to spend making corrections or slight changes.

We desperately need computer languages which offer an environment suitably robust for school use and with which a teacher can *quickly* produce educationally valid material. Some of the possibilities are discussed in Thorne (1981a). Many will not be tried until versions exist for microcomputers. There is also a need for languages wherein and techniques whereby programs can be 'tailored' by a teacher not necessarily familiar with either the language used or details of the program. Many attempts have been made at providing both of these facilities, none of them universally successful. As already indicated, some of the problems here are related to hardware.

Existing Software — Are We on the Right Track?

In the present context (and perhaps always) the most important non-technical aspect of a program is the style adopted in its user interaction, for this is the only part of the program the ordinary user of it 'sees'. Rather than attempt a straightforward catalogue of styles or offer a formal treatment along the lines of the work of Rosemary Fraser and the ITMA project, the remainder of this chapter is presented as a response to various educational inputs: Laurie Buxton's book *Do You Panic About Maths* (1981) in which Buxton analyzes some of the problems of learning mathematics; Seymour Papert's *Mindstorms* (1980) in which a particular style of classroom use of computers is advocated; and comments received and observations made on visits to twelve schools as part of the Microcomputers in Primary Schools (MIPS) project being carried out by the author and Dr David Wharry of the Department of Education, University College, Cardiff.

Papert's book, *Mindstorms: Children, Computers and Powerful Ideas* describes a philosophy for using computers in the classroom which is very different from any extant in the UK at the moment. According to Papert, our work in educational computing at present resembles that of the early car designers who failed to accept that cars were cars and not horseless carriages. He says:

> Most of what has been done up to now under the name of 'educational technology' or 'computers in education' is still at the stage of the linear mix of old instructional methods with new technologies.

In other words, we are all busy creating drill and practice programs for the three R's because that is an obvious classroom use for the computer closely allied to traditional teaching methods. What we thereby fail to observe is that in the computer we have a tool which could cause a quantum jump in the effectiveness of our teaching.

Of course Papert is not the first to offer a seeming panacea for the educational ills of the day and we must therefore venture further into his underlying philosophy. Papert himself, in part, presents his ideas not as a cure–all but rather as a cure for one of the more sickly parts of the curriculum: maths. (The evidence for the failure of our mathematics curriculum is only too often before our eyes, whether through newspaper reports of large percentages of school–leavers who can't do simple arithmetic or from watching yet another shop assistant using his/her fingers to add up two single digit numbers.) In particular, Papert emphasizes the unique phenomenon in maths of dividing people into what he calls mathophiles and mathophobes.

That this division exists will be familiar to anyone who, having been asked their occupation at a party, has said 'I teach mathematics' and received the cryptic reply 'Oh, you must be awfully clever – I could never do maths at school' as the questioner beats a hasty retreat to the kitchen. Thanks to Laurie Buxton's book *Do You Panic About Maths?* there is no need for further justification.

The Patient and the Symptoms

In his book, Buxton describes an experiment to investigate mathophobia. His subjects were all highly intelligent individuals, as their many cogent remarks recorded in the book testify. Nearly all of them were associated with the education world: one of them was a primary school teacher, one a secondary head. Buxton describes their qualifications as subjects for his experiment:

> They had mostly failed O-level maths (or its equivalent) at school. . . . There were some who were not allowed to take the exam, others who themselves refused to do so and some who had succeeded after three or four attempts. The failure in maths was specific: they had strings of other 'O'-levels and many much higher qualifications.

Laurie Buxton's book sets out to uncover some of the causes of their mathophobia and to address the question: 'How did a group of intelligent people come to have such bad feelings about the pre-eminent of intellectual disciplines: mathematics?'. (Notice that we do not say, 'How did such a group come to have so little ability at mathematics?'. As Buxton shows, when given a sympathetic environment his subjects were *able*.)

What then are Buxton's findings? Any attempt to summarize his skilfully constructed and perceptive book in a few lines cannot do him justice but, for the purposes of our main argument, we draw out four main themes:

1 Buxton's subjects often felt that the mathematics they had been asked to do had no relevance for them.

> The important distinction here is that in the classroom, maths was a matter of juggling around with symbols and numbers, where it had no meaning at all in my mind. In Physics your u's and v's represented certain quantities, and you had a purpose in working out a formula to find a focal length. In a sense because the symbol wasn't abstract, because it represented focal length or whatever, it had a reality it lacked in maths lessons.

Whether or not a mathematical topic has relevance is a complex issue. Often a topic has relevance if it relates to the outside world – thus positive and negative numbers might have relevance when regarded as temperatures above and below freezing point – but this is not necessarily the case. Many of the participants in Buxton's experiments found a discussion of whether or not there are infinitely many prime numbers interesting despite having previously expressed concern if problems didn't seem relevant to them. None-the-less, one person declared:

> No – I don't care. It doesn't matter to me or my life.

2 Time pressure put upon people to complete a mathematical problem caused many of the experimental subjects to go into some kind of panic mode:

> One of my subjects had as a child been regularly tested on the tables by her father who demanded an almost instant response. She had the highest level of anxiety and the most rapid entry into panic that I have met. When I got her to do genuine mental arithmetic she believed that she had to answer quickly, and was very soon saying, 'I can't, I can't' and clearly beginning to disintegrate. By luck I struck upon the calm phrase 'No hurry' and she managed to complete 15 × 12 in her head, no mean task.

3 Subjects often saw the maths teacher as an authority figure waiting to pounce on a purveyor of wrong answers. They made remarks to the effect that in maths you can be *found out*. It was harder to do sums if the teacher was looking over your shoulder. One of them states:

> Before you get far into it someone says 'That's wrong' and so you don't start it after that.

Notwithstanding their fear of mathematical authority subjects were *unwilling* to act as their own arbiters of right or wrong. It was not enough that they could see that they had the correct answer to a problem in geometry say, this still had to be verified by the teacher. At times the presentation of problems was seen as an attempt to trick or embarrass.

4 Maths was regarded as being about *learning lots of rules*:

> I think of maths as an attempt at remembering routines, and I gained no cohesive view of the subject.
>
> We had to learn the theorems by heart (fifty or so) and then regurgitate them.
>
> You just had to remember them ... lots of them.
>
> By learning the rules I got by in arithmetic.

Therapies

Having described the patient and the major symptoms, we are now ready to decide on a cure. We are interested in treatments which involve a computer. Others have been tried of course but the hope is that, if we are clever enough in using the computer, we may produce a cure which is in order of magnitude more effective than those which do not depend on modern technology. But this should not be without regard to the costs involved, since programs and machines to run the programs are expensive in comparison with capitation allowances.

An apparently free program copied out of a magazine can, by the general nature of things, be expected to contain at least one error. If eliminating this error takes a teacher two evenings' work, then that program has cost £20. (Two evenings to correct one error is probably an under-estimate on average, since removing errors from a program written by somebody else often introduces other errors.)

Another mistake is to write computer programs for educational objectives which are better achieved by other means. For example, none of the maths drill and practice programs reviewed in Thorne (1981b) was as well prepared as the Ladybird Workbook series (to name but one). The programs typically cost between £5 and £10, the books less than £1. Costed over five years the biggest PET computer and a maintenance contract works out at about £200 per annum. The exercise book in which the child has written his/her answers contains a complete record of what that child has done. None of the packages in Thorne (1981b) kept any such record.

In short then, we must not let our enthusiasm for the new technology carry us away. This has happened before (as we noted earlier) and the results are gathering dust in store cupboards all over the UK. Before using computer technology we should be certain that it can achieve our educational objectives either more effectively or at less cost than the other alternatives.

In the case of the mathophobia symptoms displayed by the subjects of Buxton's experiments the author firmly believes modern technology *could* offer a cure and will describe various methods of attack for each symptom.

Giving Classroom Maths Work Relevance

One possible approach is to teach the subject more or less in the same way as we did before but to involve a computer. Since children are visibly excited by the introduction of a machine into the classroom environment, they'll hardly notice they are doing maths at all. This is the approach that is adopted by the majority of educational maths programs available at the moment. Another approach, already well exploited by social science teachers and increasingly by science teachers, is to use a game to put an idea across. If the game involves a computer you double the chance of your success. A major criticism of either of these two approaches is that, if you are not careful, you end up giving children occupational therapy rather than helping them learn things.

Quality Educational Designs (of Portland, Oregan, USA) market two interesting packages based on an integration of these ideas, one called FRACTIONS and one called FACTORING WHOLE NUMBERS. Each topic is presented via two programs. The first is a presentation of the topic often requiring the children to use material other than the computer. The second program is a game designed to give additional practice and/or to extend the topic further.

By way of example, the first two programs in the FACTORING WHOLE NUMBERS package require 100 square floor tiles (or equivalent). Factoring a whole number is then presented as finding possible lengths and widths of a rectangle with a given area. By physically manipulating tiles, children are expected to see that the area remains the same if one dimension is multiplied by a given constant while the other is divided by that constant. For instance:

>XXXXXX
>XXXXXX

may become XXXXXXXXXXXX

or
>XXX
>XXX
>XXX
>XXX

The accompanying game, in effect, gives the player(s) the area and perimeter of a rectangle and asks them to find the length and width.

It is with regard to perimeter that we can best illustrate Papert's approach. Since I am not Papert and since very very few of us have access to the TURTLEs he uses, I can only hope to illustrate the principles involved.

Bigtrak is a battery-operated, electronic toy available from most large stores for about £30. It consists of a six wheeled vehicle with an electric motor and, on its roof at the back, what looks like a calculator keypad. Using this calculator keypad you control the vehicle. Pressing the sequence '↑20' will cause Bigtrak to move forward a distance equivalent to twenty times its own length. The sequence '→10' will cause Bigtrak to turn to the angle equivalent to ten minutes past the hour relative to its previous position. Thus the sequence

>↑ 20
>→ 15
>↑ 20
>→ 15
>↑ 20
>→ 15
>↑ 20
>→ 15

would enable Bigtrak to negotiate a square table. Controlling Bigtrak is therefore very similar to controlling Papert's more powerful TURTLEs. The exciting feature of either is the ability to preprogram a sequence of operations and then set it running and watch the results.

Papert and his followers believe (*inter alia*) that children have difficulties with mathematics because, generally speaking, their mathematics work has no relevance to any domain *over which they have control*. Observing children working either with Papert's TURTLEs or with Bigtrak, there can be no doubt that children will happily lose themselves inside the TURTLE or Bigtrak world. Instead of measuring distances because teacher says so or to please teacher or because it's an intrinsically interesting thing to do, distances are measured because the children want to get the TURTLE or Bigtrak to do something. If *they* have decided what this is, all the better. Learning about angles is necessary to control the robot. Children want to learn about angles because they *want* to control the robot.

Children thus learn about inverse operations: a TURTLE or Bigtrak program to go forward ten units and reverse ten units is a dramatic illustration of the equation $xx^{-1} = 1$. Persuading a TURTLE or Bigtrak to go round a table involves either measuring or estimating. (Estimation is an important scientific and mathematical skill rarely taught even though it would prohibit many children from misuse of calculators.) Having estimated a distance, tried it out and found it wrong, in comes the arithmetic drill and practice. If reversing is involved in controlling the robot, direct numbers are included in the drill and practice. The square of the hypotenuse theorem in geometry can be made empirical (rather than one of the fifty theorems for rote learning one of Buxton's subjects mentioned) by getting a robot to follow a right-triangular path.

Time Pressure

As teachers, we impose time pressure on our pupils both wittingly and unwittingly. In mathematics, of all subjects, this is hardly realistic or helpful. I know of no great theorem in mathematics which was achieved as the result of someone saying find the answer in two minutes. Yet covering the syllabus and exam pressures cause us to forget this all too easily. Buxton again:

> More than anyone the teacher tends to impose time pressures .... On balance and in most situations this is counter-productive. The awareness of time prevents the mind relaxing into the work (and thereby doing it more quickly). The constant feeling of rush is further emphasized by the need to revise material learnt only recently. This need derives from the fact that insufficient time was allowed originally; thus the urgency results in slower not faster progress.

With thirty children to occupy for more than five hours every school day the temptation is to increase the concentration of Joe Bloggs' daily ten minutes individual time with the teacher by expecting him to respond faster. As human beings, there is a limit to our patience.

Once again the computer offers a solution. Being mindless it has infinite patience and proceeds at its own rate regardless of external pressures. If a child is using the FACTORING WHOLE NUMBERS program mentioned earlier, the machine waits for the answer to each question giving out no inter-personal cues as to the required speed of answering as it does so. Moreover the machine is never distracted to participate in class control and so the child using it can maintain his/her concentration on the object of study without worrying if he or she has the teacher's attention.

The programs of Pam Fiddy of Nanstallon Primary School, Cornwall were, as I understand it, partly motivated by some of these concerns. To Pam Fiddy, a microcomputer in the infant school is another activity like the Wendy House or reading or sums but without a pressure element. She says in Fiddy (1981)

> It can ... help the children to organize a particular task. The children receive a level of unhurried dedicated support that a class teacher is not free to give. Passing some tasks over to the computer works to the benefit of the children who are using the computer, other children who are receiving attention from the teacher, and the teacher herself.

With a TURTLE or Bigtrak the problem of pace is eliminated completely since the children set their own. If they proceed too fast, the robot does not perform satisfactorily and they must start again. The teacher's role will be to suggest where they went wrong – if asked to that is.

However it must now be recorded that one of the most frequent requests from teachers participating in the University College, Cardiff MIPS project was for a program that would do maths drill and practice but would 'put a bomb under them'. I wrote down one such request:

> What would be really good would be a program ... which if you didn't type in the answer in so many seconds ... you went off the computer. Klunk.

For reasons already outlined I feel that this would not be good for the children's mathematics. More worrying still is the effect such programs might have on their attitudes to computers (and machines in general) and on their future performance as users of terminals in a computer age.

There have already been reports (for example in the *Daily Telegraph*) of family doctors treating people for hypertension caused by playing the popular Space Invaders game in which there is a strong speed element. Few of us can think *creatively* under pressure like this. At best, we respond like Pavlov's dogs which were trained to salivate on hearing a bell. Those who dislike being put under pressure will vote with their feet, as Buxton's mathophobes have done. For a society poised to enter an era where communicating with computers will become ever more essential this does seem regrettable to say the least.

Authority

As any professional programmer knows, having written a computer program the chances of it working first time are very, very slim. Certainly one should *expect* a program *not* to work first time. The net result of this is that finding errors in a program and successfully correcting them is an integral and essential part of the process of producing a working program. Papert points out that we have been trying to create such an educational environment – where making mistakes and correcting them is a perfectly ordinary event – for years.

A result of working in the programming environment is that you have to impose your own standards on the work being done. As Papert says:

> One does not judge by standards like 'right – you get a good grade' and 'wrong – you get a bad grade'. Rather one asks the question: 'How can I fix it?' and to fix it one has to understand what happened ...

As programmers, Buxton's subjects could proceed without fear of the teacher's sapiential authority, since you are not expected to get it right first time – however quickly you produce an answer. The role of the teacher would not be that of arbitrater twixt right and wrong but rather the person present who has most experience in finding bugs. Teacher would get called in when the debugging wasn't going too well, not merely to check the answers. At the same time, since the teacher would often *visibly* have as much trouble with the debugging as the taught, it would be much harder for the taught to see teacher as an infallible master, out to trick or embarrass the vulnerable.

Returning to the two approaches we have been comparing, making mistakes and correcting them is of the essence with a

TURTLE or Bigtrak. The robot does not know the answer. It has no idea how to get round the table. FACTORING WHOLE NUMBERS knows all the answers; any debugging must be done abstractly on the thought processes which got you the wrong answer.

Buxton perceptively observes that things often go wrong in teaching when the teacher 'plays to the gallery':

> There are some teachers who get trapped, as we said earlier, into seeking affection in their intercommunication in the classroom .... If the teacher has allowed his personal authority to be regarded as the main source of approval and disapproval ... he or she has done that pupil a disservice. The job is to make the work, not the relationship, enjoyable.

Since a computer is emotionally cold, there is no danger of this happening in a CAL context. Moreover no-one can accuse a computer of bias. This fact has been demonstrated to be of considerable importance in the success of computers in special schools where children can often feel that adults are cheating by 'making allowances' for them. In part this accounts for the success of the program JANE from ITMA as does the fact that the teacher doesn't know the relationship between the two numbers in advance.

Learning Rules

The vast majority of CAL programs for school use, whether they come from commercial sources or are written by teachers or from elsewhere, are of the drill and practice variety. All of them emphasize their subject matter as a collection of stimuli and responses: a computer types 'Lundi' on the screen, a person types 'Monday' etc.. As reported in Thorne (1981b), not one of six commercial mathematics drill and practice programs offered the person using the program any hint as to why the answer(s) he had just given was wrong. Even brief comments like 'I think you forgot the minus sign' or 'I think you forgot to carry one' would have made the programs more like a learning tool and less like some animal response trainer. These bad drill and practice programs are so prevalent that it is worth trying to isolate possible reasons for their propensity. By doing so we may identify more ingredients of a good program.

Drill and practice programs of the kind to which we have been referring are easy to write. Adding extra facilities which suggest where an error has occurred takes little more effort but – here's the crunch – makes the program bigger. Often what the programmer can offer the learner by way of facilities is limited by the amount of memory he assumes to the machines the programs will run on. The worst case of this is the Sinclair ZX81 which is usually purchased with very limited memory indeed. Certainly programmers try hard. I have been amazed at the ingenuity that has gone into squeezing drill and practice programs into the ZX81. But in achieving this the programmer is probably the person who does all the learning.

A moral of this is that good programs require the right hardware, so that we have by now come full circle. Small memory size can be severely restrictive. Yet it is all too easy for primary schools to be tempted into buying small machines on the grounds of the initial price. Another way in which hardware influences the programs we write has already been illustrated by the dramatic differences in approach between Papert's TURTLEs and FACTORING WHOLE NUMBERS. There is an intermediate stage, though, as yet hopelessly underexploited. Games paddles and light pens (which can be used to control a computer by turning a dial or pointing a pen at the screen respectively) are still largely unfamiliar to the majority of teachers and supplied as standard with very few machines. Yet they could be provided cheaply and would considerably enhance the variety of programs that could be written. Moreover – as we have found in an experiment at University College, Cardiff – both naïve and experienced users can *prefer* devices like games paddles and light pens for controlling certain tasks.

Conclusion

Much work needs to be done finding the equivalent of Papert's TURTLEs for other areas of the curriculum. We mustn't turn up our noses at gadgets. On the other hand, we must put our minds to the task of producing programs for teaching English, say, which exploit the facilities of a computer in an essential way. There are programs which attempt this already, using the machine as a dictionary or to examine a database held on disk. At the moment we are still, by and large, teaching the same thing but using computers to do it. It may be that, if we want to exploit microtechnology to the full, we still have to change what we teach. For example, could one adapt the methods described in Hockey (1980) *The Computer in Literary and Linguistic Studies* to give a new approach to language teaching? When Prestel is cheap enough for schools to use there will be a ready made source of data for educational computer programs. Programs will be needed to take advantage of this.

Let me finish with a plea. Since the other possibilities seem almost limitless, *please* no more drill and practice programs.

References

ATHERTON, R. (1979) 'Microcomputers, secondary education and teacher training', *British Journal of Educational Technology*, 10(3) October.

BUXTON, L. (1981) *Do You Panic About Maths?* London, Heinemann Educational Books.

FIDDY, P. (1981) *CAL81 Abstracts* University of Leeds, England.

HOCKEY, S. (1980) *A Guide to Computer Applications in the Humanities* London, Duckworth.

HORTON, R. (1980) Untitled article in *Computers in Schools* 2, March.

PAPERT, S. (1980) *Mindstorms: Children, Computers and Powerful Ideas* Sussex, Harvester Press.

SLEDGE, D.K. (1980) 'Durham Microcomputer Project (DUMP) Report', Durham, New College.

SWEETEN, C. (1980) 'MUSE software standards', *Practical Computing*, August.

THORNE, M.P. (1981a) 'Programming and learning', *Online Educational Monograph No 2*, May.

THORNE, M.P. (1981b) 'Software for teaching mathematics', *Practical Computing*, January.

THORNE, M.P. and WHARRY, D.M. (1982) 'Coping with commercial software in primary schools', *Educational Computing*, April.

Microcomputers and Marlcliffe Primary School
David Ellingham

Marlcliffe Junior and Infant School is situated in the north-western part of Sheffield. It is a school of nearly 500 pupils, and occupies a two-storey building erected in 1916. The seventeen classes are unstreamed and contain boys and girls of a wide range of ability and attainment whose average scores on standardized tests of attainment tend to be skewed above the national average.

The children come from a wide cross-section of homes where the overwhelming majority of parents are very interested in their children's education and recognize that both school and home have a joint, mutually dependent responsibility towards achieving worthwhile, educational aims.

There are several reasons why the potential of the microcomputer is being explored at Marlcliffe: there is felt to be the need to educate the school's pupils for life in a computer-based future; that it would be neglectful of the school if it didn't attempt to give the children some awareness of the increasingly important role the computer is playing in daily life; and the school also needs to do its best to ensure that the mystique which has built up about computers is dispelled as far as possible and that boys and girls are helped to understand that a computer is essentially a machine, invented by man, to help him handle information.

Leo Cherne (1977) wrote:

> The computer is incredibly fast, accurate and stupid. Man is unbelievably slow, inaccurate, and brilliant. The marriage of the two is a force beyond calculation.

If there is any truth in this quotation, then it is imperative that the fact is acknowledged by striving for not only a computer-literate society but by exploring all the ways in which the computer might help schools develop the philosophy and practice of primary education.

Looked at from the point of view of the teacher, the computer has several advantages as a teaching aid. For whatever reason, children find the computer highly motivating. It seems to demand and get from pupils a high degree of concentration. In fact, with many children, the problem is tearing them away from the computer. The computer is very patient and provides no opportunity for personality conflicts with its user. Its temperament is that of the 'perfect' teacher! Most computer-assisted-learning programs are written in such a way that the pupil controls the pace at which the material is handled, which, because of the factors already mentioned, may well be approaching the optimum pace necessary for efficient learning.

Another important consideration is that an immediate feedback to the pupil's response is possible with a computer. How often is this true in the 'normal' classroom situation of thirty pupils? Increasingly, there are programs becoming available which help reinforce the essential skills which all children should acquire. Such programs, which organize the practice of these skills, release the teacher to give extra time to the more stimulating and creative aspects of his role, particularly those where personal contact is crucial. Many teachers, who are still contemplating using a computer, often assume that this practice-type program is only to be found in the field of mathematics and, perhaps, would be surprised to discover how many programs relate to language skills such as reading, spelling, vocabulary and punctuation, as well as skills related to other parts of the curriculum.

There is another category of program which helps the teacher in a different way, acting as a stimulus to genuine learning by providing a vehicle for children to develop problem-solving, decision-making abilities and skills i.e. helping boys and girls to develop those underlying and fundamental thinking skills which are required in order to deal more effectively with whatever comes along in the future. Whilst there are not as many programs of this type as might be wished, because they are more difficult to design, it is felt that this situation will change with the realization of the need to give greater emphasis in the future to helping children handle all the information with which they will be increasingly bombarded by the information media. Amongst the learning programs already available are games demanding logic and which minimize the element of luck, simulations with a variety of settings, and programs which stimulate learning by focusing the child's attention on finding and using information related to a particular part of the curriculum.

The computer is helpful to the teacher in yet another way and that is by the help it can give to the organization of the class. Certain programs help the teacher give a class lesson more effectively, where the computer is connected to a twenty-six inch TV set and what is shown on the screen is more immediate and of a higher quality than a blackboard or overhead projector. For example, we use a program called 'Co-ordinates', which shows the vertical and horizontal axes and allows for points to be plotted, which is far more efficient than any other method.

There are other programs which provide the opportunity for the individual to work, whilst others are more suitable for use by a group of three or four children. Thus a computer can be organized as a valuable aid for all children within the classroom, from the most able to the least able. Within our own experience, it has been found to be particularly useful for 'stretching' the more gifted children in our unstreamed classes.

These are the chief reasons why we are trying to develop the computer as an important teaching/learning tool at Marlcliffe but, before this is described in more detail, it might be helpful to say something about the beliefs and attitudes we hold about microcomputers and primary education.

It needs to be said at the outset that everybody is at such an early stage in the development of computers in primary education that nobody is yet in a position to give any definite answers on the topic. However, we feel that our experience at Marlcliffe is giving us a glimpse of the exciting potential of the computer and that this is sufficient to make us want to continue to explore, develop and extend the use of the computer with young children. As a teacher's aid, the computer can be an important part of primary education as we know and understand it, but the school must not become so absorbed with the computer that it loses sight of the fact that the machines' use should be part of the whole philosophy of primary education and not a 'trendy' something added as an afterthought to that which already exists.

Effective learning using computers in primary education will stand or fall by the quality of the software that is available and, in the final analysis, the computer is simply a vehicle for running the programs. If the software is to be of the highest quality it needs to be designed by teachers and not by computer programmers. However, it is probable that most teachers will not have the time and/or knowledge to encode their teaching or learning programs and it is therefore important to try and find ways of blending the expertise of the teacher with that of the computer programmer. In this situation, the initiative and final responsibility should rest with the teacher, who will be using the program and the programmer's role should be that of writing a program precisely to the teacher's instructions.

All of the foregoing adds up to the fact that it is the teacher, and not the technology itself which is the key to computers in primary education and that it might be better for all if the current expression 'Computer-Assisted-Learning (CAL)' was resisted and we gave the proper emphasis by a virtual reversal of the phrase to 'Learning and Computers' in primary education.

This view of the teacher's overwhelming importance resulted in the decision to call three staff meetings to discuss computers in general and computers in education. It was felt that whatever emerged from these meetings should determine the starting point for any staff in-service training as well as provide ideas as to the content of such a course.

The meetings were lively and the points raised were wide-ranging. The questions asked by the Marlcliffe staff on the subject of computing were, of course, only representative of themselves, but it is important they should be stated because of the fundamental issues they raise. They are set down here in the same order as they were posed.

1. What is a computer?
2. Are all computers the same?
3. How do they work and what are their capabilities?
4. What is a program?
5. How is one made?
6. Can I make my own program or do I have to enlist the help of a computer programmer?
7. What information must I give to the programmer if he is to make a program for me? What problems could this entail?
8. Once a program has been made can it be altered?
9. How can I keep a record of a child's progress?
10. Can a child, by accident, progress too rapidly through a program without true understanding?
11. How much personal attention from the teacher will the child need whilst using the computer?
12. Most of us have a lack of knowledge about computers so we are unqualified to use them, therefore will instruction be given?
13. How much instruction will be necessary?
14. How will this be arranged and where?
15. Is it intended that every teacher is given computer training?
16. At what age will children begin to use computers?
17. What proportion of the school day will a child spend on the computer?
18. Are all children capable of using them? If not, what about those who are incapable of using them?
19. How many computers will be available per school?
20. What about their cost?
21. What subjects will be taught by the computer?
22. If each child follows his own personal programme in a specific subject, when will the teacher have the time to work out these programs?
23. How will the teacher's role change?
24. Will there be the same degree of job satisfaction for the teacher?
25. Will there be a change of emphasis in the teacher's role?

26 How will the increasing use of computers affect children's *social* development?
27 Will computers encourage an introverted society?
28 Will personal communication one to another become a dying art, for example, children finding it difficult to express themselves in conversation, art, music, dance, etc.?
29 How will increasing computer use affect individual personality development and the development of relationships with others?
30 How will individuality and creativity be encouraged when children will be spending *less* time interacting with other children and adults and spending *more* time alone at their computer?
31 Will computer use encourage lazy, static individuals – expecting answers at the press of a button rather than producing men and women of action and initiative?
32 Much experience of life comes from mistakes made – if we eliminate mistakes are we depriving children of the experience of how to act in a crisis?
33 It has been said that computers will make endless information available – what must we as teachers do to ensure that children know how to use that information properly?
34 How much of the current methods of teaching will be retained in the future?

Permeating many of the questions can be felt a deep concern about the quality of life both inside and outside school in a computer-based society. Is it going to be better or worse? There is clearly a great deal of anxiety not only about the relationship between teacher and computer but also about the effect that using the computer, in the classroom, will have on the children of the future. This all added up to an obvious need for knowledge about the subject, particularly when regard was given to the order in which the questions were posed, and so it was decided to put on a talk/demonstration for staff, which would try to provide a few answers about matters of fact and, hopefully, a glimpse of the potential the 'micro' had as a teacher's aid.

The entire staff of twenty-one heard the talk and when asked afterwards if there were any who would like to investigate any further, seventeen expressed a willingness, although for a number of them this was tinged with a mixture of scepticism and some apprehension.

It was felt that there should be as much 'hands-on' experience as possible for this next step, and so with the help of the Science postholder, who had done some work on computing as part of an Open University course, there began a number of after-school meetings for the three J4 teachers only. These sessions consisted of learning how to load, run and list programs and generally become familiar with the 32K Commodore PET microcomputer and cassette recorder. There was also plenty of opportunity to interact with, and discuss, a cross-section of CAL programs and find out just a little about BASIC language by tackling a worksheet of simple routines. Once these three teachers had gained sufficient confidence, then the same exercise was repeated with another three teachers and so on, whilst, at the request of the teachers who had come this far, arrangements were also made for the PET to be borrowed by them at the weekends and during the holidays whenever they wished.

Parallel with this school-based INSET work it was decided that the three J4 teachers would be helped in their classrooms with experimental work on Computer Literacy for Upper Juniors. The timetable was arranged so that the Science post-holder worked with one J4 teacher and the Headmaster with the other two teachers, for one hour per week, on developing the present scheme which covers flow charts, the binary number system, punched cards, how a computer works, some very simple ideas on programming, sets, attributes, elementary logic, educational toys (i.e. 'Little Professor', 'Dataman', 'Speak and Spell', 'Spelling ABC') electronic calculators, a project on the History of Communication, and the computer today and in the future. In the next academic year it will be possible for the J4 class teachers to 'go it alone' as far as Computer Literacy work is concerned and allow the Science post-holder and Headmaster time for helping to develop other computer work felt to be worthwhile.

Right from the beginning, it was also decided that the first attempts at Learning and the Computer would be with J4 children and as experience and, hopefully, resources grew, it would then extend downwards to the younger classes. The current situation is that computer-assisted-learning and computer-assisted-instruction is regularly timetabled for seven classes (three J4, three J3 and one J2), for from two and a half hours to three hours per week. Additionally, because of the children's great enthusiasm and the wish to give them as much 'micro' time as possible, a Computer Club has been formed for the ten and eleven-year-olds. This meets four lunch times per week plus one weekly session after school. Approximately seventy-five children have been involved with the club during the past year, in groups of from ten to twenty-five in number. At these meetings the boys and girls can play computer games, use any other available programs of their choice and have the opportunity to do a little more programming than is possible within the classroom.

The way the 'micro' is used within the classroom seems to vary according to the views of the teacher, the needs of the children and the nature of the programs. As it has been already stated, sometimes the teacher uses the 'micro' and the twenty-six inch TV set as an electronic blackboard on which will be run a program suitable for a teacher-controlled class lesson with a better quality of presentation than by other means.

Such programs can also help stimulate lively discussion on a variety of topics, from mathematics and science through to language work. One member of staff has concentrated on using the 'micro' on a one-to-one basis with pupils and feels like the rest of us that, provided the program is matched to the pupil, there are benefits for all children irrespective of their level of attainment. One of his children surprised him by the effective way he tackled some of the language programs on sentence order and 'cloze' work whilst, at the other extreme, more able children have asked to stay in the classroom at playtime in order to carry on with a program that was stimulating them. At another level, for a very few children, the novelty impact of the computer is relatively short-lived but, for the vast majority, the motivation which is produced and the concentration which is demanded by the 'micro' seems to have only a marginal fall-off. Only time will tell whether these important characteristics of the computer will prove to be permanent features, but at the moment the signs are good.

Probably the most valuable way to use the computer is with a group of children. Initially the idea behind this arrangement was to provide access to the 'micro' for as many pupils as possible. Experiments were conducted as to the size and composition of the group and it was eventually concluded that from two to four, or even five children was the size for most occasions and that the children within the group should be roughly the same level of ability for the chosen program.

Observing the groups in action it was noticed that this organization provided other advantages than just more children interacting with the 'micro'. It encouraged cooperation, since the group was collectively responsible for interacting with the program, and it certainly encouraged and developed a great deal of valuable discussion, whose general direction, point and purpose was controlled by the program.

Within the seven classrooms the teachers keep their own records of the programs used by different children. The children are responsible for loading and running their programs which they do very efficiently without the help of their teacher. For the teachers' part most prefer to have the computer in the classroom for an hour at a time three times a week. It is usually located in a corner of the room and, in two rooms, is separated from the rest of the room by a blackboard or desk. One teacher however, prefers to put the 'micro' in the corridor outside his room and this seems to work just as well.

The problem of the teacher knowing when the computer program has been finished by the group has been tackled in one of two ways. In some classrooms, the children are instructed to tell the teacher when they have finished running a program. In other rooms, the teacher keeps a close eye on the group at the 'micro' and intervenes when he sees the program is finished. One teacher has suggested an audible signal be built into each program, which would then attract the teacher at the appropriate time but others have argued against this and, as yet, no final decision has been made.

Our experience to date in these situations has confirmed the original decision to use a Commodore PET microcomputer in the school. In fact, we now have two 'micro's – the original 32K PET and a recently acquired 16K machine, both with cassette recorders using ordinary magnetic tape on which the programs and data are stored. This method of memory storage was chosen because it is so much cheaper than the alternative magnetic 'floppy' disk system and this compensates for its relative slowness in transferring data in and out of the microcomputer.

At one time the experiment was tried of 'consumer-testing' an Apple and a Sharp MZ-80K as well as the PET by giving some of the children a brief opportunity to use all three and then noting their reactions. At the same time a set of criteria was built up which was thought appropriate to microcomputers and primary education. The criteria decided upon were as follows:

1 Reliability
2 Good keyboard with large, well-spaced keys
3 Interface for using with TV set
4 Graphics capability
5 Reasonable cost
6 At least 16K memory
7 Rugged construction
8 Compact and mobile
9 Good back-up service from suppliers
10 Availability of software
11 Relative simplicity of operation

The school's assessment, which involved noting the children's reactions, produced the following results when all eleven criteria were finally considered:

	PET	SHARP	APPLE
1	XXX	XXX	XXX
2	XXX	X	XX

3	XXX	XXX	XXX
4	XX	XX	XXX
5	XX	XXX	X
6	XXX	XXX	XXX
7	XXX	XXX	XXX
8	XX	XXX	X (separate units)
9	XXX	XXX	XXX
10	XXX	X	XX
11	XXX	XXX	XX

The fact that there are far more PETs in schools countrywide than any other 'micro' and that, consequently, far more programs are being produced for the PET is a very important factor when a school is trying to develop the computer as a learning aid.

Whilst it is true that those programs which are available are variable in quality, nevertheless even the poorer ones do provide a start as well as a stimulus to producing something better. It is a very healthy situation when class teachers criticize a program and, at the same time, suggest modifications which, in turn, lead to ideas being put forward for entirely new programs.

Because the PETs are compact machines they can be moved quite easily from one room to the other, usually by one of the male members of staff. However, it would be quite feasible, if their use was confined to one floor of the school, to move them on a trolley, which would be taken to each classroom when it was required. The sturdy design of the PET has given us no anxieties for the safety of the children or the 'micro' itself and the need for maintenance seems to be minimal. The school was warned that dust was a potential enemy and so the use of dust covers and the occasional cleaning of the computers became an automatic feature of their care. The machines have proved to be extremely reliable with the additional comfort of having an extremely good specialist 'microcomputer' retailer in Sheffield who would quickly come to our aid if something did go wrong. The value of the two computers and programs requires that the school makes definite arrangements for their security. The Science post-holder is responsible for storing everything in a secure room at the end of the day and a record is kept whenever a 'micro' and any programs are borrowed by a member of staff.

Whilst hardware is an important consideration, in the final analysis the key to the computer's value to the teacher is likely to be the quality of the software available. The range of software is restricted by the unfortunate fact that, at the present time, many programs written for one make of microcomputer will not necessarily run on another make without the program being modified. All of this takes time which, for most teachers, is at a premium and means that schools almost of necessity, tend to ignore worthwhile programs written in a different 'dialect' of BASIC to the one recognized by their 'micro'. Nevertheless, Marlcliffe School has now accumulated over one hundred and seventy programs suitable for primary school use and know that this number will continue to grow.

It is important that teachers have sufficient information about these programs in order to make effective use of them and it was felt to be especially important to indicate not only the nature of the program but the level of the learning experience presented to the pupil so that the teachers knew whether or not the software met their particular needs. Therefore, at the outset of the project on learning and computers, it was decided that an attempt would be made to classify all computer programs in order to provide this information. After considering a number of alternatives, it was decided to make use of a modified version of the hierarchy of learning levels developed by R.M. Gagné (1965) in his book *The Conditions of Learning*. Every program is therefore examined to see which is the highest type of learning it demonstrates in the following six-level range from the most simple to the most complex:

1 *Stimulus – Response Learning* – This is known to many as trial and error learning and requires that the child make the appropriate response to a particular stimulus.
2 *Chaining (Motor and Verbal)* – This level of learning is reached when a series of stimulus-responses is linked together in a sequence to form a chain. An example of this would be the correct saying or writing of a multiplication table.
3 *Discrimination Learning* – At this level the pupil has learned to differentiate or discriminate between two different, but similar, stimuli, for example, 'b' and 'd', a '5p' and a '10p' coin.
4 *Concept Learning* – This relates to classification and the child being able to generalize by seeing what characteristics are common to a group of things whether they be people, places, things etc., etc..
5 *Principle (or Rule) Learning* – This level of learning is about the relationship between two or more concepts. For example 'Lions are carnivores' is a principle because it is a statement of a connection between the concept 'lion' and the concept 'carnivore'.
6 *Problem Solving* – This is the highest level of learning and is about combining two or more principles in such a way as to solve a problem.

Since it is a hierarchy, it follows that the higher levels of learning require that the pupil has previously learned the lower levels, elements of which are usually contained within the new learning situation. This analysis is, of course, applicable to all methods of helping children learn and encourages us to remember that each level is built on the foundation of earlier levels. As an illustration, it can be seen that there is little point in a teacher helping a child learn about a *Concept* until he is sure that the child can *Discriminate*.

It was also decided that, within Gagné's hierarchy of learning, an attempt would be made to indicate some of the more important thinking skills identified by Edward de Bono and the Cognitive Research Trust. This was felt necessary in order to highlight the principle that what was important about some programs was not the subject matter as such, but rather the underlying thinking skills developed within the context of that subject.

It would have been possible to provide this information, about each program, within the program but it was felt that it should be more immediately available by being written up on a five inch by three inch card (see figure 1).

Figure 1

Title		Dewey No
Author		
Publisher		
Reading Level		
Location		

This lay-out matches the card index-system already developed in the school for other resource material such as books, pictures, plans, film-strips, filmslides, audio cassettes and LP records. The card is blue in colour, which helps distinguish it as computer software, distinct from other colours which relate to other categories of resource material. The space for Reading Level is used to indicate the reading-age required by the pupil to enable him to interact effectively with the program. The Location space provides information about where, within the building, the program is stored. On the back of each card there is an indication of which of Gagné's six levels of learning is reached, as well as information about the thinking skills which are practised when the program is in use. There is also a brief description of the overall content of the program to help the teacher decide whether it is relevant to his purpose.

Some of the programs in the software library enable a teacher to alter the data statements to meet his specific needs. Wherever this is possible, the fact is indicated on the back of the card along with details about the location of the data statements within the program's listing. As more programs are now being used it is becoming apparent that there is a need for fuller documentation and it has already been decided to give this topic due attention in the immediate future and provide more educational and technical information than at present.

There is also a need to develop an effective system which will enable teachers to initiate the production of worthwhile software. To this end a Program Design Specification Form is already available for teachers to complete as the necessary first step. This will be followed by a detailed check-list to help analyze the educational content of the original idea. Much very valuable work along these lines has already been done by the Humberside Project and their ideas will form the basis of our checklist.

Another firm intention, in the near future, is to make more information about the school's work with the microcomputer available to the parents. The first step along this path has already been made when a talk/demonstration was provided for the school's Board of Governors at the outset of the project. This provided an opportunity for the parents' representatives on the Board to pass on some information about what the school was hoping to achieve. The next step will be to talk to all parents, through meetings arranged by the PTA, and give them an opportunity to run some of the school's programs. It is worth mentioning, at this point, that one parent who is professionally involved with computers has already given us occasional help by volunteering his expertise in the subject.

Parallel to the work within the school has been the development of INSET courses for the LEA on Microcomputers and Primary Education with the intention of achieving the following aims:

1 To increase awareness of the implications of the microcomputer for society in general and education in particular.
2 To remove anxieties about microcomputers in primary education.
3 To ensure that microcomputers are used effectively in primary school by:
   a) Providing a groundwork of knowledge sufficient to encourage a willingness among teachers to use microcomputers in their schools.

b) By encouraging teachers to look critically at programs.
c) By providing guidelines for the future production of ideas for software by teachers.

This work is seen to have three stages. The first is to provide a general lecture and demonstration for groups of headteachers and other teacher colleagues. The second stage has been to run a series of one-day familiarization courses for groups of ten to twelve teachers. These courses have included a general lecture on learning and computers, a look at educational toys (such as 'Speak and Spell', 'Dataman', etc.) followed by a discussion on their possible uses. There has been an opportunity for teachers to examine critically some existing programs and the ways they might be used and everybody has been given an introduction to BASIC language, by means of a demonstration and working through an elementary 'learning-type' worksheet. The third stage, in the INSET series, will attempt to build on the previous stages by a course of sufficient length which covers the following topics:

1 Computer literacy.
2 Elementary explanation of how a microcomputer works.
3 The first elements of BASIC — including the encoding of a simple program.
4 Learning and computers, including an examination of Gagné's hierarchy of learning and thinking skills.
5 Computer appreciation work for primary children
6 The use and organization of the computer in learning and teaching situations.
7 The examination of existing software.
8 The development of software, emphasizing educational aims and objectives.
9 The detailed development of ideas for a number of programs by the teachers on the course working together, in pairs, on topics of their own choosing.

In conclusion, all that has been written above is only the beginning of one school's efforts. Many other schools throughout the country have done a great deal more but much much more remains to be done by teachers everywhere in order to realize the full potential of the computer in education. Papert (1980, viii) wrote,

> The computer is the Proteus of machines. Its essence is its universality, its power to simulate. Because it can take on a thousand forms and can serve a thousand functions, it can appeal to a thousand tastes.

It is to be hoped that everybody concerned for children will feel something of that same sense of excitement about the computer and will be thus encouraged to do all they can to improve the primary child's learning experience in the computer-rich world of the future.

References

CHERNE, L. (1977) *Creative Computing*, quoted in AHL, D.H. (1976) *The Best of Creative Computing* Vol. 1, Creative Computing Press.
DE BONO, E. (1976) *Teaching Thinking* London, Temple Smith.
GAGNÉ, R.M. (1965) *The Conditions of Learning* New York, Holt, Rinehart and Winston Inc..
PAPERT, S. (1980) *Mindstorms: Children, Computers and Powerful Ideas*, Harvester Press.

Managing the Micro
Ronald Jones

Anticipating the Problems

There is little doubt that the microcomputer is a sophisticated piece of equipment, despite its easy use by both the teacher and the taught. It is probably the most sophisticated educational tool ever to have been brought into the school environment. However, like most things new, its early uses were developed by keen amateurs, enthusiastic pioneers who can so easily be enamoured by the technology and, thereby, often unwittingly arouse unrealistic expectations in others.

There is little doubt in my mind, that the microcomputers will eventually find their way into most Primary/Middle Schools in this country within the next five years, if for no other reason than the fact that we have entered the microelectronic age where even the most traditionally based schools will find themselves in the situation of 'Change without Choice'. It is therefore imperative that, having overcome the natural caution and reserve present in many school staffs, those staffs should be aware of the many problems which enter a school with the introduction of the technological miracle – the microcomputer. This chapter sets out to describe some of the problems discovered, often painfully and expensively, by schools who entered the microelectronics field early on. There will be other problems, as yet undiscovered, but to be forewarned is at least to be fore-armed.

Management problems associated with the introduction of the microcomputer occur in three main sectors – in the school itself, within the microcomputer system used and thirdly the problems associated with management. Each of these sectors is discussed in some detail.

Management Problems Arising from the 'Chemistry' of Primary Schools

> No matter how favourably set are the microcomputer factors (equipment, software, and support), it is the complex chemistry of the school itself that will ultimately determine the outcome of the microcomputer in the school.
>
> (Sledge, 1979:44.)

The 'chemistry' of the school is the complex interaction between the school's philosophy, its physical environment, and the school's curriculum, as well as its staff, its pupils, and their parents. Each one of these 'elements' must be considered – for each can present particular problems.

The School's Philosophy

Each school has its own philosophy which, in many schools, means the philosophy of the headteacher. Each school has to decide how best to use the computer: whether or not to concentrate its use among a few staff and in a narrow field of the curriculum – thereby making quite an impact in that subject area; or to let its use spread thinly over a much wider area, encouraging all the staff to put it to some use – thereby illustrating to staff and pupils alike the computer's use in many areas of the learning environment. It is, therefore, important at the outset for the head *together* with his/her staff fit the computer into the school's philosophy. The real problem to be faced is trying to achieve a balance between studying the computer as 'content' (that is, as in a computer studies course) and its use as both a teaching aid and as an aid for the learner. It is a problem of emphasis and the solution lies within the individual school. Seeking the answers to the following questions may be of help.

> Are there sections of the school's philosophy which need to be changed to fit the needs of a technological society based upon microelectronics?
>
> At which points in the school's philosophy does the computer fit most easily thus causing the least inconvenience?
>
> Should the microcomputer be used for computer studies – if so within which age group?
>
> Should the computer be introduced across the curriculum and throughout the age range?
>
> Should the computer be used in a concentrated way within one or two areas of the curriculum?
>
> At what stage should complex programs be introduced which demand more interaction from the pupil?

Such questions are for each school to discuss openly – the answers will be affected by and will undoubtedly affect the school's philosophy.

The School's Environment

The Buildings   The physical environment of the school can lead to several problems. The microcomputer has made its impact because of its portability – the ease with which it can become part of a child's normal learning environment. It can very easily be moved to the class of children rather than be firmly fixed into a computer room. However, some schools prefer a fixed base, and the system moves the children to the computer for convenience. Other schools with more favourable physical layouts – that is, few changes in level, single storey etc. – load the system onto a large wheeled trolley, and even when linked to a twenty-six inch TV (for CAT) still retains the portability. A staff needs to decide how it intends to use the microcomputer system from the beginning, in view of the physical layout of the school, because this can ultimately determine the type of system to be purchased.

Secure Storage   The microcomputer can represent, depending on the size of the school, a substantial capital investment and, as such, requires secure storage arrangements. A really portable system, whilst being convenient for the staff and pupils, is also portable for a thief! The equipment is far too attractive and expensive to be left openly in a classroom. It is a problem needing a solution, and one that is closely linked to insurance, which should include the use of the system outside school hours. Some schools prefer staff to take the system home for familiarization and program development rather than leave it unattended in school.

Classroom Accommodation   Until each classroom is equipped with its own microcomputer, it is only an occasional visitor and this can lead to 'best location' problems. It certainly needs to be located close to a power source (a 13 amp socket) and it needs to be sited in a position so as to cause the least disturbance and distraction if used in its computer-assisted-learning mode (CAL). It also requires a situation away from reflections from windows. This is obviously a problem for the classroom teacher to solve. However, there is a need to be aware that the problem does exist, in that a microcomputer's location within a learning environment does affect its proper use and impact.

Size of School   Size is a factor – to maximize the use of the microcomputer within a very large Primary/Middle School, calls for very careful management and organization. There is an optimum number of pupils where it becomes necessary to purchase a second, third, or even a fourth unit. Smaller schools, whilst not having the same problem associated with size, also need to maximize their investment in an expensive piece of hardware if the maximum number of children are to benefit. The easy solution is to limit its use to certain age groups – and within a narrow band of the curriculum – but that is really dodging the problem. Good organization can ensure maximum use by the maximum number – it needs thought, organizational skill, and good-will on the part of the staff.

The Staff

Attitude Undoubtedly the key factor to the proper use of the microcomputer within the primary school sector of the educational service lies within the attitude of the teaching staff. Sympathetic understanding of the problem, backed by careful structure in-service training courses are essential if staff trained and brought up in the Industrial Era are to be absorbed painlessly into the Information Technology Era. Duncan Sledge (1979: 56) lists a number of problems associated with staff attitudes – the ones relevant to the primary school situation are reproduced below:

> A teacher's attitude towards computers in general and their use in education in particular.
>
> A teacher's level of knowledge or awareness of computers and computing both in general and in relation to his/her own subject discipline.
>
> The level of previous training/experience in computer related work.
>
> A teacher's extra-curricular commitments.
>
> A teacher's professional outlook.
>
> A teacher's relationship with, and feelings towards, other members of the staff.
>
> A teacher's willingness to undertake in-service training.

A headteacher certainly needs to ask these questions of himself and then of his staff. No doubt some of the attitude problems can be solved by good in-service training but some are, sadly, so ingrained that training, however good, will not erase them. Fortunately, the media, especially television, are doing sterling work to increase computer literacy amongst the general population and this should result in a more positive attitude developing within the teaching profession.

Senior Staff In order to solve the problems associated with

MANAGING THE MICRO

individual staff a positive attitude is essential from senior staff – for it is they who must give the lead. If this is not so within a school then there is little point in introducing a microcomputer, for the whole process will fail. However enthusiastic an individual class teacher might be, little can be achieved without the support of the senior staff, especially the headteacher. To carry this argument to its logical conclusion, this also applies to the advisory staff, and inspectorate. There must be a lead from the top, for it is only their enthusiasm and leadership which will enable the microcomputer to be successfully absorbed into the school. Without that condition, the expensive, sophisticated system will end up unused and dusty in the proverbial cupboard, to the detriment of both staff and pupils. There is no doubt that a school needs a high level of staff commitment.

The Pupils The great advantage that primary school pupils have over their teachers is that they have been born into the Information Technology Era and have enviable open-mindedness towards all things new. Their natural curiosity and excitement about the future make it much less a problem to introduce them to the computer – indeed the opposite is true – the problem is finding efficient and fair ways to satisfy the demand. They have a will to master the system and this adaptability and flexibility, together with their powers of absorbing quite complex concepts, all help to create a positive attitude towards the computer – they are not in awe of the system. Where, then, are the problems? The following questions associated with pupil problems are in need of answers:

> How do you introduce the computer to pupils of differing ages and abilities?
>
> At what age should pupils be introduced to a computer?
>
> How do you create an attitude of respect for the computer as a powerful tool rather than as an expensive toy?
>
> Should you create a team of computer-monitors to supervise extra-curricular activities, or does this create an élitist group?
>
> How do you organize maximum access to the machine for the maximum number of pupils?
>
> How do you encourage those pupils who wish to write programs for themselves, and ensure that such work is carefully recorded?
>
> How do you encourage pupils who wish to use rather than develop programs?

It is obvious that pupils do raise problems!

Parents Many primary schools now involve parents as partners in the education of their children and, indeed, in some schools, it is the parent body that wishes to supply the microcomputer in the first place. Problems do arise from such involvement. In fact, the worst problems arise when a parent presents a school with a microcomputer, especially if the school is unprepared for the unsolicited yet generous gift. Even if such a gift is not contemplated, there are problems which need to be faced; these are as follows:

> Parents are adults, and as such have many of the attitudes shown by the staff of the school.
>
> How does a school justify to parents the expenditure on a microcomputer system in these days of financial stringency?
>
> How does a school show parents that the computer will not reduce the teaching of numeracy and literacy?
>
> How does the school aliay the natural fears of many parents that the children will be taught by a 'cold' calculating machine, which lacks the 'warmth' and understanding of a teacher?
>
> How does a school overcome the fear of some parents that their child is too young to be exposed to such sophisticated equipment?
>
> How does a school overcome the fear of the 'knowledge gap' developing between parents and their children?

Management Problems Associated with the Microcomputer System

The Hardware Problem

A school needs to select the best possible system at the outset – one which will perform the tasks *as defined by the school* – USPEC 32, available free of charge from the Council for Educational Technology, will be of great help in making the choice. In many areas, the choice is being made for the schools by the Local Authority. Nevertheless, schools should be aware of the problems associated with the system. Some are detailed below – there are probably many more.

Maintenance If a school chooses a system recommended by its LEA then maintenance can usually be arranged free of charge through the authority. Expensive systems can break down, although the solid state electronics are such that the systems are becoming extremely reliable and almost child- and teacher-proof in their robustness. It is, however, a factor which should not be overlooked when considering the introduction of a microcomputer into a school. Maintenance contracts offered by hardware suppliers can prove very expensive because they are usually based on business and commercial usage – lower rates for schools which do not necessarily require such immediate attention as commerce can often be obtained.

Mobility If a school decides to move the computer into the classroom and not set up a separate computer room, then it is vital that the system is kept as portable as possible to ensure that it is easily transported from classroom to classroom or wherever the user-space is located. This is best achieved by purchasing a suitably *large wheeled* trolley – preferably one which can also accommodate a twenty-six inch TV for its use with large groups. Some schools have successfully converted the old type of school desk, suitably modified. The main concern is to keep the system as neat as possible, preferably with the minimum number of cables visible – a spaghetti-like mass of wires is off-putting to the most enthusiastic teacher and it does nothing at all for the less enthusiastic!

Printers Printers are still very expensive but, if a school decides that it is a necessary part of its system to obtain hard-copy for its children and as an aid to programmers, it must be carefully considered. There can be a noise factor which is most distracting if used in a classroom, however well disciplined. Then there is the additional cost of paper and the problem of proper loading and storing to ensure a steady feed-through. This can outweigh its advantages if the system is to remain portable. It may, of course, be used outside the classroom for specific purposes, the advantage then being that it is easily detached. The great danger is over-sophistication at the Primary School level, thereby anchoring an essentially portable mobile facility.

Software Problems Whatever system is chosen by the school or selected by the LEA, there is at the time of writing insufficient software (that is, programs) to support it. There may appear to be a large quantity available for certain systems, and this will be widely advertised as a selling point, but it will probably be of a disappointing standard. We are in a 'lock-in' situation at present because there are too few Primary Schools generating good programs and, because there are too few good programs, there are too few schools with microcomputers. The problem is exacerbated when schools use the computer across subject boundaries – the broader the base the worse the software problem becomes – and yet this is the only way to establish the computer as an interdisciplinary tool and not merely an extension to the mathematics syllabus.

The problem will ease in the near future as one or two systems begin to dominate the market. The Micro Electronics Programme (MEP) is doing a great deal to lessen this problem of software and, as the regional organization begins to flourish under MEP, good quality software will begin to flow. Organizations such as MUSE and MAPE (Micros and Primary Education) are also tending to concentrate on solving this problem by offering library facilities to their members.

Other Management Problems

These are discussed under two main headings: the problems of management within the school as a whole; and those arising from the use of the microcomputer within the specific 'user area'.

Management Problems within the School

Problems associated with management are directly related to those arising from the individual school's philosophy which does, of course, determine how the microcomputer will be used, for these create problems of organization. Some of these are as follows:

> How should the headteacher organize the use of the computer to ensure a fair distribution of time between classes, and between departments (in Infant and Junior combined schools)?
>
> Which member of staff, if any, should be given responsibility for the system and how should this be rewarded?
>
> How does the headteacher encourage *all* members of staff to use the system?
>
> How does the headteacher ensure that all members of staff have equal opportunities for access to the system?
>
> How does the headteacher create 'in-service' time for those staff who are interested in developing programs for use within the school?
>
> How does the headteacher create a balance in use between children and staff?

MANAGING THE MICRO

How does the headteacher create a balance in use between subject areas?

Should the system be anchored in a computer room, or should it be moved around the school in such a way as to minimize movement yet give accessibility to the maximum number of children?

How does the headteacher ensure that safety standards concerning the use of electrical applicances are maintained in every 'user area'? (for example, use of extension cables etc.).

How does the headteacher arrange for the proper organization of software? (that is, catalogue systems etc.).

Management Problems within the Classroom or 'User Area'

The problems listed below are those which should concern every class teacher who intends to use the microcomputer and teachers should be made aware of them before committing themselves:

Where should the teacher position the system within the classroom, so as to cause the least disturbance yet give easy access to the user, or users, yet be in view of the teacher?

How does the teacher ensure adequate safety precautions are observed when children are using electrical equipment within the classroom (length of cables, position of switches etc.)?

How does the teacher avoid a computer-users élite and ensure equal access by all pupils within the class?

How does the teacher ensure that the children receive maximum benefit from using the system with the minimum of teacher interference?

How does the class teacher manage the software (that is, care of tapes or disks)?

Should the teacher train the children and use them as 'monitors' to prepare the system for use by other class members?

How does the classteacher plan for the computer's impact on the children's other work?

What is the best classroom layout to maximize the attributes of the computer – remembering that it is probably not a permanent feature of any one classroom?

How does the teacher ensure that careful records are kept of its use?

How does a teacher best evaluate its use by the children?

In Conclusion

This chapter set out to make headteachers and others interested in introducing a microcomputer into a primary/middle school aware of the very many problems which they will face. These problems are often made light of by the aggressive selling techniques used by hardware salesmen who, of course, base their sales on the marvellous attributes of the computer system. Computers will be in schools, nothing can stop the trend if children are to be properly equipped for life in the age of Information Processing. However no computer system will provide the panacea promised by some enthusiasts. Introducing a micro into a school, as has been shown, also introduces many problems of management and organization. This chapter has offered no easy solution, rather it has raised many questions – but often to have questions raised is all that is required for a professional teacher to be able to find a solution which fits neatly into the local situation of the individual school. For a teacher to examine the question and to seek a solution is the first step towards meeting the challenge of the future – an exciting challenge and one that must be met for the sake of the children now in primary schools at the foundation level of our Education Service.

Reference

SLEDGE, D.K. (1979) Durham Microcomputer Report (DuMP), Durham County Council Education Committee.

A Role for the Microprocessor in Infant Education

Marjorie Holloway

Using the Curriculum in the Infant School

The microcomputer has entered our everyday world and the toy cupboard of the child is becoming transformed by automated toys, talking and dancing machines and addictive, sometimes noisy and emotive electronic games. How many experiences now has the child? We remember experiences and learn by using remembered experiences. The microcomputer in all its various forms is invading the world of the teachers who are challenged by technological progress. Children with parents who are over anxious zealots in the course of education could easily become the recipients of ill-designed and badly chosen 'learning packages'. How then will the teachers deal with this hitherto unknown situation?

On taking a closer look at the whole situation, it is clear to see that infant teachers are, in fact, preparing children to grow up in a world dominated commercially, industrially and socially by the 'micro'. Many teachers of older children have already seen the repercussions of the first computer revolution and its effects on the world of mathematics due to the capacity of the computer to perform rapid calculations. Some teachers were fascinated by this new tool, whereas others ignored it and buried their heads back in text books to the exclusion of all else. Many teachers feared redundancies, should the microcomputer take over some of a teacher's duties and so reduce the number of people required to teach the children. They quite overlooked the important fact that it is the programmer and not the machine itself which presents the challenge. Should teachers allow themselves to become the acolytes to an exclusive force of programmers and systems analysts then the body of professional programmers and analysts could become a very powerful professional body indeed.

As the era of the micro revolution gathers momentum, a period of great change in social and practical living modes will occur which will display the need for educationalists to master the processes required in order to maintain some control over the programs produced for learning.

As the micros become more commonplace, the processes of

manufacture will produce cheaper machines. Teachers will be placed in the position of choosing a particular machine in order to fill their specific needs. Therefore, primary school teachers need to be trained in the ability to judge both machines and software as well as informing suppliers regarding the needs of the pupils educationally. The evaluation of machines and of software is a lengthy process requiring both educational and technological knowledge and trials in the school situation.

In order to make efficient evaluations, teachers will need to be discerning, analytical and critical in their viewing of the structures of each program, bearing in mind the curricular structure of that particular subject in individual schools. I would suggest that small groups of teachers from the same area should form evaluation groups before the primary schools are presented with a *fait accompli* by educational suppliers. These groups could work together to formulate plans which could lead to the use of the micro in a mode approved by teachers and so produce guidelines of acceptance with which to face the suppliers at the planning stage.

Primary school teachers could gain their knowledge by way of in-service training, studying the microprocessor, the software, and the relevance of using the combination as a classroom tool in order to perform both evaluation and creation of programs. If one can design a program for a micro by using the English language and flowcharts, this information could possibly be handed over to a teacher who is also a trained programmer to be translated into the language of the micro with the original teacher providing the basic elements of the program.

We have many questions to settle regarding the use of the micro in infant schools and the questions will be answered in the main by experiment and experience in order to build up a background of knowledge for all teachers.

As long ago as 1912 this statement was made by an educational psychologist whilst considering some aspects of educational psychology:

> Just because personal teaching is precious and can do what books and apparatus cannot, it should be saved for its peculiar work. The best teacher uses books and apparatus as well as his own insight, sympathy and magnetism.
>
> (Thorndyke, 1912)

Amongst the 'apparatus' to appear recently in our field is the microcomputer which can in no way be dismissed as a gimmick, rather it should be treated with respect. It is important that education should remain in the hands of skilful educationalists who will ensure the attainment of potential skills and creative thinking by as many

THE MICROPROCESSOR IN INFANT EDUCATION

pupils as possible. Children of a very tender age are quite able to turn the TV on or off and to change choice of channel to suit individual tastes. Our youngest generation are 'button pushers' and 'switchers' from a very early age by the very design of children's toys. In every home, children gain experiences of many patterns of behaviour, both natural and electronic. We should not assume that we know the effect that experiences have on children. Every child has a past and has formed attitudes and associated emotions with event; the present experience will be interpreted in the light of this unique and personal history. If we accept these statements as true then we ought to consider the importance of providing a rich variety of experiences as a background to all activities within the curriculum. A child may then build onto a secure, familiar but developing concept, providing that his linking experiences have familiar aspects and emotive or attractive elements. The formation of new skills, therefore, needs to be linked in a secure and attractive manner with already known and experienced skills. In other words, we must use the skills already present in the child in order to form a basis for new skills.

We now consider evolving a method by which we can link the microcomputer to the skills presently prevailing in the classroom situations of infant schools. We shall for convenience call these links 'pre-computer skills' and will attempt to define the nature of some of these skills. Pre-computer skills should be adequately developed in order to form strong links between present classroom experience and anticipated future experiences which involve use of the microcomputer. These experiences can be compared to the rungs on a ladder, each of which allows a further advance to be made in the ascent of developing skills. We start at ground level and progress from the known experience and skill to the new experience. The new experience will, in turn, form the basis for the next progressive step in the ascent of developing skills. Assuming that the new skill to be learned is the efficient use by children of a microcomputer, then the linking elements to present experiences already remembered well by the child are open to the following questions:

1 do the children require additional skills at all?
2 if the answer is 'Yes' then how do we identify these skills?
3 having identified the skills, what experiences are required in order that the child may master these skills?

The conclusion appears to point to a 'half-way house' between human input/output and electronic input/output, which brings us to the field of audio visual activities by the children, both with and without machinery of some description.

Let us now go to the stage in which the child has first entered school.

The Teacher

The child's first learning relationships in school are in the main formed with the help of experiences which are linked to the teacher, almost to the exclusion of any other person except his peers. The dependence of child upon teacher, who is always fairly close at hand to give help, guidance, reassurance and affection, gradually grows into a firm relationship based on trust and security which increases with the various experiences in which many children and the teacher are involved. Once the teacher/child relationship is firmly established, the teacher dependence must eventually be transformed into the confidence and security of a reasonably independent child.

From Personal Relationships to Visual and Audio Aids

At this stage, the first intermediary link is to be established between child and teacher. Puppets are very good intermediaries especially if they are able to 'speak' through a small three inch amplifier hidden inside the clothing of the puppet. These amplifiers are cheap and simple to install by using a soldering iron and a length of wire, plus a jack plug. When wired for sound the puppet is linked to a cassette recorder which can be disguised to complete the illusion. Having accepted a recorded voice the child will readily transfer from puppets to another type of recorded instructor. Listening skills have been encouraged by use of the puppet and verbal responses encouraged and extended. At this point it is quite natural for the child to move onto another machine which does not involve any other person: the language master or card reader for example. This machine involves a recorded verbal instruction accompanied by a pictorial illustration which moves from left to right whilst the instructions or requests for action are transmitted by the machine. Obviously, this requires the skills of concentration, due to the time factor of recording and also the ability to press a response button at the correct time. The child is at last controlling a machine to a limited extent and can repeat any section of his work if he is not sure of his answer. The teacher is at hand, but not all the time, so the child is working independently unless help is required. Also at this stage, because the child likes switches and needs to be able to manipulate them, a row of small coloured bulbs controlled by small hand switches may be used for mathematics in the field of number bonds.

THE MICROPROCESSOR IN INFANT EDUCATION   61

Audio Response

As he reaches a more demanding stage of audio response the child is given practice on a more specific machine. At this stage the child will commence to use an audio cassette combined with personal earphones and a response microphone. These materials can also be combined with work cards or work sheets. This represents quite a comprehensive system which can be linked to classroom schemes of work by the teacher.

My favourite machine, which I use for individualized learning, is a Sony Audio Comparative Mini Language Laboratory which measures about seven inches by ten inches and is approximately three inches deep. This machine looks like an audio-cassette recorder and player but has added facilities which enabled the instructor to design:

1 recorded instructions on track one;
2 a recording track for the pupil use which enables the pupil to listen to instructions and record the response audibly;
3 an inlet for a headset to which is joined a microphone. This headset enables the child to both listen and respond;
4 with these facilities the pupil's hands are free to write or to physically manipulate any apparatus as required.

Thus, a child may take a work card or sheet and listen to instructions for carrying out the work on the sheet. His hands are free to follow instructions for written or physical activity, or he could respond audibly. Should a work card related to classroom activities be related to such a machine, then the answers to problems, puzzles etc. or the observations by the child in the field of comprehension of pictures or English language work could be evaluated by the teacher following activity with the machine. Areas which could be covered include both mathematics and reading/language, as well as the 'check list' type of questions used to test levels of competence in certain areas. This type of plan allows the child complete privacy, even in a crowded classroom and gives a facility for playback to both teacher and child. He can learn and respond quite confidently, alone, working on material designed specifically for the satisfaction of his needs.

Thinking of the VDU

In preparation for the use of the visual display unit – the VDU or screen – the child is next introduced to projected light via the overhead projector. Multi-media packages may now be designed that link past and future experiences. Using a roll of acetate, which is much cheaper than single transparencies, a teacher can draw and illustrate a story on a continuous strip. This piece of material can then be used either with an audio-cassette to record the story with sound effects and then to play the cassette whilst a child reveals the story frame by frame, or as stimulus for a story to be told around the class by all the children. Children can also usefully use the table of the projector in order to manipulate solid materials such as small templates, counters, small pictures drawn on one inch squares of acetate. The images produced fill a large screen and the child feels particularly pleased when he can actually write a few words for other children to read from the screen. There are lots of delightful activities which can be designed for use in this media in which response and motivation gain maximum experiences and the interplay and dialogue are very rich: experiences which will lead we hope to a happy acceptance of the VDU on the microcomputer eventually.

Keyboard Practice

Up to this stage, the child has been carefully guided to use media leading toward VDU, the worksheet and tape recorder as these are elements that will be associated with the microcomputer. However, one element remains that we have not yet explored and that is the computer keyboard. It will be essential for the children to gain some experience of typing in order to use the keyboard on the microcomputer. The jumbo typewriter is an ideal agent for practice in typing, as it has keys compatible in size with the microcomputer keyboard. One creative way of using this skill is to give the child acetate on which to type his story or poem which can be illustrated with coloured pens made especially for OHP work. This work forges a link in a creative way with both the VDU and the written materials displayed.

The 'Link' of the Machine

Through all other stages, the children have been coming to terms with machines and educational technology. Some adults have a built-in barrier to electronic machinery and, in turn, communicate this barrier to their pupils by refusing to use the machines in a natural and creative manner. It is important that in an era of technological advance teachers should be able to step forward and accept the challenge of the machines. On the other hand, once a child has enjoyed the initial experience, it is probable that he may possess a great affinity with electronic learning devices.

The atmosphere during the use of the 'link' machinery should be a sociable, friendly and happy set of learning experiences. Each child should be carefully introduced to a well programmed machine which is related to other media or materials with which the child has remembered experiences and secure happy moments.

Social interplay and repartee are important at all stages: learning should take place together, in small groups, where enjoyment of experiences together is the main ingredient. If children are involved with educational tools as members of a supportive group then leaders have a chance to shine and the nervous child is well supported and happy.

Establishing the Relationship

Assuming that the child has benefited from his experiences with audio visual machinery and materials then we can conclude that at this stage he will have a happy relationship between himself and the machines. Once the various elements mentioned earlier have become related to the child in various combinations he should be ready to accept the final combination of these machines – that is, the microcomputer.

Evaluation

Of course, finally, the only satisfactory evaluation is to take a small group of children to a microcomputer and to introduce them to their first relationship with this friendly and cleverly contrived machine. It is important that, initially, programs remain linked to classroom experiences, including the beneficial chatter and dialogue of the classroom. The child can start simply by having fun typing in his own name and those of his faimly. Above all, it must be remembered that the teacher still controls the program content produced by the machine and that it is up to us all to look very carefully now at the next development in our system – that is, the actual microcomputer programs. The micro processor programs will, initially, be associated with classroom display sheets such as card vocabulary sheets for classroom activities before and possibly following use of the microcomputer. Following correct work by the pupil rewards would show on the VDU such as ... 'good. Take a gold star' or alternatively ... 'No. sorry. try again'. This little dialogue between machine and pupil will reinforce the motivation of the child, especially if popular catch phrases are used in a joking way.

Sealey and Gibbon (1962: 16) state:

> Working backwards from the stage where growth or learning has taken place, we find that this has stemmed from experience which was absolutely bound up in communication.

From this statement I conclude that communication is essential if learning is to occur. It would seem sensible, therefore, to consider the following question: 'In the light of the last statement how effective then is the microcomputer as a communicator?'. Computers and infant-aged children appear to have common elements. Primarily, both will only accept input under the criteria of their unique known experience (in the case of the microcomputer, a known language; and in the case of the child, at a language-level suitable to his perceptual and conceptual development). Secondly, instructions must be in simple, logical steps because neither children nor computers can anticipate the instructions to follow nor can they correct ambiguous or misleading commands. However, the computer will carry out all correct commands and will report command errors with direct error messages. It will never forget the data stored away in its memory. The computer is an accurate, rapid calculator, obedient and predictable. The child, however, finds instructions hard to remember and is only as precise as his emotional and intellectual development allows him to be. The computer, when programmed in simple steps, can help children to remember instructions by using encouraging remarks or pictures. It never tires of repeating a program in order for learning to occur.

From these statements a conclusion may be drawn that, providing the links between the elements of a child's development are carefully considered when the program for the computer is written and also providing the language displayed is at the level of and attractive to the child, then a happy relationship can be formed between the computer, child and teacher.

We are now able to consider which areas of the curriculum could be suitably linked to computer programming. We must assume that we have a good knowledge of the child's present learning environment, including teaching materials, apparatus and media available in his particular school situation. We should also have some idea of the attainment level and learning speed of the children as individuals. At the present time we also assume that audio-visual machinery may be in use but not the computer. The audio-visual machinery can engender recorded response either written or verbal from the child. Our objective is to produce a series of responses which will be made by the child manually pressing buttons and be displayed on the VDU of the computer to be read back by the children. The responses we have obtained so far have been recorded either manually or verbally, yet the new type of response is remote and controlled by a button. It would seem reasonable under the circumstances to go from the known to the unknown via the link of the classroom materials, teacher and computer; a trio of elements to reach our objective. With these thoughts in mind I will now explain how I 'invaded' my infant curriculum with the help of pre-computer skills linked with simple programs.

My first area of programing was the linking of a piece of classroom material with a simple computer program in the area of mathematics (see figure 1).

Figure 1   Classroom Material

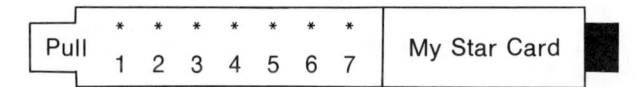

```
┌─────────────────────────────────────────────┐
│        *   *   *   *   *   *                │
│ Pull                          My Star Card   │
│        1   2   3   4   5   6                │
└─────────────────────────────────────────────┘
```

Stars were stuck on a card which in turn slid in and out of a cover which could either conceal or reveal stars and number symbols by manual control. In the classroom this card was used in order to identify groups of stars by matching and later to add or take away stars in learning number bonds. Allied to this piece of material the computer was programmed to display random groups of stars in a box up to a maximum of ten stars. The display on the VDU invited the child to press a number symbol to match the group in the box. This typing was then displayed on the screen. If the response was correct, the computer displayed 'Well done ... clever kiddo ... try another'. and if wrong an appropriate remark to encourage the child to try again. Initially the teacher was present and indirect supervision followed at a later stage. The link was formed whenever the two media were used together – the children discarding the card as they were ensured of the validity of their answering skills. This technique worked well in the following areas:

1 *Early mathematics*
group to group matching to ten;
addition and number bonds to ten;
subtraction from ten
2 *Happy sums*
A program offering addition and subtraction sums at choice from

one to one hundred: levels to be chosen by the child – that is, E = easy sums; H = harder sums; S = subtraction sums. The classroom materials used in this case were a 100 square number card or a 100 counting line.

3 *Bullseye*

A competitive game which can be programmed to fit the level of the child. A bullseye board is shown, followed by a small sum. If the child gets the sum correct, a bullseye is given. The computer flashes up the score each time a sum is done. Children take so many turns a piece and the highest scorer is the winner. This game reflects the speed and accuracy of the children's learning. The competitive nature of the game adds excitement and motivation.

4 *Early reading and writing skills*
   a) word matching
   b) letter matching game
   c) cloze procedure linked with reading scheme
   d) quiz on project work in order to increase vocabulary words

Word Matching

This program used the class readers and words used in bingo or flash card games. The words were listed on one side of the screen in a list of ten words. On the other side of the screen the word to be matched is flashed on in isolation. An arrowed line, which completely underlines each word singly, moved down under each word in turn. As the match occurred the child pressed the space bar and a 'tick' appeared beside the word if it was correct. If the word was wrong, the same word was presented again – for example (using words from *Kathy and Mark*, Book One):

bed	
mother	Find
came	
he	
run	run
———	
go	

Five to six-year-old children manage this game with confidence. It is also a good group game as a change from flash cards with the teacher because it is highly motivating, each child working at his own level.

Quizzes

These are very popular and involve single word response only. The origin of the material is the topic work occurring in the classroom at any time. This first one was 'Christmas'. We made a list of Christmas words as we talked about the things we would do at Christmas and wrote the words in a list on a large sheet of card which we illustrated in colour and put up on the classroom display to use for word games and creative writing. We then made a smaller card of A5 size and put the words in both upper and lower case letters with smaller pictures. I had to make up my mind at the very onset whether or not to use both upper and lower case letters and as I have so often said that the children learn by experience, so have I. I have discovered since using the microcomputer with the children that they have very little difficulty in relating 'A' to 'a' or 'B' to 'b'. They realise that the typewriter has upper case letters and usually call them 'big letters'. The concept of an upper case letter to a child appears to be that it makes the same sound as a lower case letter but it is also used to start a sentence or to start somebody's name. In my opinion, the concept of the old fashioned 'Alphabet Letters' verbalized as 'AY' 'BEE' 'CEE' whilst children were shown the upper case letters is what caused and still causes the confusion which occurs in the minds of infant aged children. In towns, on buses, on public buildings and on TV, children read upper case letters which form words and can do so with ease. I try to teach that 'A' and 'a' both say 'aaaa' and are both bearers of the 'name' ay; after all, how do you verbalize when you say 'Andrew'? This, I hope, will explain to you my reasons for designing the card to display both lower and upper case letters. Let us now return to the work card. This card was used by the child to answer the quiz on the microcomputer, as the upper case letters were the same as the keyboard on the micro. The children had no difficulty in relating the card to the machine and accepted the fact that both types of letters were valid when using the microcomputer.

By using these programs I have tried to reinforce some of the skills required across the curriculum by the children. For instance: reading left to right and down a page; the concept of a word; the construction of a sentence; recognition of single letters; the creation of stories. As I have no audio channel on my computer at present, I am often the added voice that reinforces and encourages the more difficult work. When slower children are around the microcomputer we often discuss what an answer to a problem displayed on the VDU might be before one of the group pushes the button for the answer. In theory any routine repetitive tasks can be computerized. One needs to observe closely in the classroom in order to identify the areas of need with which adapted materials could be filled adequately. Specific skills could be identified and checked for each child and programs written in order to give practice and experience by a combination of classroom materials and computer programs.

We now move away from specific curriculum work to make some general remarks regarding the microcomputer in terms of motivation and group work. We shall take an example of motivation first.

Allan is five years old. He has a speech defect and has become bored with doing his speech exercises. Allan is a child whose mother does not want him to grow up too quickly and therefore his baby like speech does not worry her at present. Allan enjoys using the micro and is able to type in letters to see if the collective sounds can build up into a word that he knows. We have great fun together, especially when Allan types nonsense words and then tries to verbalize. It is easily possible at these times to correct the functioning of his tongue and teeth in order to clarify his speech. Allen thinks he is very clever to be able to use the micro, consequently, his self image and motivation have improved as well as his speech and general behaviour.

Darren is six and a half years of age. He was unable to perform simple computation to ten. Classroom observations indicated that his difficulty appeared to occur when he tried to write the numbers down. His pencil control was so poor that his recording became minimal; greater and more mischievous gaps of time and inactivity were seen to occur in between each number experience. It became obvious that Darren would in no way gain a sufficient number of mathematical experiences working at such a slow pace. The difficulty he experienced in recording would overshadow any motivation which he needed in order to work. With insufficient experiences Darren had no hope of building up the experiences necessary in order to recall number bonds. We designed a combination of classroom counting line card and a simple micro program for him. On the micro he used the program Happy Sums. This program showed a smiling face and instructed the child to 'take a gold star' when the correct response was given. As Darren had no writing to do, he was able to absorb himself completely in his number work and eventually he had so many number experiences that he easily recognized the number symbols. As Darren became confident his recording in the classroom improved and the improvement continues.

Phillip is seven years of age and a highly intelligent child. He was

THE MICROPROCESSOR IN INFANT EDUCATION

a great trial to his teacher who had difficulty in producing enough work for him to consume, whereupon, Phillip would become mischievous. Phillip enjoys doing the hard sums from the program Happy Sums. He can also type stories on the keyboard when the machine is put in the lower case mode. These stories can be saved on cassette and may be read by other children at a later date.

A number of children are just starting to experiment with the graphics symbols on the micro. They are reaching the stage where they can use simple co-ordinates to plot a mark without realising quite what they are developing. For instance you will hear a child say 'His nose will be about sixteen across and fourteen down'. This is when the children are attempting to draw a face on squared paper and transfer the marks to the VDU. This work is both creative and logical.

I now find that children aged six and a half to seven years are capable of loading the computer and of changing programs under indirect supervision. One of my teaching staff is attending an evening course for teachers on computer programming and we shall develop our computer activities further as opportunities arise. It is, however, no easy task to institute new procedures and techniques. We must remember that the teacher will remain an essential and vital element within the system however many computers are in use. The skills involved in teaching a child to handle the computer will be acquired at different speeds by individual children. If the necessary audio-visual machinery has been used in order to provide the child with pre-computer skills, then his feeling toward the micro, his facility to understand communication by machine and VDU display and his ability to respond to the machine will have been developed through his own experiences.

We, as teachers, should realize that we have to plan activities that will build on the child's experience and eventually enable him to respond effectively and intelligently to media. Perhaps one of the most effective and simplest means of communication with the young child is the ever loved hand puppet, an inanimate object which appears to the child to be alive. When a puppet is given the power of speech by the addition of a small concealed internal loudspeaker it becomes a very powerful motivator and stimulator to the child. The potential field of inventiveness is enormous and highly motivating to both child and teacher alike.

I have attempted to illustrate the ways in which a learning programme becomes more meaningful to the child when previous experiences of the child are taken into account and related to the developing learning situation. Most simple teaching machines can of course already be related to materials or apparatus reflecting prior experience by the child. When we plan a program for young children we should never be slow to realize the value of a return to concrete materials for a while, as an important element of a whole program. From previous comments which I have made you will realize that I see a place for the microcomputer within the multi-media programmes at present existing in our schools. As developing curricula are planned to fill the needs of children in the world as it is today and as it will be tomorrow, surely this is the opportunity to decide on the media appropriate and most effective for specific learning situations. We need to plan our techniques to match the media to the learning objectives clearly in mind. Gagné (1965) has made most helpful suggestions on the ways in which multi-media packages might be developed: his ideas are relevant to anyone adopting the approaches suggested in this article.

Having considered the children, the programs and the possible criteria to follow in relation to curriculum development, I would recommend the following areas as possibilities for developmental computer programming as a part of multi-media packages:

1 checking the child's response to a given stimulus and responding appropriately to the child;
2 guided practice work in a variety of modes with monitored responses;
3 matching, differences and setting;
4 building up deductional skills by use of small developing steps of strategies and answers – that is, if x happened to a y would you be happy or sorry? or a hypothetical type query;
5 the pacing of learning to help slower or quicker children. All steps to be reinforced where required by practical classroom experiences.

I trust that I have made it clear that I have a respect for the place of the teacher in the midst of all our technology. As teachers we must become active participants and not passive receptacles in a world of change. The challenge is already here and we must seize it to the advantage of us all.

References

GAGNÉ, R.M. (1965) *The Conditions of Learning* New York, Holt, Rinehart and Winston, Inc..
SEALEY, V. and GIBBON, V. (1962) *Communication and Learning* Oxford, Blackwell.
THORNDYKE, E.L. (1912) *Education* New York, Macmillan.

The Primary Curriculum/ Micro Interface: Implications for In-Service Education and Resource Provision

Peter Davies

Micros and Society

Any discussion on the introduction of micros into the primary school begs the question, 'why micros?'. There are enough problems even now in coping with an already overcrowded syllabus, without advocating an additional burden. We have seen many other ephemeral educational fads before. Is this merely another one?

Views are varied. To some, micros are a challenge, to others they are a threat to the smooth running of a well tried and tested system. Others are simply not concerned with them and evince not the slightest interest one way or the other.

It is interesting to see how often those who are for involvement with the micro technological expansion assume what might best be described as a more than mild attachment to their beliefs. In the same way, those who are opposed to the new technology show a similar attachment to their beliefs. This attachment tends to make them somewhat monodirectional in their outlook. Forecasts on the changes the new technology will have on society likewise tend to be polarized. One extreme view is of a world of leisure and mankind emancipated from the drudgery of toil. The other view is of mankind denied any say in his destiny, a tool fit only for servicing production robots, exploited and snooped on by a vast secret data bank.

While evidence for both views can be found already translated into fact, the middle ground seems to be conspicuous for the lack of interest it generates in the media. It is my view that this middle ground is probably the most significant. Mankind throughout the ages has demonstrated a tenacity to survive and adapt his environment to suit his own purposes. The so called 'primitive' peoples of the Nile of a few thousand years ago, the Greeks, Romans and European medieval writers left evidence which indicates that the people of those times were recognizably like ourselves. They took their neighbours to court, they worked, fought, loved and died, often for ideals as worthy as any we could conceive of today.

When Alvin Toffler (1970) spoke of the world being overwhelmed by accelerative change, it appears that he was referring to the small minorities he mentioned who are either acutely for or against it, since their reactions are not typified in the majority of people most of us meet day by day. If Toffler's predictions on the dangers of accelerative change were valid, then today, eleven years later, we should all have succumbed.

Concerning micros, it might therefore be helpful if the extreme views of those for and against are seen as holding opposite ends of a single continuum, with varying degrees of attachment to either viewpoint lying somewhere between. The whereabouts of any individual on that continuum will be dependent on his commitment to a certain viewpoint. It will not necessarily be fixed but will shift from one point to another depending on the variety of tasks the person is engaged in, and in those contexts for a host of reasons: personal, professional, political, ethical, moral and so on. Some tasks will be differently affected than others by the use of micros. Passing time will also affect the position for, as the technology proliferates more widely, so the points of view of people will change. With increased familiarity will come greater understanding and strategies for coping with its potentials, advantages and disadvantages. These, in turn, will affect people's viewpoints and, like perhaps the wheel, micros will have ever widening applications and efficiency through all time to come, thus continuously modifying people's attitudes to them. From now on we shall have to acknowledge in some form or other the presence of micros.

And what of those who are disinclined either one way or the other, who do not see themselves at any point on the continuum? They are, likely as not, unconcerned about the wheel. It gets them to work in the morning as part of a larger system – a car for instance. In this context it is accepted as an indispensible part, a mini-system that contributes to a more easily recognizable whole system – the car. Nevertheless it is there and does influence their style of living in many different ways. In order to survive, however, it is not necessary for them to become knowledgeable wheelrights.

What Are Micros?

Before you accept micros into your school, you would do well to remember the Trojans and beware of Greeks who come bearing gifts, until you have some idea of what they are. The question then might best be answered in two ways.

The first is to examine what they are sometimes mistakenly

IMPLICATIONS FOR IN-SERVICE EDUCATION

thought to be. It is felt that many teachers view them as synonymous with mathematics and calculators. Looking at some of the writing widely available reinforces this. For instance Coan (1977) says in his preface:

> In addition to other topics, the applications chapters cover co-ordinate geometry, area, sequences and series, polynomials, graphing, simulation and games ... these topics evolve from or build on the ground of a second course in algebra and beyond.

The editorial in *Electronics and Computing* Magazine (July 1981) states:

> There can be few parallels ... when there has been so much enthusiasm shown by pupils to learn a mathematically based subject.

There are many other instances. Such views are enough to turn a non-mathematician right off at the preface.

Micros are also associated with programmed instruction and teaching machines similar to those that emerged with much ambitious promise in the late fifties and the sixties. Where are they now you may well ask. Perhaps buried under the tons of paper that were filled in arguing the case for and against the behavioural objectives that generally guided their use.

Less applicable at the primary school level perhaps, micros are thought to be concerned with electronics and high technology. As such, they come within the domain of specialist teachers who are at home with machine tools and other scientific mysteries.

The second way to answer the question is to try to formulate what they are. This is necessarily a personal interpretation based on a limited period of experience that I feel I share with many other teachers:

> They are indeed all of those things mentioned above in the first answer to the question.
>
> They are computers and computers are microcomputers and microcomputers are microprocessors and they all contain chips and chips are microchips and microchips are miniature large scale integrated circuits and for our purposes here almost anything else is a black-box with a button that switches it on and off. This black box is part of a computer system that, in addition, generally includes a TV screen and a cassette tape recorder for storing programmes or data. Tape storage can be replaced or augmented by a

disk storage machine. A disk provides much greater memory or data storage which is available for very fast and easy access. Finally there is a printer. That basically makes up a computer system. The minimum requirements however are the computer, the tape recorder and the TV screen.

They are information processors of 'real word data'. (A synonym for what you are reading now – that is, text.) Many of them also offer coloured and moveable (animated) graphics plus sound effects.

They are able to interact with other machines – for example, model railways, telephones, in addition to those mentioned above – TV set, etc..

They are stores of vast quantities of data ready for almost instant display in a variety of forms.

They are empty depositories waiting to store pupils' or teachers' input of data for later processing by them.

They are suitable for individual, group or whole class activities.

They are able to test, plan, report on and record an individual pupil's progress.

They can act as a personal guide through a store of information, prompting a pupil and responding to his responses.

They are able to act as a sympathetic tutor or as a neutral or collaborative researcher with pupils.

They can be a playmate, they are mostly courteous, humourous even, endlessly patient and mostly fun for pupils to be with.

They can assist in the management, planning and running of the school.

They are able to swell the coffers on Open Days. (Arcade games at 10p a go.)

Problems Concerning Hardware

There is a bewildering choice of computers on offer. This choice is growing almost monthly. The various claims for each system are very confusing to what is generally an unsophisticated market of first time buyers. There is little experience to draw on in the teaching profession and what guidance there is, is sketchily co-ordinated for sharing with others. Generally it is either tentative and discreet or

IMPLICATIONS FOR IN-SERVICE EDUCATION 75

wildly optimistic. Things are improving but only slowly. One thing that is clear and more pertinent to primary teachers is that without adequate software of good quality even the best hardware is going to have limited value.

Before purchasing equipment, ask the distributor what is available to support the hardware. Since his interests will not necessarily coincide with your own, check out his information concerning quantity and quality with others who have already committed themselves.

Problems Concerning Software

As indicated above, much of what is on offer is of variable quality. Essentially, programs need to be designed by teachers and especially those working at the level of the pupils for whom the programs are intended. An example of a mathematics program currently on offer from a commercial distributor shows some of the drawbacks. It is very attractive in its graphical presentation. It covers the four rules in number. It sets a sum. If the pupil gets the right answer it smiles and goes on to the next. If the pupil gets the wrong answer it looks miserable. It will go on looking miserable at the pupil until he makes a correct response. It is not courteous in the way that programs can be. It should give two or three attempts, maximum, a 'Never mind!' message, the correct answer and move on to the next. It has a more serious educational drawback. The addition and subtraction sums it offers are quite suitable for use with infants. The multiplication and division exercises are more suitable for middle juniors upwards. The requirements of the two different levels are not met within one program.

Some companies are making headway in this respect. One has appointed an Education Manager. Amongst other things, it has encouraged schools to submit programs that have stood the test of classroom use for inclusion in its contributed software catalogue. These are on sale to other teachers.

There is a bewildering number of languages available for programming the machines. Each emphasizes a different function. Some are incredibly different from others and, in like manner, to our own use of everyday language. For example, a useful little subroutine from C. Phillips in *Liverpool Software Gazette* (November, 1979) written in machine code with Assembly language:

```
0300   A2 00         LDX   # $00
0302   20 IE FB      JSR   $FB1E
0305   8D 30 C0      STA   $C030
0308   4C 00 03      JMP   $300
```

The last two columns are the Assembly version of the machine code instructions contained in the first four columns. It produces tones of varying pitch by altering PADDLE 0. To demonstrate the difference, here is a Pascal language example from John Stout in *Liverpool Software Gazette* (December, 1980)

```
(SIC):
    type MIMIC = record
                 case boolean of
                 true:(INTFIELD:integer);
                 false:(ARRAYPNT: ↑arraytype)
                 end
```

Not being into Pascal, this has no meaning for me. It is evidently a way to handle scrolling for memory mapped displays. The differences are quite starkly represented here. The first has line numbers followed mostly by a series of coded digits. The second has no line numbers and uses mostly coded words.

The universally accepted language for microcomputers is called BASIC. The language names are nearly all acronyms for some process or other — this list of nine will suffice to give you some idea:

BASIC
ASSEMBLEY
FORTRAN
FORTH
COBOL
PASCAL
PILOT
CESIL
COMAL

There are others, with more in the pipeline.

Unfortunately, there are many versions of BASIC. One that works in one machine is not likely to work in a different type of machine. In my own machine there are two versions of BASIC. These are not compatible with each other either. One BASIC is resident in the machine, the other optional BASIC has to be loaded in and takes up nearly half the available usable memory of a medium sized 16K machine. The new improved resident BASIC, incredibly, does not possess all the functions of the old. Some of these functions are exceedingly useful and crucial to the operation of software developed for the old version. If a car manufacturer rightly decided

IMPLICATIONS FOR IN-SERVICE EDUCATION

to introduce a Mark II with improved steering because, although the Mark I had good brakes its steering was inadequate, and the new version then had inadequate brakes there would be cause to wonder. If there is a logic behind this incompatibility concerning languages available in the same machine, it is very difficult to isolate from the customer's point of view.

Another problem primary schools are going to have to come to terms with unless things change, is the format in which the computer displays its messages on the monitor. Generally these are counter to what is considered the norm for procedures in the teaching of reading and handwriting. It should be mentioned that pupils find no difficulties in adapting to an all capitals presentation. Zeros are written as 'ø' multiply (×) is written as an asterisk '*' and divide is an oblique stroke '/'. With so much unused capacity on the keyboards on a number of machines, it is surprising that more facilities are not made available. Others can do it. One crams all manner of functions onto its keyboard and still has room to allow some for user specified functions.

> THIS PARAGRAPH IS WRITTEN IN THIS STYLE
> OF FORMAT TO DEMONSTRATE THE MAXIMUM
> DISPLAY OF TEXT AVAILABLE ON A NUMBER OF
> MACHINES. THE MOST YOU CAN GET ONTO A
> LINE LIMITED TO FORTY COLUMNS IS SHOWN
> HERE. THE MAXIMUM NUMBER OF LINES ON
> DISPLAY AT ANY ONE TIME IS TWENTY FOUR,
> BUT THAT IS ONLY IF YOU CAN ACCEPT THE
> LINES RUNNING INTO EACH OTHER ABOVE AND
> BELOW. IF YOU WISH TO SEPARATE THEM
> WITH SOME SPACING AS USED HERE, YOU
> ONLY REALLY HAVE TWELVE USABLE LINES.

The above paragraph shows the actual limits of text available. Some machines provide 72 columns while others provide as an option 80 columns. Coming out soon is a new improved machine that has reduced the number of columns to 22. For this machine, no doubt, you will be able to purchase at some cost a plug-in adapter that will convert it to a higher number of columns. You can buy a lower case adapter for many of the machines now. Others have the facility resident in the machine when you buy it. With these there may still be some drawbacks for primary schools since some of the systems do not make provision for letters with tails below the line (descenders). Consequently the word 'put' appears a bit odd with the 'p' the same size as the 'u' while the 't' is printed normally. The same style of printing often applies to the printers for obtaining 'hard copy'.

A final word on format. Since most of the essential bits of the micro originate abroad, the dialect is American. Thus 'color program' is the norm for the machine. It will not accept 'colour' as an instruction. This same dialect will usually be found in most of the software but you can alter that if you wish.

On the subject of dialects, the whole computer world abounds with 'buzz words'. A small fortune is waiting for the person who can rewrite the 'in-language' so that it is translatable for use by the layman. You will come across such things as a DATA BUS which in essence is little more than a complex cable. A BUFFER seems to be closely related to a plug and socket. An I/O PORT is even closer to a socket that things are plugged into. Abbreviations and numbers are as thick on the ground as manna from heaven. Unfortunately, the uninitiated, who are the majority, find it difficult to swallow. Common terms you will be expected to know are Z80, 6502, IEEE, C/PM, ASCII, RAM, ROM, PIA, PIO, BCD, CPU, LSI, CMOS, VMOS, HEXADECIMAL, NIBBLES, BITS, BYTES, DOS, BOOT-STRAP and so on.

Books on or about computers and programming are even more profuse and confusing than the machines themselves. It is very easy for the novice to be encouraged to buy several books at around £7 a time, in order to get the best return from an investment in equipment approaching £1000. Generally very little of the contents are suitable for any particular computer on offer today. Those concerned with programming the 6502, and there are many, are more suited to the technically minded who are prepared to build accessories with a soldering iron. Sizeable and essential parts of these books are devoted to making lights go on and off on a small light board. Most computer systems nowadays tend to operate through a TV monitor which makes the construction tasks unnecessary. Furthermore, it is common for computers to incorporate many supporting systems for a variety of functions within the machine. It would be appropriate for someone to write a book on programming in machine code, for that is essentially what 6502 programming is about, bearing in mind the type of machines popularly coming into use.

There are one or two books that are worth their weight in gold for the novice. One, which is worth mentioning perhaps above all others, is by Alcock (1977). You can judge its popularity by the number of issues in the libraries. This also gives some idea of the price too. The best advice you can get is to ask others what books they think are suitable in the light of your own expertise and requirements.

All computers have a limit to the size of their memory. Briefly, memory is measured in units of 1024 BYTES rounded down to 1000 for convenience and called a 'K'. Thus a 16K machine would have 16384 BYTES or data storage units. There is no guarantee that this

IMPLICATIONS FOR IN-SERVICE EDUCATION

amount of memory will be available for your use though. Certain routines in some machines can require large chunks of this memory for its own operating procedures especially if you are using high resolution graphics programs.

The guiding light in deciding on the minimum memory requirements for a primary school might benefit from a consideration of at least two factors:

1 Young pupils may need to have their programs accompanied by heavily detailed descriptions or explanations.
2 Teachers, unfamiliar with the structure of programs will need them well documented with explanatory REMark statements if they are to be able to modify the programs slightly to suit the needs of their pupils, or to overcome minor 'hiccups'.

All of this can take up a fair bit of memory. Also many bought-in programs are written for medium sized memories. If graphic routines, which are an important element in primary school programs, are taken into account then a minimum memory requirement could reasonably be put at 32K.

The provision of taped software is declining in favour of disk software. Many programs are only available and will only operate through a disk. This additional facility will cost in the region of £500 but it will, of course, increase the size of memory available on its own, thus reducing the need to 'RAM' up the actual machine's memory.

The Primary Curriculum

It would be as well, at this juncture, to establish what exactly is meant by the term 'primary curriculum' before going on to discuss its interface with micros. Limitations in space only allow a description in rather simplistic terms. However, many years in a teachers' centre have made me aware of criticisms by my teacher colleagues of the way in which some people describe teaching situations theoretically, without attempting to mirror their theories in practical teaching situations that are recognizable as such by teachers. If theory is not drawn from and does not inform practice, it holds little value. To avoid this discourtesy I shall give concrete examples to support the initial descriptions and pray that attempts to economize in length do not too seriously distort the picture, though some distortion will be inevitable.

It goes without saying that the description is a very personal one based on understanding that has developed over many years of intimate involvement in it. From this experience, I have broken it down into two separate but interdependent components. For me, the primary curriculum essentially is concerned with:

1   The acquisition of the basic skills in numeracy and literacy. These form a necessary framework for,
2   An enquiry based programme of education in which the skills acquired in the first component assist as tools in the process of learning and are themselves increased, modified and adapted by their application to meaningful activities by pupils. These activities in Douglas Barnes' (1976:148) terms should be geared to suit the 'interests and purposes' of the pupils.

Possession of the first is the right of every pupil. It is the duty of every teacher to ensure that every pupil has sufficient opportunity to develop fluency in them. This is not to be interpreted as a requirement for every pupil to succeed in the acquisition of skills, especially to the exclusion of all other educational activities. As already stated, though separate, the two components are interdependent.

Translated into practical terms, it seems reasonable that primary pupils should have varying degrees of fluency in handling number bonds, in the four rules of number; they should be familiar with positional and relational values in notation – for example, 5 is between 4 and 6, standing at 9, 6 is 3 in that direction (minus) and so on, moving either way in steps of 3 from 12 gives . . . etc.; they should be developing a fluency in their tables and an ability to interchange decimals, percentages and simpler appropriate fractions; they should be growing more familiar with units of measurement, weights, length, time, volume, capacity, area, etc.. A better and fuller description can be found in DES (1979) *Maths 5–11*.

Literacy skills include such activities as developing fluency in phonetics, word recognition, word building, letter clusters, initial sounds and blends, the identification, understanding and learning of 'content' words in reading passages prior to the actual reading task. They need opportunities for extending their vocabularies through discussion and natural or contrived experiences. Other skills are to be found in spelling exercises which highlight the different families of words, that emphasize similarities and meanings in word structures. Reading skills should fulfil different aims, for example, enjoyment, skimming for information, reading for understanding. Handwriting has its place alongside creative writing.

The two lists are obviously incomplete, they can only briefly indicate the flavour of what is involved. What is done with those skills, however, is more problematic in practice. In the second

IMPLICATIONS FOR IN-SERVICE EDUCATION 81

component, I indicated that enquiry based learning, geared to serving the interests and purposes of pupils, should predominate.

Enquiry is deliberately distinguished from discovery here. Enquiry involves active participation. Discovery, in contrast, has passive overtones in which pupils discover or not from the evidence before them. Manipulating the evidence does not necessarily lead to direct discovery but it does involve a deliberate intention to pose questions of the evidence. The choice is between verification of data or acceptance of data, between interactive learning or passive learning.

How free are pupils to be in their enquiries? It would be wholly unrealistic, indeed irresponsible for teachers to put the onus for their education on the pupils, to leave them countless open-ended opportunities to enquire into whatever took their fancy without any guidance. That is not what is being advocated. Rather, in such a curriculum model, the teacher's role is to define the parameters of a selected study area (for example, school pond, postal services, jewellery making), previewing and becoming familiar with the possibilities in it. The varying pathways of investigation within those parameters, however, are open for interpretation by the pupils. They are more likely themselves to adapt the work to suit their own interests and purposes. The teacher now becomes the manager of education rather than a transmitter of educational content, a facilitator, resource agent, collaborative researcher with the pupils.

In these conditions it will be easier for pupils to draw more readily on the values of their own cultural backgrounds. These are the values that all pupils bring to school with them. Unfortunately, schools find all too often that they cannot fully capitalize on these values especially when they are heavily engaged in the process of transmitting a school-selected body of knowledge which, in the school's opinion, has intrinsic worth. Only in the area of skills acquisition is transmission suitable as the dominant mode of teaching. It is in the varying viewpoints between pupils and schools on what things have intrinsic worth that there is likely to be found a degree of mis-match, for they involve value judgements.

Within the school any such dissonance is likely to be resolved in favour of the school's cultural values rather than the pupil's. In this way the school is exercising judgement and a judgement which finds pupil's cultural values wanting is not exactly complimentary to those values and, by implication, it is not complimentary to the pupils either. In Carl Rogers' (1954) terms it does not create that psychologically safe environment which enhances self-actualization or achieving one's potentials. He listed three associated conditions necessary for this to occur:

1 Accepting the individual as of unconditional worth. (78)
2 Providing a climate in which external evaluation is absent. (79)
3 Understanding empathetically. (80)

The conditions likely to encourage pupils to realize their potentials are not met where judgement as described above exists. If education is essentially about self-actualization, wherein lies the value of a school's work that actively prevents it?

It was attempting to overcome this problem that led to my adopting the second component of the curriculum as the necessary prerequisite for education in the primary school. In an earlier work (Davies, 1973), I described this in practical terms, drawing on a five week project with forty third year juniors. The following is a brief resume of it.

A small group of pupils were trying to write an opera about Henry VIII. A Lebanese girl had brought some very large medallions and cheap metal jewellery from her former home. This was thought to be ideal for the costume props. Unfortunately there was not enough to go round. It was suggested that they might make some of their own at school, which raised the question of working with metals. When asked, it was evident that few had much experience or understanding of such skills. One boy said his dad was a welder. (He was to prove very useful in the later stages of the project.) It was made clear that, beyond opening a tin of beans, their teacher had no expertise to offer them in the field of metals.

Before attempting to manufacture the artefacts it was suggested that it might be profitable to know more about the types and qualities of different metals, their cost and how easy it would be to obtain them in sufficient quantities. Such knowledge would assist in making the final decisions. This approach emphasizes science as the servant of technology, informing and restricting it by the application of the natural scientific laws discovered. In schools with pupils from wide cultural backgrounds, it is preferable to a study of science as a body of knowledge, isolated from practical applications, for in this sense its main value is directed towards serving those middle class cultures that generally operate on the principle of deferred gratification – that is, passing examinations in order to succeed in later life. Evidence shows that the majority of pupils in schools do not come within this category and that instant gratification is their preferred mode. This condition was more closely met in the work described here.

When asked to identify different metals the pupils came up with: tin, iron, copper, brass, lead, gold, silver, platignum and aluminium. One of the girls informed us of a local metal dealer who proved to be

IMPLICATIONS FOR IN-SERVICE EDUCATION

very sympathetic to the project. He supplied, at very low cost, a wide variety of metals in different shapes and sizes: rod, sheet, gauze, block and strip of every metal previously mentioned (not precious) plus zinc, bronze, nickel and magnesium from a war-time incendiary bomb. (Lovely for firework effects.)

A copy of Schools Council (1972) *Science 5–13:Metals* was at hand. This the pupils dipped into, working on topics that either appealed to them or that seemed to offer insights that could be applied to their needs. The aims and objectives, comprehensively provided in later editions, were fortunately unobtainable. In their work the pupils defined for themselves their own levels of development without the need for the teacher to limit their work to a falsely imposed formula. Their enthusiasm and cross talk deepened and extended their conceptual understanding, while the motivation driving them had its roots in being allowed to interpret the work according to their own or their group's particular interests. The work spilled over into their homes and their homes into the school. Parents came in to demonstrate welding. They contributed to a temporary collection of metal articles. They came and worked with pupils. They took groups on exploratory visits to collect evidence of metals being used in the local environment. The evidence of parental involvement in the finished artefacts in my view only enhanced their educational value; it did not detract from them.

The entire scope of *Science 5–13:Metals* was covered: corrosion, elasticity, malleability, hardness, joining, heat and electrical conducting properties, expansion, polishing and magnetism. From an informed position, they produced an astonishing variety of metal artefacts which went far beyond meeting the original requirements of costume jewellery – an all metal electric toy car, decorative wall plaques, a fish-paste jar light-house, some mobiles, an electric buzzer game for Open Day, a door opening (headmaster) alarm, a perpetual-motion magnet driven car, necklaces, rings, pendants, brooches and ear-rings in a profusion of shapes, different metals and combinations with other materials, shiny and dull, chased, beaten and otherwise worked upon or joined together.

Accompanying all this work were many folders containing analyses of procedures and results, tables and graphs displaying relationships, data on physical and chemical properties, the geographical location of deposits, the influence of metals in history. There were numerous collections of experiments executed on crude home-made equipment but answering pertinent questions nevertheless.

The amount of work generated in language development, writing and researching in other books was enormous and purposeful. They had to interpret charts to obtain data. They were involved in a variety of forms of measurement, often having to devise their own measuring instruments. They needed to demonstrate an understanding of the outcomes or applications of their work in order to convince others to get their work accepted as relevant to the aims of the project. Putting it kindly, the opera was a mild success in comparison.

The Primary Curriculum/Micro Interface

To what extent do micros detract from or serve to enhance the two components of the curriculum described in the section above? The ways in which they are used in schools can broadly be categorized under three headings:

1. They can be used for learning about computers, how they work and their application to other things.
2. They can be used for learning with computers. Rushby (1980:11) isolated four styles, three of which usefully describe this category:
    a) Tutorial. Drill and practice in the basic skills.
    b) Simulations. Analogue of real world systems (that is, analogies of real world situations.)
    c) Modelling. Analogue constructed by pupils (that is, analogies representing certain aspects of world as they see it.)
3. They can be used for learning to program computers, or replicate, improve or expand existing programs.

Critchfield (1976:13) interpreted these categories more fully in her 'Taxonomy of Educational Computing'. Her list of categories is divided into two modes which are summarized as follows:

A in the Dual Mode

1. The constraints operating on pupils are the program designer's concepts of a subject and the ways of learning. (Therefore the program designer needs to be an educator.)
2. Minor programming skills are required by the pupil. Major skills are required by the program encoder. (But not necessarily the program designer.)
3. a) Author-directed computing mainly emphasizes:
    Drill and practice.
    Testing and recording.

IMPLICATIONS FOR IN-SERVICE EDUCATION

b) Learner-directed computing mainly emphasizes:
Decision making through simulations.
Game playing.
Information retrieval (processing).

B in the Solo Mode

1 The constraints operating on pupils are limited to the capability of the machine and the pupil's own imagination and skills.
2 Increasing program encoding skills are required of pupils. Guidance and similar skills are required of the teacher.
3 a) 'Hands on' computing emphasizes writing or encoding programs and/or 'debugging' existing programs.
   b) Learner organized computing includes all those skills in Modes 'A' and 'B' above. Mainly it is concerned with programming for the needs of others (implying the inclusion of Systems Analysis).

Combining the initial three categories above with Critchfield's Taxonomy, plus other items included in the description of micros above, the following list of computer uses in school emerges:

1 Drill and practice
2 Testing and recording.
3 Simulations.
4 Games.
5 Programming.
6 Modelling or information retrieval/processing through DATA BASES.
7 School administration.

Having isolated the possible uses, we are now able to examine their interactions within the framework of the curriculum as described above.

1 Drill and Practice

'Sums' by Morgan in *Computer Age* No. 12 (1980:27–28) – Morgan says in his program description that large numbers of children with a wide range of ability make the marking of arithmetic a tedious and time consuming task for teachers. It is also prone to occasional errors – 'The situation is crying out for a degree of automation'. Drill and practice are still considered to be one effective way of gaining fluency in the mechanical skills of numeracy. Number work, for example, learning the four rules on a computer, can be more interesting and a lot more fun for pupils than perhaps the more traditional methods. With a machine, failure on the part of the pupil is a private affair between the pupil and the computer. It is not so exposed to a more public audience. This encourages a pupil to try again with less embarrassment. His work is then, in Carl Rogers' terms, focused on an internal locus of evaluation (76) and is thereby non-threatening. A further advantage is contributed by the intimate and informal quality of the program itself. An example of a computer RUN that I adapted from Morgan's program will illustrate this more fully. In the following example, only the first and last responses are given. The first illustrates the worst condition obtainable, the last shows the exit procedure. (Note. The '?' is this particular machine's way of prompting the user to make a response – it does not always imply a question.)

SUMS

```
HI, WHAT'S YOUR NAME?   HANNAH
OK HANNAH, WHAT KIND OF SUMS DO YOU WANT
1   ADDITION   ADD   PLUS                           +
2   SUBTRACTION   TAKE AWAY MINUS                   –
3   MULTIPLICATION   TIMES                         * ×
4   DIVISION   SHARING                              /
CHOOSE 1, 2, 3 OR 4 AND TYPE IT IN? 6
OOPS! YOU GOOFED HANNAH
CHOOSE 1, 2, 3 OR 4 AND TYPE IT IN? 3
FINE! DO YOU WANT THEM TO BE
1   EASY
2   HARD
3   VERY HARD
CHOOSE 1, 2, OR 3 AND TYPE IT IN? 2
```

```
RIGHT, HERE ARE SOME HARD MULTIPLICATION
SUMS FOR YOU HANNAH.
I WILL GIVE YOU TEN SUMS. IF YOU GO
WRONG, DON'T WORRY. YOU WILL GET THREE
GOES AT IT. AFTER THAT, I WILL TELL
YOU THE ANSWER AND WE CAN GO ON TO THE
NEXT SUM. I WILL GIVE YOU YOUR SCORE
AFTER EACH SUM AND THE TOTAL OUT OF
TEN AT THE END.
    (TO CONTINUE, PRESS ANY KEY ...)
```

```
HERE WE GO THEN HANNAH.
1   9 × 6 = ?   15
```

IMPLICATIONS FOR IN-SERVICE EDUCATION

```
OH BOY! YOU'RE KIDDING!
TRY AGAIN HANNAH
1  9 × 6 = ?  45
DON'T MUCK ABOUT!
TRY AGAIN HANNAH
1  9 × 6 = ? DON'T KNOW
HEY! YOU ARE ONLY ALLOWED TO GIVE
NUMBERS HANNAH.
NEVER MIND, LET'S SKIP THAT ONE.
THE ANSWER WAS 54
(A few bars of the 'Death March' are optional here.)
YOUR SCORE IS 0
```

```
10  8 × 7 = ? 56
(A few bars of 'Dixie' are optional here.)
GREAT YOUR SCORE IS 8
OUT OF TEN SUMS YOU GOT 8 RIGHT.
WELL DONE HANNAH.
YOU MIGHT LIKE TO CHOOSE HARDER SUMS
NEXT TIME. DO YOU WANT TO PLAY AGAIN (Y/N)? N
BYE THEN HANNAH.
SEE YOU AGAIN SOON I HOPE.
```

The casual use of the pupil's name, the chatty style and use of the word 'play' suggests that it is a fun activity. Though they tend to advertize success or failure and intrude upon the class the melody routines are nevertheless very popular with pupils.

This program could easily be adapted for use as a group activity with each entering their name and taking a turn. Similar programs on number bonds for instance have proved to be stimulating by the addition of gaming techniques – for example, 'Hangman' in glorious technicolour. Again it is suitable for individuals or groups. Graphical point scoring techniques can be employed in a number of mechanical skill or fact learning situations. It is limited to the teacher's imagination in adapting them to the desired content of the curriculum.

Other programs are suitable for use with very young pupils too – for example, number, letter, shape or colour matching games are some that I have written and tested quite successfully with pre-school children. In these games practically no supervision is required. Frequently another youngster will intervene to get things going again if the user gets stuck.

This aspect of children learning from and with other children is not without significance. The trouble might be to stop informal assistance from becoming dominance. This can reduce the intended user's role to that of a passive observer. The greatest advantage of computer assisted learning is in its *interactive* qualities, a quality that would be denied to a passive observer.

Many of the literacy skills are suited to a degree of automation. Spelling lists can be stored in the computer either by the teacher or pupils. These would probably be entered as INPUT DATA statements – for example, using the LEFT $ and RIGHT $ functions, the spellings could be practised as an 'I Spy' game with points or graphical scoring.

Programs to reinforce the learning of prefixes, suffixes, initial blends are simple to construct. The computer asks pupils to add an appropriate ending to the prefix given. It then prints the completed word for them to judge whether it makes sense. This is a group or individual activity, but greater value comes from pupils sharing their interpretations in groups.

Dealing more directly with nouns and verbs is an amusing little program by Larry Press (1976:202) called 'Insult'.

```
RUN
HEY STUPID! WHAT'S YOUR NAME ANYHOW?
? LARRY
RIGHT THEN LARRY
WHAT'S YOUR FAVOURITE NOUN?
? COW
IT FIGURES!
SO, WHAT'S YOUR FAVOURITE VERB
? PAINT
SAY LARRY, HOW WOULD YOU LIKE
TO PAINT A COW?

(TO CONTINUE, PRESS ANY KEY . . .)
```

A program that makes much greater use of 'content' words and is suitable for juniors is David Ahl's (1976:272) adaptation of 'Mad-Lib Stories'.

```
RUN
WE ARE GOING TO MAD-LIB OR MAKE UP A
FUNNY STORY TOGETHER. YOU SUPPLY THE
WORDS, I SUPPLY THE PLOT.
FIRST I NEED TEN NOUNS. THESE ARE THE
NAMES OF THINGS LIKE FROG, CAKE, ETC.
1   ? FROG
2   ? CAKE
```

3 ? DOOR KNOB
4 ? TURNIP
5 ? JELLY
6 ? NAIL
7 ? BIKE
8 ? SCHOOL
9 ? BALL
10 ? BUCKET
OK, NOW GIVE ME TEN ADJECTIVES. THESE
DESCRIBE WHAT THINGS ARE LIKE.
E.G. RED, NASTY, WOBBLY, ETC.
1 ? RED
2 ? NASTY
3 ? WOBBLY
4 ? SILLY
5 ? BEAUTIFUL
6 ? NICE
7 ? TWISTED
8 ? CRACKED
9 ? BURNT
10 ? TORN
FINE. NOW FIVE ADVERBS. THESE DESCRIBE
HOW THINGS ARE DONE. E.G. BADLY, STIFFLY,
SUDDENLY (HINT! THEY OFTEN END IN 'LY').
1 ? BADLY
2 ? STIFFLY
3 ? SUDDENLY
4 ? QUICKLY
5 ? SLOWLY
HOW ABOUT TWO BOY'S NAMES?
1 ? GEORGE
2 ? ADAM
AND A GIRL'S NAME?
? MARY
AND SOMEONE'S SURNAME (LAST NAME)?
? THOMPSON
AND TWO PLACE NAMES?
? AXMINSTER
? WATERSHIP DOWN
NOW A KIND OF LIQUID
? COCA COLA
AND FINALLY A COUPLE OF EXCLAMATIONS LIKE
GEE WHIZZ!
1 ? GEE WHIZZ!
2 ? HELLS BELLS!

GREAT! THAT JUST ABOUT DOES IT.
NOW. WHAT WOULD YOU LIKE
1   ? A NEWSPAPER ADVERTISEMENT
2   ? A WESTERN STORY
3   ? A STORY ABOUT THE ARMY
4   ? A STORY ABOUT A WATER-BED
CHOOSE, 1, 2, 3 OR 4 AND TYPE IT IN? 1

EXPRESS AND ECHOE SMALL ADS.
FOR SALE. 1966 SALOON CAR. THIS RED
CAR IS IN A NASTY CONDITION. IT WAS
OWNED BY A WOBBLY TEACHER WHO ALWAYS
DROVE IT BADLY. THERE IS A SILLY
FROG ON THE BONNET. IT HAS A BEAUTIFUL
COLOUR SCHEME, NICE TYRES AND THE BACK
OPENS INTO A TWISTED CAKE.
WILL CONSIDER TAKING A SLIGHTLY USED
DOOR KNOB IN TRADE.

LOST. IN THE VICINITY OF AXMINSTER,
A CRACKED POODLE WITH BURNT HAIR AND A
TORN TAIL. IT ANSWERS TO THE NAME OF
GEORGE. WHEN LAST SEEN IT WAS CARRYING
A RED TURNIP IN ITS MOUTH.
A NASTY REWARD IS OFFERED.

WANT ANOTHER STORY (Y/N)? Y
SAME WORDS (Y/N)? Y
CHOOSE 1, 2, 3 OR 4 AND TYPE IT IN? 2
   ... etc.

The other three stories in the program make use of all the variables (the words INPUT by pupils) in turn, using the DATA ... READ instruction. They can be selected randomly but many of the words then get omitted while others are repeated too frequently. Some of the stories generated in this way can descend well below the vernacular. To the pupils, the machine appears to participate willingly in this 'illicit' behaviour. Even without lewd elements the results can be and often are hilarious. Pupils have been seen with tears of laughter streaming down their cheeks which is not so general an occurrence when working through their school primers. Such extraordinary emotional responses are a powerful motivation for others. The same enthusiasm follows the computer into other areas of the curriculum too.

One observed outcome with 'Mad-Lib' was the desire by pupils to compile lists of words for later use with the program. They swap

IMPLICATIONS FOR IN-SERVICE EDUCATION

words with each other like football cards. The prepared lists speed things up so they get to the stories quicker.

Larry Press' (1976:203) 'Poem Generator' reveals a more creative side to the computer, extending the pupil's use of vocabulary. Here is a short descriptive extract:

```
TO WARM UP, TRY PLAYING WITH COLOUR WORDS.
FOR EXAMPLE, WHAT COLOUR DO YOU THINK OF
WHEN I SAY APPLE? GREEN. HOW ABOUT SKY?
BLUE. YOU KNOW, YOU DON'T ALWAYS HAVE TO USE
THE REAL COLOUR OF SOMETHING IN A POEM.
YOU CAN USE ANY COLOUR YOU FEEL LIKE EVEN
IF IT SEEMS FREAKY OR SILLY. IF YOU
DON'T COUNT RED OR GREEN, WHAT COLOUR
SEEMS LIKE APPLES? SILVER. CLOSE YOUR
EYES AND SEE IF YOU CAN IMAGINE A BIG
SILVER APPLE. SEE IF YOU CAN MAKE IT
GROW OR DANCE OR DO SOMETHING SILLY.
JUST TYPE 'OK' WHEN YOU ARE FINISHED.
? OK
THINGS LIKE APPLES ARE NOT THE ONLY
THINGS THAT MAKE PEOPLE THINK OF COLOURS.
FOR EXAMPLE, JOHN THOUGHT THAT THE
SOUND OF A CAR ENGINE WAS SCRATCHY RED.
WHAT COLOUR IS THE SOUND OF A WHISTLE.
? BRIGHT BLUE.
THE WHISTLE SOUNDS BRIGHT BLUE. TRY
MAKING THE SOUND OF A BALLOON POPPING.
WHAT COLOUR IS THAT? ORANGE ... etc..
```

The program goes on to use first, short descriptive words and, later, whole sentences INPUT by the pupil to create poetry.

Summarizing those aspects of skills acquisition through Drill and Practice suited to automated learning techniques we could perhaps envisage:

Matching skills.

Positional and relational notation.

Four rules in number.

Tables of numbers and measures, and equivalents in other forms.

Lists of formulae.

Rules in mathematics, language and science.

Lists of facts and figures constructed and INPUT by pupils and teachers.

Sorting information alphabetically or numerically.
  Spelling lists,
  word families by sound, meaning or association,
  letter clusters,
  initial or ending blends,
  dipthongs and digraphs,

Content words in reading schemes to accompany pictures in books.

Punctuation exercises.

Poem and story generators to extend vocabularies.

Experimentation in your own school and contacts with others will reveal many more applications as you become more experienced. Develop the habit of sharing with other schools and getting feedback on your programs.

2 Testing and Recording Progress

This is closely allied to 'Drill and Practice' in many ways though not exclusively so. The computer, if so programmed, can keep a record of the score logged against the pupil's name. This can be either as a one off record or a cumulative one and in a number of different subjects, giving a record of progress over a period of time. The total scores can be averaged and possibly 'norm-referenced' with the rest of the class or year/ability group. (If that sort of thing turns you on.)

3 Simulations

Generally these are exercises in logic. A large number of them is numerically based, 'Hamurabi' (Apple contributed program) being an interesting example in question. The program begins by defining the parameters of the game:

  20 BUSHELS OF GRAIN REQUIRED PER PERSON ANNUALLY.
  $\frac{1}{2}$ BUSHEL OF SEED REQUIRED PER ACRE.
  10 ACRES PER PERSON MAX FOR WORKING.

The new Hamurabi (player) is initially allotted a store of 2500 bushels of grain, 1000 acres and a population of 95. At this point he is told of his harvest yield, how much was eaten by rats, the change in his population and the trading price of land in bushels per acre.

IMPLICATIONS FOR IN-SERVICE EDUCATION 93

Within that equation and the given parameters he must decide on how much land he wishes to buy or sell, how much grain to feed the tribe and how much seed to plant. A RUN produces this kind of outcome:

YEAR 1

LAND TRADING AT 26 BUSHELS PER ACRE
RATS ATE 0 BUSHELS
ACRES TO BUY? 0
ACRES TO SELL? 12
2812 BUSHELS IN STORE
988 ACRES OWNED
95 POPULATION
BUSHELS TO FEED? 1990 (i.e. pop. × 20)
822 BUSHELS IN STORE
ACRES TO PLANT? 950 (i.e. pop. × 10)
YEAR 2
HARVEST YIELD = 1 BUSHEL PER ACRE
LAND TRADING AT 19 BUSHELS PER ACRE
RATS ATE 0 BUSHELS
1297 BUSHELS IN STORE
988 ACRES OWNED
95 POPULATION

Not a happy position from hereon in. What with the variable size of population, the rats, the variable price of land and the harvest yield it is easy to end up as an 'Imperialist Pig' or be impeached and thrown out of office branded as a 'National Fink'. Other numerically based simulations that quickly come to mind are 'Boat Race' and 'Ski Jump'.

The one thing that is often missing from these programs is graphics. People like to see where they are and what is around them. Even the addition of bar graphs in 'Hamurabi' would have added greatly to its impact as well as giving pupils valuable experience in interpretation. The popular machines of today tend to handle graphics rather well, some in brilliant colours. In primary schools, graphics have an important function to 'play'.

An example that does use graphics well and is not so heavily number oriented can be found in 'Saxon Settlement' if my memory servies me well. It is obtainable from the Grimsby LEA. and is a program from their Humberside Project. In it, pupils have to make decisions from the data presented to them, to establish and sustain one of four tribes. War, co-operation, diplomacy and trade are some of the options open to them. The same options are likely to be mirrored in the actual classroom transactions. With the addition of a neutral chairman this in itself could yield fruitful discussions.

Another example along these lines is 'Transpots' from the ITMA Project under the direction of Rosemary Fraser at The College of St. Mark and St. John, in Plymouth. It may be significant that both of these excellent examples were designed by and for teachers.

There is a contribution to Social Education from Sally Richards (1976:211) in which she describes a 'value strategy' game. In this, pupils are given a list of activities which they are asked to grade according to their cost, how frequently they do them, whether they would have done them, say, three years ago, alone or with others and so on. The computer analysis at the end can be very revealing. It then asks the pupils to analyze their reactions to specific outcomes.

4 Games

Within many games are hidden subtle forms of calculations not to mention the more obvious reading requirements. Other gaming activities can involve pupils in working out 'x, y' co-ordinates in a matrix, predictions and developing skills in manual dexterity. Games like 'Space Invaders' have their educational critics. The sharpest reflexes fare best generally but there is more to them than that. They satisfy competitive instincts. Strategies can be worked out that are more beneficial than others, certainly better than having no strategy at all. To youngsters learning to gain control of developing bodies and possessed of a competitive spirit, these attributes are not insignificant when consideration is given to the total being and development of the child in the school.

5 Programming

This activity is not as some may think the prerogative of secondary schools. One five-year-old was delighted with a programme she wrote. It endlessly printed her name on the TV screen. Here is the LISTing:

```
10 ? 'HEATHER' (The '?' is shorthand for 'PRINT')
20 GOTO 10
RUN
```

She frequently repeats the program, sometimes entering other words she has learned, at other times she enters 'keyboard finger-walking' garbage.

An eight-year-old girl wrote a program, notionally to assist with

IMPLICATIONS FOR IN-SERVICE EDUCATION

her tables. She found this LISTing in Dwyer and Critchfield (1978:18):

```
10 ? 'MULT TABLE FOR 9'
20 FOR K= 0 TO 12
30 ? K*9
40 NEXT K
50 END
```

She typed it in and on the command RUN it gave:

```
MULT TABLE FOR 9
0
9
18
.
.
.
99
108
```

She decided she did not like the second line since it was not her practice to include the '0' in her tables. She looked at the LIST and typed:

```
20 FOR K = 1 TO 12
```

She then decided that she wanted the numbers to be listed slowly enough for her to say them as they were printed on the screen so she added a further line:

```
5 SPEED = 0
```

The next time she LISTed the program after a RUN she was taken aback to discover that it LISTed slowly. She typed:

```
50 SPEED = 255
60 END
```

After a RUN it LISTed at normal speed. Then she wanted the program to print the 5 times table. After a brief look at the LIST she typed:

```
30 ?K*5
```

On RUNning that, she counted in fives as fast as she could and had reached 75 when the program stopped at 60. She said she wanted the program to stop at 100, her normal limit when counting in fives. After another searching look at the LIST she typed:

20 FOR K = 1 TO 100

The following RUN took her with some amusement up to 500 in fives. When asked what would be needed to stop the table at 100 she said

    It should be 40.
    T: Why 40?
    G: Because 60 (where the original program stopped) from 100 (the number required) leaves 40.
    T: OK Try it.
    20 FOR K = 1 TO 40

This of course printed fives up to 200

    T: Still too many eh?
    G: Yes
    T: 40 gave 200, but 200 is twice what you want. What do you think?
    G: Hmm! Yes. Ah, I know ...
    20 FOR K = 1 TO 20

This worked out fine for her. One point that needs to be stressed, and that proved to be a surprise for the teacher, was that this was the first formal attempt at programming made by the girl. Her previous experience was limited solely to playing games on the computer and watching older and more experienced people encoding or debugging programs. All the modifications she made were drawn from memory. Her analysis of and amendments to the logic and arithmetical processes were more remarkable for the fact that she was not previously considered to be capable of such a level of understanding.

There seemed to be a link between the process (programming) and the content (tables) in which each element contributed to modifying and deepening understanding. Programming is an attempt to process information but, in processing it, there is a demand for greater clarification of the information itself in order to understand more clearly how the processing shall best be achieved. Even at this basic level, there appears to be a valuable advantage in programming activities and at relatively early ages.

IMPLICATIONS FOR IN-SERVICE EDUCATION

6 Information Retrieval and Processing through DATA BASES

This is a useful function of the computer. It can make a valuable contribution to project work in primary schools. The raw data collected by pupils from their field studies can be fed into the computer and classified under a variety of categories and sub-categories or files, hence DATA FILES.

Handling some aspects of the 'Metals' project described above with DATA FILES could produce this kind of model:

    Main title page:
      Metals
    Main categories:
      1 Kinds of metals.
      2 Costs of metals.
      3 Properties of metals.
      Sub-categories:
      a) Hardness.
      b) Shiny or dull.
      c) Elasticity.
      d) Malleability.
      e) Expansion.
      f) Corrosion, tarnishing.
      g) Joining them together or to each other.
      h) Weight.
      i) Conduction of electricity.
      j) Conduction of heat.
      k) Magnetism.
      l) Colours.
      m) Burning.
      n) Melting.

As pupils begin to feed in more of their data, certain qualities of the different categories can be called up for comparison with one another. Insufficient data may point to the need for more or possibly new categories to be established. From file 2 'Costs', they may then wish to know how much and what kinds of metals are already available in school or easily obtainable from home. A new category could be added:

      4 Metals in stock or available.

This might lead some pupils to ask where they could get further supplies and create yet another file:

5   Suppliers of metals.

and so on. The information fed in becomes interactive with pupils when they explore what they have. It encourages them to pose questions of the accumulating data, directing them towards new fields in the project study area.

The computer can not only assist in designing the shape of the project, defining more clearly its possible parameters, it can also assist in the actual analysis of the results of experiments already established. For example, in attempting to use the information they have on the different properties of metals, they may wish to ask which single metal is shiniest and softest so that they may cut, bend or chase it easily. Calling up files 3a) and b) would indicate which metal scored highest in both these properties. If they concluded from the evidence before them that gold most adequately fulfilled their criteria, it is likely that other comparisons on cost and availability would be needed.

The ability to rank order metals from the hardest to the softest could be handled by the computer's sorting facility. In the actual project, the experiments to establish the different hardness of metals involved squashing a 1/8 inch diameter ball-bearing between two different metals in a vice. The softer metal had the bigger indentation. This had to be done as a permutation with about nine different metals. Longhand it proved to be a tedious task for the pupils and the sorting results were prone to errors.

Working things out longhand tends to limit the number of activities pupils undertake because of the tedium factor. Generally children enjoy pushing buttons. In doing so with the computer, they are able to compare lots of different categories of data at the same time. There is a better chance in this of their discovering relationships that might not otherwise have occurred to them. The computer encourages a 'brainstorming' approach. It accommodates that quality endemic in most children, 'Let's try it and see what happens'.

The development of my first DATA FILE program is still in the embryonic stage. It was inspired by another program by Roy Garland and Bernard Lane described elsewhere in this volume. Their description gives a much fuller account of the value of DATA FILES in promoting project work in primary schools and in a different context.

7   School Administration

A computer will handle many of these functions – for example, time tabling, pupil's records and examination results, school's accounts, staffing, library, meals and inventories, to name but a few. Programs to support these activities can probably be bought off the shelf commercially.

The worrying drawback concerning school administration is the likelihood of the machine becoming too exclusively a part of the administrator's domain, thus denying full opportunity for pupils to take advantage of it. If there is a heavy demand on the machine's time for administrative purposes, a separate machine should be purchased out of appropriate funds, if and when they are available. Otherwise it would be better if such tasks did not take priority over learning tasks. To do so implies to teachers and more importantly to pupils the wrong values of what schools are about.

Trivial or Worthwhile Applications

Computers are sometimes referred to as 'artificial intelligence' machines. The intelligence they have is more apparent than real. A chicken even can outstrip them easily in the arena of decision making. A computer will process any information fed into it without discrimination since it has not the wherewithal to decide on what has worth and what is trivial. In a learning situation, it partially becomes the responsibility of the teacher either to direct which tasks shall be performed or to query the value of tasks pupils are carrying out on the computer.

On discrimination Edward James (Nov. 1980:86–87) in *Practical Computing* says that schools should emphasize the applications aspects of computers in terms relevant to the kind of situation pupils are likely to encounter. Programming, he says, should be seen *essentially* as a means to a purposeful end and not an end in itself. Too frequently he feels that pupils are led directly into programming on fairly trivial subject matter (for example, maths calculations) with not a word by their teachers about the purpose of the program. There can be difficulties in pursuing James' aims in the initial stages of programming. Furthermore, as indicated above, the actual task of programming is often concomitant with the process of learning itself. This, however, does not devalue his overall intentions.

In similar vein David Ahl (1976:6) provides a list of observations on learning which has a bearing on the application of computers in schools. Some are summarized as:

1   Kids learn best from other kids, probably out of school.
2   Text books don't often get stolen.
4   Motivation is more important than teaching style.
7   Learning by discovery, doing it, sticks better than reading it.

8 Learning to learn is more important than learning data

It is possible to take issue with some of Ahl's points. After all, schools do enlarge the opportunities for kids to meet other kids, though I take his implied point. The fact that books are text books is seldom the deciding factor in determining whether they get stolen compared to the interest they generate. On this criterion a large proportion of them are not worth stealing. Motivation can be as much a part of the style of teaching as other factors. What does appear to be emerging is that working with computers is often more enjoyable for pupils than working with teachers and, when that happens, teachers usually find their work more rewarding too. If this point is coupled with working with other kids on the computer, it is a point worth making.

The concept of learning to learn being more valuable than learning a body of knowledge needs qualifying more fully. Those who already possess a body of knowledge, and use it in earning their living, tend to view advocates of this concept as 'wets'. If we are to be professionally responsible as advocates of educational innovation, the case needs to be argued in full. The doctrine 'learning how to learn' as a curriculum specification is not in itself exclusive. It is not that particular doctrine to exclude the learning of a body of knowledge. If it were it would be valueless. A student skilled in the art of learning but possessing no knowledge would be a very odd creature. From experience, it is my view that when pupils learn to become, say, geographers, rather than learning geography, they do, in fact, become knowledgeable in the subject matter itself. The knowledge they have, however, is an informed and tested knowledge based upon relevant aspects of the practical world with which they have had intimate contact. If the knowledge turns out to be somewhat limited it will, in recompense, likely be deeper. This quality could increase their confidence in the subject, leading to a better self-image as 'geographers', leading in turn to a greater commitment to geography as a body of knowledge. This could create a tendency to increase further the breadth of understanding within the discipline. It is those, who emphasize the acquisition of knowledge as the salient issue at stake in education, who themselves are in danger of becoming exclusive. This exclusivity denies access to knowledge for many pupils because too often they see no relevance in possessing it and, therefore, that doctrine becomes counter productive.

Pupil interaction with the computer is an essential element in its use in schools. When pupils interact with teachers they are more likely to be put in a position where the teacher can exercise an element of judgement on them. This external judgement is less

IMPLICATIONS FOR IN-SERVICE EDUCATION

preferred to an internal or self-generated judgement in the continuing development of the child. The way in which computers are used, therefore, needs to be exercised with some sensitivity and demonstrations of computer use by experts to audiences of teachers need to be exercised with even greater sensitivity.

Avoidance of demonstrating the computer as a blackboard or as a work card should be two of the salient points to bear in mind when demonstrating its application in schools to, as yet predominantly uninitiated, teachers. It is wrong to stress these models at the outset. Postman and Weingartner (1969) were highly critical of things like text books, black-boards and work cards for the way in which they facilitated a teacher's control over learning, thereby opening the way to introducing irrelevant knowledge into the curriculum that is unrelated to the interests and purposes of the pupils. The new electronic blackboard can merely replace 'chalk and talk' with 'press and address'. It would also be undesirable to see demonstration programs as the forerunners of a new breed for continuing the 'loneliness of the long distance (electronic) work card!'.

In-Service Training and In-Service Education

There are some, even in high office, who have not yet learned to distinguish between the two. For their sakes the following distinction is put forward.

In-service training can be likened to the first component of the curriculum described earlier. It has been described as manipulating or doing things to teachers. In this mode, teachers are passive recipients of a body of knowledge or transferable skills. It is probably what this book is mostly doing, but INSET (training) generally requires an audience of teachers with a brought/bought in expert. They are then either given a message and sent on their way with the expectation that the message will be translated into practical terms in the classroom (for example, talks on giftedness, Bullock, local history, etc.) or they are given the opportunity to practise certain skills for passing on to pupils, or assisting teachers in other ways (for example, guitar, batik, AVA handling and certain aspects of some 'Science 5–13' courses).

Opportunities to challenge the relevance of the knowledge or to challenge the knowledge itself do not loom large in this mode. Discussions on the implications imbedded in the use or value of the skills contributing to furthering the overall aims of the curriculum are minimal and seldom lead to any significant shift in attitude or performance.

However, those who decry INSET *per se* need to examine more carefully their own position. When teachers try to operate from too narrow a base of knowledge or skill, they are more likely to limit the choice of activities available to pupils. A tightly framed curriculum is then likely to result. There are other side advantages offered by INSET, including professional social contact or building up professional self-images, to name a couple. Havelock (1973:138) discussing this aspect of in-service training refers to 'Marco Polo' teachers. They keep coming home with new 'goodies'. Less kindly it could be said that the 'goodies' are little more than nine day wonders. They seldom result in the discovery of gun-powder.

In-service *education* in contrast to in-service *training* can be likened to the second component of the curriculum. In another context (Davies 1979:18) I used the term INSEED to distinguish it more sharply from INSET, since this term overtly contains the germ of what educational *growth* should acknowledge.

At a wardens' meeting late in 1980, the view was expressed pragmatically that the curriculum development movement is dead. The drawback with pragmatism is that it is only concerned with a workable proposition. That proposition is not necessarily the best one. In this context, is it not a little curious that those charged with the responsibility for the efficient functioning of the service, for encouraging and enabling teachers to adopt classroom innovations which amongst other things emphasize an enquiry-based curriculum or the Plowden philosophy, are generally fairly reluctant to adopt the same philosophy themselves in educating teachers? Up till now there has been too heavy a commitment to INSET at the expense of INSEED and it is this which allows the pragmatist to say that the curriculum development movement is dead. Rather, like Plowden, curriculum development has not really failed, it has never really been tried. Mostly, they have been using all the wrong models.

If the classroom is where changes are to be made, surely that is also where the emphasis of curriculum development should find its expression. Recognition of this fundamental tenet is emerging: from Lawrence Stenhouse (1975) with his 'Teachers as Researchers' model, the Ford project and the fairly recent 'IT: INSET' project of the Open University. There is little documented evidence on the number of local initiatives which have taken this approach but indications are that they are growing.

The subject is too complex for a full explanation here, so at the risk of doing a grave injustice to Stenhouse's comprehensive analysis, suffice it to say that often this approach initially involves teachers accepting a curriculum proposal on provisional trust. (Unless they put forward their own proposal.) Such a proposal, in the terms of this book, would be concerned with computers in the classroom. Secondly, teachers would assess whether the proposal had intelligence for them. This would be gauged in a heuristic way but guided by the assistance of a collaborative outside change agent, adviser, working alongside the teacher for a short period each week. Thirdly, their subjective views on the way they implemented the proposal and the observed outcomes, would be offered for the critical appraisal of their colleagues at a local centre, at fairly regular intervals. The discussions arising from these meetings would either refute the proposal utterly or indicate modifications necessary, either to the proposal or the teaching methods employed. In this way, small accumulative insights could be accommodated into the classroom transactions. Where subjectivity is the keynote in the analyses, the changes brought about will fit the interests and purposes of each unique and individual teacher in the context of each unique and individual classroom.

Attempts to isolate those less attractive or unproductive traits in classroom transactions unaided and alone can be very difficult. This is why offering the work for the critical appraisal by other colleagues is so important and potentially, of course, uncomfortable. To reduce this discomfort it is also essential that the outside collaborator takes an equal responsibility with the teacher for the teaching load. In this way a genuine equality of discourse is more likely to be established between the two. It will also serve to establish the credentials of the outsider as being someone who is prepared to show that he knows what he is on about.

There is greater promise of actual change taking place when INSET and INSEED are seen as two sides of the same coin. They complement each other and any attempt to allow the acquisition of skills, the function of INSET, to dominate, will not lead to any significant 'paradigm shift'. Thomas Kuhn (1962) described this as dissatisfaction in the light of experience with the old beliefs, practices or rules (paradigms) which in our eyes 'no longer define a playable game' (34) and although faced with uncertainty and a host of problems there is faith that the new paradigm offers a better alternative for creating another and more appropriate set of rules. Perhaps the clue to accepting this difficult task lies in the word 'create' – a self-fulfilling activity.

The appropriate tasks for INSET (training) in connection with computers could address themselves to training teachers in computing skills.

> About computers, that is, what makes them tick and how to service or add to their facilities.
>
> About becoming skilled program encoders and computer operators.

About aspects of managing them in schools to maximize their efficient use.

About acquiring skills in the compilation, storage and retrieval of software and add-ons.

The appropriate tasks for INSEED (education) could address themselves to developing a deeper understanding of the ways in which computers are and can be used in schools including:

The theory of applications allied to the theory and practice of education.

The theory of applications allied to society's needs.

The evaluation of current computer practice in meeting the overall aims of the curriculum.

Outlining designs of programs that will give expression to different curriculum aims. These will be for later encoding by a skilled programmer. The programs will then be subjected to detailed evaluation in the classroom with feedback for additional modification or approval.

The sharing of reports or case studies on computer use and outcomes amongst groups of schools in an area (including those schools not equipped with computers).

The establishment of a meaningful channel of communication with commercial providers and national and international bodies concerned with educational computing.

The lists under the above categories are by no means intended as a definitive statement on them. They do, however, serve to indicate the different emphases each has. As part of its function, the latter category implies the need for an Association of Teachers of Educational Computing (ATEC) on similar lines to many other subject associations already in existence. The kind of activities ATEC could promote might usefully include:

Issue of a bi-termly news-sheet along the lines of most good independent user group magazines.

Hosting exhibitions and workshops of software and hardware.

Trying out programs, writing or debugging home-brews and adapting existing programs to user specifications.

Reviewing software and hardware and reporting the outcomes to schools.

Involving themselves in liaison meetings between infant, junior, secondary and HE establishments.

Offering a program copying service.

Building up and being responsible for a software library with loan facilities to schools in the area.

Organizing trips to places of relevant interest and purely social activities.

Seeking to maintain a balance of software applicable to every subject on the syllabi of most schools.

Establishing contacts with commerce, colleges of HE and other LEAs.

Again this list is by no means exhaustive or necessarily prescriptive.

Provision

To what extent the needs of training and education are being met and the provision of hardware and software is being made are not all that easy to judge accurately. There is no, one, national co-ordinating body to which reference can be made.

The central government's position is not very clear. It vacillates between emphasizing either training or assistance with the provision of equipment. For the want of firm evidence to indicate that one policy is preferable to the other, it seems to be coming round to the logical position that it will financially support the provision of hardware on condition that schools commit themselves to a programme of training. The government's desire to promote British private enterprise has led to an, as yet untried, machine being advocated as the only one eligible for a grant. This policy has been received with strong and mixed views by many teachers. There may also be problems concerning the financing of teachers' release for training and finding a sufficient number of computer experts to man the training programs. This can result in cutting back the demands on government provision.

The form of training recommended may or may not include education. Past history indicates it will not be included, which leaves the phenomenon of 'innovation for no change' facing us as a real and expensive possibility of limited value. However, in the early stages, the development of skills through training might have a priority over applications. This, for reasons already stated, has the drawback of teachers trying to operate from too narrow a base of knowledge or skill. To implement a widespread programme of computer in–service education would need a large number of education experts familiar with computers rather than computer experts *per se*. Such numbers are only to be found in the advisory service of LEAs, schools and institutions of HE. It is to these sources that we must turn, as experience develops over the next few years, to implement fully a policy of in-service education that will offer a better chance of changes taking place in schools.

What other sources of provision are there? Apart from an individual school's fund raising and capitation resources and the occasional commercial and industrial competitions, the only obvious remaining providers are the LEAs.

It is well understood that these have hardly enough money to spare for current essentials, let alone additional demands. While it would be nice to think that the central government would give at least part of the money it has set aside for educational computing to the LEAs for them to decide how to spend it to meet local needs, it is unlikely that such a step will be taken. A case for provision by LEAs needs to be made. It might be helpful if this covers both the long and short term benefits that can accrue. Research into this appears to be the remit of the education officers and their staff.

There are other things the LEAs can provide with probably very little extra expenditure. Expertise and encouragement would go some way to meeting needs, for example,

> Using their expertise in negotiating bulk purchasing to reduce the initial cost to schools and affording them some protection from the sharp practices of some suppliers. It would also benefit schools if the savings from bulk purchasing could actually reach them without being eroded by the imposition of 9% on cost handling charges made by some LEAs.
>
> Setting up an advisory service to co-ordinate and inform the ATEC groups and schools.
>
> Re-allocating already existing premises to house a central library and locally dispersed libraries of software.
>
> Providing typing and printing facilities for ATEC newssheets.
>
> Accommodating and encouraging the workshops and exhibitions.
>
> Locating and advertising national events of interest to schools.
>
> Liaising with and seeking opinions from national and international movements in educational computing.
>
> Encouraging and assisting institutions involved in research

IMPLICATIONS FOR IN-SERVICE EDUCATION

and development to use their schools for trials and pilot runs of projects.

Disseminating the outcomes of local individual initiatives (successes and even some aspects of failures).

Encouraging maximum participation in programs of in-service education and training (and learning to differentiate between the two and their functions).

Negotiating free trials and sampling of hardware and software prior to recommending their take up by schools.

Some additional expenditure will be inevitable to make all of this cost-effective. Program encoders are a must. Their task would be to develop programs from specifications submitted by teachers. The successful programs can realize a return on investment in the region of £5 to £10 each when advertised and sold to schools in other LEAs. Programs can be contributed by schools within the LEA on a credit system. These credits can be spent in purchasing other programs from the LEA library. This will in some way encourage schools to write their own finished programs.

The programmers will need the support of technicians to service the schools' hardware at nominal materials cost only. Other tasks might include copying locally produced programs onto tape as requested, making hard copies on paper of tapes or disks submitted by schools, testing and developing peripheral add-ons for machines.

Another possible source of programming lies within the schools themselves. Given the notion that programming should be purposeful and concerned with the needs of society, there is much to recommend pupils writing programs for pupils in other schools. They would have a legitimate audience for their work. In collaborating with the other school they would clearly be able to see the value and applicability of their labours. It would provide the foundation for meaningful self-evaluation. This would most widely be applied to secondary pupils who have passed the initial stages of learning to program.

A final point on provision concerns research and other institutions which are in a position to view the scene nationally and further. These include:

Council of Educational Technology
Universities
N.F.E.R.
Schools Council
C.E.R.I.
British Computer Society
National Computer Centre

and there are others. I have omitted MUSE (Micro Users in Secondary Education) for obvious reasons and MAPE (Micros and Primary Education) for its restricted audience.

These are already making valuable contributions in one way or another to the debate on using computers in schools. What is lacking is a sense of real direction. No one body seems to be charged with the responsibility for disseminating the findings of research or the potentially useful advances being made in any particular area. There is a lack of co-ordination at a national level. Pop into any primary school and see if there is a broad understanding of what computers can offer them. Dig deeper and see if recommendations have reached the members of the staffroom, specifying in practical curriculum terms ways of using the computer to enhance their teaching. It would be pleasant to think that these doubts could be substantially refuted. Until they can, the national bodies should be addressing their energies to deciding how best to bring about this state of affairs and who should shoulder the major responsibility.

Conclusion

Some would have us believe that radical changes caused by the widespread introduction of computers into schools are imminent. In the light of what has gone before there is room to doubt these opinions. Not even a few gowned robots splatting kids with laser beams for running in the corridors! Those teachers who fear they will be replaced by automation should jolly well move over for those who know they cannot.

A more realistic view can perhaps be obtained by looking at past attempts to introduce innovations on a broad educational front. Where, for instance, is 'Junior Nuffield Science'? Alive and doing well in Canada we are told. To what level is 'Science 5–13' being implemented nationally in our primary schools? A very low level indeed according to DES (1978). And what of Plowden? Not a lot, as we have seen.

In a shrinking economy, costs will, of necessity, reduce the impact of any widespread introduction. Indications are that prices are bottoming out now. Further improvements will probably lean more towards providing extra facilities for roughly the same price. Schools wishing to purchase a single bare-bones system – computer, TV monitor, cassette recorder plus supporting software – will be committing something in the region of £750 to £1000 of their resources, depending on the system they choose, with a probable addition of £500 for a disk facility.

For a school with several hundred pupils this leaves unanswered many questions on the wisdom of such an outlay for one piece of equipment. It is not necessarily true, as is sometimes thought, that only one pupil at a time can work with the machine. This is more true probably when they are actually writing programs, but for the purposes of language development, learning basic skills, simulations and project work, group and even class work offers a better alternative. With careful planning it should be possible for the majority of pupils in a two form entry junior or infant school to benefit from using the machine each week.

What is potentially most heartening about micros in the primary schools is the chance they offer to decrease those less attractive situations that can occur in learning the basic skills. They can also make a valuable contribution to project work. They can assist in extending pupils' logic by allowing them opportunities for the formulation and testing of hypotheses. They can broaden the pupils' understanding by giving them a wide selection of data from which to make their decisions. Also, if we are prepared to face it, when micros come into the classroom, education becomes more light hearted and enjoyable for both pupils and teachers and that cannot be a bad recommendation. At least it goes some way to answering the question posed in the opening paragraph. So, in the style of the little five-year-old girl:

```
10 ? "HAPPY COMPUTING."
20 GOTO 10
30 END
RUN
```

References

AHL, D. (1976) 'Mad-Lib: A game.' in AHL, D. (Ed) *The Best of Creative Computing* Vol 1. Morristown N.J., Creative Computing Press.

ALCOCK, D. (1977) *Illustrating BASIC* Cambridge, Cambridge University Press.

BARNES, D. (1976) *From Communication to Curriculum* Harmondsworth, Penguin.

COAN, J. (1977) *Advanced BASIC* Rochelle N.J., Hayden.

CRITCHFIELD, M. (1976) 'Recent trends in Mathematics curriculum research.' in AHL, D. (Ed) *op. cit.*

DAVIES, P. (1973) 'Child generated science.' in BIRD, J. and DIAMOND, D. (Eds) *College Curriculum Science Studies* Nuffield/SSRC Science Teaching Project. University of London, Chelsea College.

DAVIES, P. (1979) *'INSEED: Serendipity'* unpublished M.A.

Dissertation, University of Sussex.

DEPARTMENT OF EDUCATION AND SCIENCE (1978) *Primary Education in England: A Survey by H.M.I.* London, HMSO.

DEPARTMENT OF EDUCATION AND SCIENCE (1979) *Mathematics 5–11: A Handbook of Suggestions* London, HMSO.

DWYER, T. and CRITCHFIELD M. (1978) *Basic and the Personal Computer* Mass., Addison-Wesley.

HAVELOCK, R. (1973) *A Change Agent's Guide to Innovation in Education* Ann Arbor, University of Michigan.

KUHN T. (1962) 'The structure of scientific revolutions.' in WORSLEY, P. (Ed) 2nd edn *Modern Sociology* Harmondsworth, Penguin.

POSTMAN, N. and WEINGARTNER, C. (1969) *Teaching as a Subversive Activity* Harmondsworth, Penguin.

PRESS, L. (1976) 'Computers in the English curriculum.' in AHL, D. *op. cit.*

RICHARDS, S. (1976) 'What do you value?' in AHL, D. *op. cit.*

ROGERS, C. (1954) 'Towards a Theory of Creativity.' in Educational Training and Counselling *A Review of General Semantics* 11 (4).

RUSHBY, N.J. (1980) 'Computer based learning in the UK: The direction of the art.' in Journal of College of Preceptors *Education Today* 30 (3).

SCHOOLS COUNCIL (1972) *Science 5–13:Metals:Stages 1 and 2* (Trial Edition) London, Macdonald Educational.

STENHOUSE, L. (1975) *An Introduction to Curriculum Research and Development* London, Heinemann Educational.

TOFFLER, A. (1970) *Future Shock* London, Pan.

Using Microcomputers across the Curriculum in a Primary School
John Dodridge

A General Introduction

On hearing the news of the invention of the telephone and a friend's remark that 'Now California can speak with Florida', Mark Twain is said to have replied: 'But what has California got to say to Florida?'

This section will look at the applications of the microcomputer both within the classroom and across the curriculum. Although there are no hard and fast boundaries between subjects, nevertheless it is convenient to identify those areas that can gain from using a computer. The humanities, geography and history, call upon large data-bases of information that can enhance, but not replace the conventional library. The computer, as its name implies, was originally a number machine, but it is now a powerful tool in economics and business management. Mathematics can call upon many routines, adding to tasks done by sophisticated pocket electronic calculators. Music is now produced electronically and recorded digitally. Kinetic and op art can call on computers to produce periodic patterns in colour and movement.

The study of encryption or coding becomes even more important in protecting individual and personal freedom gradually being eroded by electronic surveillance in one form or another. And finally, recreational games such as Space Invaders are the motivation behind the persistence of learning that can be capitalized upon for the reluctant pupil. Teaching programs can be made more 'user-friendly' by a conversational style that allows children to put their own names into the computer's memory and at suitable intervals produces what appear to be human responses. The computer is complementary to learning systems that already exist, from the mathematics or reading scheme, to the library of maps or the written-out hymns projected on the hall wall both for readability and in order to save the handing out of individual song-sheets or hymn-books.

Good Housekeeping

All the classical rules of good management apply to machine-oriented learning, and care must be taken to discover the most effective place for the computer. In the entrance hall it is an invitation for all children to participate, but time must also be set aside for the teachers to explore its use in the staffroom. The rejection of programmed learning in the early nineteen-sixties has been replaced by a greater faith in the prospects for classroom learning. There still remains the fear by some teachers of electricity and hesitancy of using even a slide projector, but children are less likely to have had such inhibitions. This is one reason why it is important that careful observations are made of how the children relate to and interact with the computer. The intention in this chapter in looking at program possibilities, is to underline the use of those computer facilities not possessed by other devices, which can be utilized in all stages of microcomputer education.

Language and Communication

The study of 'informatics' and the total nature of communication must, by implication, include the development of language. The understanding of any form of symbolism involves the recognition of consistent patterns in the information given. Learning to read involves the internalization of letters of all shapes and sizes occupying many different positions in space.

People talk to each other in differing ways depending on their relationship. Children use different vocabularies in different circumstances. Children will come to realize that, in talking 'with' a computer, they will not be able to rely on normal body gestures and other clues in human communication.

Spelling is a skill that depends on the repetition and recall of patterns of symbols. A computer can check on spelling by comparing the string of letters put in by the child with the 'proper' spelling which may have alternatives. The use of words can be developed with a bank of synonyms and opposites, and alternative expressions can be encouraged by the recall of useful phrases. Sentence completion can be tested and records kept of performance in the choice and variety of selected words, and the computer can make selections of letters quickly and easily. The English word capable of the greatest number of anagrams is the word 'misrepresentation' (McWhirter and Greenberg, 1978:92). It is a good idea to give the children a likely word for, say, a week to try to find as many different subset words which make sense. The accumulation of crossword possibilities will increase their word-power.

The alphabetic search that the computer uses to find words in a passage of writing is similar to human word-search, but, of course, it cannot recognize the 'shape' of the words. Creativity in writing might be encouraged by the use of a data bank of key words. In formal poetry a range of rhyming words could prove very useful and in older poetry forms such as the Japanese 'Haiku', the English sonnet form or the 'limerick', could be stored.

Structure in a Language

The idea of a 'machine' for carrying out operations either on words, numbers, or sentences can be used in all areas of the curriculum. The 'match-box' model of a computer with the information stored in each tray can be used to demonstrate both the steps needed in doing a sum and also the break-down of a sentence into its component parts. Strings of single words used in primitive communication have a simple form, but as soon as branches and relationships multiply, as in the syntax of developed language, then a considerable amount of computer memory is needed.

The readability of a book can quickly be measured by the children using one of a variety of formulae that the computer will work out.

The learning of French, even in its early stages, requires many different ending to verbs and these, combined with tenses and masculine and feminine nouns, involve some very complex patterns of thought. The computer may enable us to learn more about children's use of language.

Mathematics

Whilst many primary teachers are likely to equate mathematics with work in number, mathematics is treated separately since it is here that the possibilities of help in the curriculum are greatest.

Many of the major developments in Primary Mathematics over the last twenty-five years are not easily understood by the non-specialist. There are relics of many movements, ranging from the 'practical' classroom of the nineteen-thirties to the Nuffield Guides of the mid-60s, later to be incorporated in the current work-card and work-book schemes that sometimes degenerate into a treadmill of silence. One of the weaknesses of the text-book approach lies in the inherent cultural lag (Wilder, 1978:170). The delay between conception of the author's plan and subsequent publication ensures that the piecemeal appearance gives the children a patchwork of mathematical ideas.

Sorting into sets is a necessary fundamental human and, therefore, mathematical activity. Instructions in some of the activities with attribute blocks can be given by the computer but one must be careful not to exaggerate the qualities of computers in learning. The computer can show the major methods of sorting using Venn, Carroll and Tree diagrams and their interrelationship and relative efficiency. Function machines can both indicate the idea of what a transformation is and the nature of chains of operations as in the attribute-difference games of Zoltan P. Dienes (Seaborne, 1975:32).

The major problem of two-dimensional presentation lies in the difficulties in trying to copy the three-dimensional world. Television or slide film show photographic images of natural objects but computer shapes are limited in their representation. Newer ideas for measuring area can be shown. The most useful unit for measuring the surface of an orange is the unit triangle, but the majority of books perpetuate the idea of squared paper or grids for area measurement.

As in the paper-folding of, say, a hexagon, the relationship between the triangle as a sixth of the hexagon, as half a rhombus and a third of a trapezium is seen directly. By looking 'inside' a skeleton of a shape a child can see its structure. Tessellations of regular and irregular polygons turned into birds or faces can be shown to cover two-dimensional space as in the work of M.C. Escher (1961).

Graphs of all kinds can indicate the differences in relations. Straight-line graphs originate from linear relationships, parabolas from square relationships and hyperbolas from inverse functions. One of the main advantages of the computer lies in its ability to provide the overall conceptual framework that, if properly programmed, will ensure that there are no gaps left in the child's mathematical experience.

Number

Memorized number relations, bonds and tables can be recalled at a quicker rate than keying the equation into the computer, hence the value of 'mental arithmetic'. The computer is good at generating sums, but it can also keep scores of right and wrong answers and diagnose difficulties.

Visual Images for Number

Structural apparatus is only one aspect of the history of counting devices which should be available to the children – such as rods of proportional length like those of Cuisenaire, Colour-factor and Stern.

Adding lengths gives the result of adding numbers or, in other words, the rods act as an analog computer. A good computer program is capable of showing the relationships between the different images for counting.

Patterns Due to Lay-out

The cycle of ending in the '2 times' table – 2, 4, 6, 8, 0, 2, 4, 6, 8, 0 – is the result of an inherent pattern due to the modular nature of number systems. In later number work, the endings of the square tables – 1, 4, 9, 6, 5, 6, 9, 4, 1, 0, 1, 4 ... can be seen to be 'palindromic', and also they appear in cycles. Such patterns when written down depend on column layout on squared paper. Children calculate sums better in vertical form than horizontal form and so the programmer must ensure lining up of digits on the screen, in order to emphasize place value.

Place-value and Number Bases

Place-value is a principle which involves the operation of grouping. It comes as a surprise to many children to learn that Base 16 (hexadecimal) is more important to the computer expert than Base 2. This emphasizes the need for as early work as possible to Multibase Arithmetic (Cheshire LEA, 1980:24). It can be seen that points on the number line are part of a continuous system and also that the line can be stretched to include other numbers.

Fractions, as points on the number line, can be inserted and seen to be part of the sequence of numbers. Traditional approaches often treat fractions as quite different in nature from whole numbers. Fractions can also be demonstrated as the results of the operation of dividing one number by another. The equivalence of fractions can be animated to indicate that $2/2 = 3/3 = 4/4 = \ldots$, and that $2/3 = 4/6 = \ldots$. The succession of the integers can be 'proved' by generating:

1, 2, 3, 4 ... 21, 22, 23, 24 ... 1001, 1002, 1003, 1004 ....

Calendar patterns can be picked out by the computer for closer inspection and the modular nature of the weekly cycle can be seen to form equivalence classes. If Sundays, for example, in a particular month are 1, 8, 15, 22 then the Mondays are 2, 9, 16, 23, etc..

The different methods of generating magic squares can be compared and explained (Van Delft and Botermans, 1978:86). The nature of leap-years and the cyclic nature of time is shown by those programs that generate calendars and also calculate the weekdays on which children were born. (The number patterns of Pascal's famous Triangle are given as Example 5.1 in appendix.)

Numbers missing within a sequence can be checked against the correct answer. In this way children can both explore the nature of number and, at the same time, acquire the necessary basic number skills. (An example of a semi-open-ended investigation is given in the 'Seaweed numbers' of Example 5.2 in appendix.)

Puzzles and Secret Information

> It is only by observing carefully what children do in problem-solving situations that we can come to realize the degree of high-level thinking of which they are capable. The roles of trial-and-error and of insight vary with the type of problem and possibly with the characteristics of the solver but observable behaviour can only be significant when the intellectual weighting of the problem matches the children's thinking. (Robinson, 1979:25)

The computer offers such a learning situation where the child is interacting with the display and is able to match his intellectual skills.

Alcuin of York published a booklet called 'Problems for the Quickening of the Mind' in which he gave the puzzle of the Wolf, the Goat and the Cabbage. The ferryman in order to transport them across the river was constrained by the wolf's hatred of goats and the goat's fondness for cabbages since the ferry could only hold one item at a time. How did he carry them across the river? Although this puzzle was posed in 775 AD, it still recurs in the many puzzle books that can be translated into suitable computer form.

Secret Information

The use of codes during times of war has always been a subject of extreme importance for safety, and electronic surveillance is part of the background of modern warfare. This scrambling of messages has come to be known as 'encryption' – the two main methods being substitution and transposition. An example of the latter was the Spartan 'scytale' of 450 BC which entailed the helical winding of parchment around a cylinder. The message written on it required an identical cylinder for the decoding. Braille is an example of a substitution cipher. The game of 'Hangman' involves attempts to uncover a hidden word.

Passports in the reign of Louis XIV were coloured according to the country of origin. Ambassadors carried a circular one if under twenty-five, an elliptical one if twenty-five to thirty and octagonal from thirty to forty-five. Special lines under the man's name gave a description – wavy parallel lines meant that he was tall and thin whilst other variations showed that he was tall, fat or short (Beal, 1973:56). Punched cards with large holes can be used for storage of information for children to use in class surveys (Young, 1972:42).

Bar codes on goods in a supermarket are a way of transmitting secret information which can also include stock levels and price increases. In a similar way children can identify their own programs by labelling them using their own name. They can also protect the use of their programs by introducing hidden control characters into the title only known by them. Such control symbols would need to be remembered by the user and convenient ones would include initials, date of birth (for example, 1972), or number of their house. A program labelled 'Caroline' could have these letters hidden anywhere along the string. The teacher, of course, would have the unlocking program to discover the keys!

Science, Geography and History

Science

One of the major contributions of Linnaeus was the idea of a binary classification of living things (for example, Homo Sapiens). He proposed that each plant and animal should have a generic and a specific name and that they could be grouped into families according to common characteristics – for example, colour of flowers, number of petals and sepals and so on. The program called 'Animals' is an interactive one that 'learns' from the wrong and right answers that are fed in successively, again using the yes-no binary-search method in a similar way to popular flower dictionaries.

The majority of impressions gained through touch, smell, hearing and sight and sound cannot possibly be reproduced by any mechanical device. The important scientific process of making hypotheses, then investigation, followed by generalization cannot be carried out by the computer.

Electronics

There is now a number of reliable and well-produced kits for micro-electronics and it is not a daunting task to show very simple logic circuits. The Ladybird book *How it Works – The Computer* provides a very good introduction (Carey, 1979). The clear illustrations indicate the main components of Arithmetic Unit, Processor and Memory. For the very skilful ten-year-old there are more complicated circuit layouts in *Adventures in Electronics* (Duncan, 1978:9).

The outlet ports or the game paddle sockets of microcomputers can be used in control technology and the computer programmed to operate the sequence of a set of traffic lights.

The more ambitious electric train layouts use a microprocessor control for addressing individual locomotives on the same track. Alternative interactive systems use light pens for their input control and the understanding of the nature of photo-sensitive cells can be acquired through this real life practical application.

Geography and History

In producing maps and diagrams, lines can represent rivers and railways and areas can represent mountains. On the map of a country the major towns can be indicated by dots. A simple overlay of tracing paper can be used by the children to put their answers on as a cheap permanent record or 'hard copy'. The game of 'Treasure Island' is invaluable as an introduction to both co-ordinate map-references and compass bearings (see Example 7.1 in appendix).

Once the main structure of a quiz is worked out, then the questions and multichoice or specific answers can be put as data statements at the end of the list of the program instructions.

On both the pictorial and statistical sides in history and geography, block and line graphs can be plotted accurately and quickly. Children can be encouraged to access large data-bases in imaginative programs in history. A typical program is that of the census of 1851 of Welsh Row, Nantwich, Cheshire which enables the children to derive occupations, ages, surnames and other interesting social facts from the last century (Crookall, 1980:14). 'Disraeli and the Eastern Question' is a good example from the Schools Council of role-playing in History.

Art and Computer Music

'Painting by numbers' is a technique which is, in its simplest form, the carrying out of instructions to put colours in pre-determined patterns. In a similar way, this can be done with many picture routines in microcomputer programs.

If a graph is drawn line by line and the points placed by tabulation at calculated intervals to give a picture scrolling downwards, then the illusion is of a composite picture but the minimum line width limits the quality of the picture – as in the somewhat coarse definition of some of the Snoopy calendars.

Drawing a picture by hand is very much easier, cheaper and quicker than trying to persuade a computer to do the same job, quite apart from the aesthetic pleasure. What then has the computer to offer apart from being an expensive crayon?

The computer can reproduce identical pictures very rapidly and there may come a time when it may be easier and cheaper to store pictures for support, work-cards or related research documents in the computer rather than in other forms.

Animation

If each point in space in a vector display is operated on by a triple matrix, the picture can be changed at about five times a second, giving an illusion of movement. An excellent example of this is the 'flight simulator' of the Apple II in which the computer user is in the cockpit of a World War I Sopwith 'Camel' flying at about 60 mph over a 'world' represented by a six by six grid of 10 mile squares (Artwick, 1980:1).

The speed of screen refresh is made possible by the clever use of two pages of high-resolution graphics which means that one page can be up-dated in memory in a similar way to the cartoons of Walt Disney.

Music

Sound recordings are now made digitally and the task of editing tapes is therefore made much easier. Nevertheless, electronic music made by a computer is only a pale reflection of the sound of traditional instruments. The idea of musical notes being related to each other on a mathematical scale, although it is logarithmic, can be conveyed through the idea of numerical frequency. The number of vibrations for Middle C is only half that of the 'C' one octave above it.

There is now a number of exciting programs that allow a tune to be composed in parts for different 'instruments' which can be altered, added to or deleted from the computer file.

Ear training skills can be encouraged through well-devised tests. An appreciation and love of traditional music may come to children who are able to put electronic music in its place.

The learning of a musical instrument such as the guitar can be made easier by the use of a visual prompt as in the beginners' 'Guitar' program (see Example 8.1 in appendix).

Prospects for Recreation

The dividing line between work and play is difficult to define, simply because they are woolly-edged sets. A game of football is regarded from quite different points of view by the players and the spectators. A game of noughts and crosses requires the formulation of a strategy for 'best moves' at particular points in the game.

Chess requires the ability to develop a plan that can look ahead in order to anticipate situations where advantages can be taken. In most board games that can be translated onto computers the nature of the programming ensures that it is possible to predict how a computer program will behave. This gives children the facility to analyze sequences of patterns, which will improve their quality of play. It is possible that some children may be able to relate to a computer in a more positive way than to adults. War-gaming has rapidly developed as a hobby, and many strategic war situations can be recalled and simulated. Eighteenth century naval warfare mainly took place between French and British fleets (Taylor, 1971:38). One variable chosen in a game could use size or rating of ships:

Ships	Guns	Full Crew
First Rate	100	350
Third Rate	74	275
Frigates	28	100
Schooners	12	75
Merchantmen	28	75

Another variable in sea-battle could be the wind scale devised by Admiral Sir Francis Beaufort:

1. Calm Sea
2. Light breeze, small waves
3, 4 Choppy seas
5. Strong breeze, rising swell
6. High wind, heavy seas

Business games can be used to give an understanding of buying and selling shares on the Stock Exchange, or calculating profit or loss in running a lemonade stall.

In golf, it is possible to 'play' against oneself. In a similar way children can play a game in order to better a previous 'best' score, and many teachers will see this as one solution to the problem of avoiding comparison between children. Children persist in a task that they enjoy and the endless patience of the computer can be used to best effect when linked with a strong recreational element.

Organizing Information

Operating the System

Many of the operational problems of children are dependent not only on difficulties in writing programs but on the often complicated rituals that are necessary for accessing data. Good-quality wallcharts alongside the computer can give clear indication of which buttons to press and which are the more important or most frequently needed commands.

Help Commands

Within any program there should be the opportunity for the child to call upon some form of assistance, commonly called 'help' commands. If there is a standard way of asking for help in as many of the programs as possible, then this is likely to increase self reliance and to develop self confidence. Mistakes in input could also default to a help routine that would diagnose the fault and indicate where the mistakes lay.

Libraries of Programs

Colour-coding of cassettes or discs and sequential numbering seen in many work-books is essential for ease of management and mental ordering of the pattern of work. A catalogue of software available on an alphabetical search system can be streamlined by the use of a master catalogue. This would be a program that not only would list the program, but would indicate its length, level of difficulty and appropriateness to a stage of learning. Alongside the library of program names would be listed the materials necessary to extend the work.

Libraries of Routines

If the children are encouraged to make their own programs then they can use the idea of concatenation. Catenary means 'chain' and the chaining together of smaller sub-programs can be made with some of the merge programs now available.

The lines of a particular program are renumbered from a high location point, say 1000, and the program held in high memory. A second program can then be merged with the first, care being taken to ensure no overlapping of the line numbers. In this way routines for calling up shapes or noises can be used in much the same way as a library of recorded sounds on a cassette player. A bouncing ball may have a suitable accompaniment and other musical responses could accompany success or failure in solving a problem.

A standard trailer or a series of housekeeping commands could be put in the 'menu' at the beginning of all programs to give a coherent house style to the presentation (Beynon, 1981:109) (see Example 10.1 in appendix). In this way, personalizing programs will provide the opportunity for the children to be creative programmers.

Appendix: Example Programs Referred to in the Text

Example 5.1.

```
100  CLEAR
110  PRINT "THIS PROGRAM GIVES PA
     SCAL'S"
120  PRINT "TRIANGLE UP TO ANY LI
     NE"
130  PRINT:PRINT
140  PRINT "WHICH LINE WOULD YOU
     LIKE?"
150  INPUT X
160  IF X = 999 THEN END
170  PRINT
180  N = J:A = 1:M = 1
190  PRINT A" ";
200  K = K + A:T = K + 1:T = T/2
210  A = A*N/M
220  N=N-1:M=M+1
230  IF A = 0 THEN 250
240  GOTO 190
250  PRINT
260  IF J = X THEN 290
270  J = J + 1
280  GOTO 180
290  PRINT
300  PRINT "TOTAL IN ROW ";J;" IS
     ";T
310  PRINT "TO END PROGRAM HIT '99
     9'"
320  GOTO 100
←RUN
THIS PROGRAM GIVES PASCAL'S TRIANGLE UP TO ANY LINE
WHICH LINE WOULD YOU LIKE?
?8
```

```
1
1  1
1  2   1
1  3   3    1
1  4   6    4    1
1  5   10   10   5    1
1  6   15   20   15   6    1
1  7   21   35   35   21   7    1
1  8   28   56   70   56   28   8   1
```

TOTAL IN ROW 8 IS 256
TO END PROGRAM HIT '999'
THIS PROGRAM GIVES PASCAL'S
TRIANGLE UP TO ANY LINE

WHICH LINE WOULD YOU LIKE?
?12

```
1
1  1
1  2   1
1  3   3    1
1  4   6    4    1
1  5   10   10   5    1
1  6   15   20   15   6    1
1  7   21   35   35   21   7    1
1  8   28   56   70   56   28   8    1
1  9   36   84   126  126  84   36   9    1
1  10  45   120  210  252  210  120  45   10  1
1  11  55   165  330  462  462  330  165  55  11  1
1  12  66   220  495  792  924  792  495  220 66  12  1
```

TOTAL IN ROW 12 IS 4096
TO END PROGRAM HIT '999'
THIS PROGRAM GIVES PASCAL'S
TRIANGLE UP TO ANY LINE

WHICH LINE WOULD YOU LIKE?
?999

Example 5.2.

```
100  PRINT "PROGRAM FOR'SEAWEED NUMBERS"
110  PRINT "THE SEPARATE NUMERALS OF EACH"
```

124 J. DODRIDGE

```
120  PRINT "ARE SQUARED AND THEN ADDED"
130  PRINT "TOGETHER TO GIVE A FRESH NUMBER"
140  PRINT "IT COUNTS UNTIL IT REACHES 1 OR 89"
150  PRINT "PUT IN THE FIRST SEAWEED NUMBER"
160  INPUT S
170  N = 1
180  T = 0:D = 1000
190  K = 0
200  IF S < D THEN 240
210  S = S - D
220  K = K + 1
230  GOTO 200
240  D = D/10:IF D = .01 THEN 280
250  A = K * K
260  T = T + A
270  GOTO 190
280  PRINT T;
290  PRINT "=>";
300  IF T = 89 THEN 350
310  IF T = 1 THEN 350
320  S = T
330  N = N + 1
340  GOTO 180
350  PRINT
360  PRINT "SEAWEEDS="; N
370  N = 0
380  PRINT:PRINT
390  GOTO 150
```

←RUN
PROGRAM FOR SEAWEED NUMBERS THE SEPARATE NUMERALS OF EACH ARE SQUARED AND THEN ADDED TOGETHER TO GIVE A FRESH NUMBER IT COUNTS UNTIL IT REACHES 1 OR 89 PUT IN THE FIRST SEAWEED NUMBER? 123
14=>   17=>   50=>   25=>   29=>   85=>   89=>
SEAWEEDS = 7

PUT IN THE FIRST SEAWEED NUMBER? 567
110=>   2=>   4=>   16=>   37=>   58=>   89=>
SEAWEEDS = 7

PUT IN THE FIRST SEAWEED NUMBER? 6789
230=>   13=>   10=>   1=>
SEAWEEDS = 4

Example 7.1.

```
100  CLEAR
110  HOME
120  N = 5
130  PRINT:PRINT:PRINT
133  INVERSE:FLASH
135  PRINT "TREASURE ISLAND"
137  NORMAL:PRINT:PRINT
140  G = 10
150  PRINT "BURIED TREASURE LIES ON"
160  PRINT "A 10 KM. SQUARE ISLAND."
170  PRINT "CAN YOU GUESS THE CO-ORDINATES?"
190  PRINT
210  PRINT "YOU WILL GET CLUES ..."
220  A = INT (G*RND (1) )
230  B = INT (G*RND (1) )
240  FOR K = 1 TO N
250  PRINT:PRINT "GUESS #";K;
260  INPUT X, Y
270  IF ABS (X − A) + ABS (Y − B) = 0 THEN 380
280  GOSUB 430
290  PRINT
300  NEXT K
310  PRINT
320  PRINT "SORRY, THAT'S ";N;" GUESSES,"
330  PRINT "THE TREASURE LIES AT ";A;", ";B
340  PRINT
350  PRINT "I WILL HIDE THE TREASURE AGAIN ..."
360  PRINT
370  GOTO 220
380  REM
390  PRINT
400  FOR N = 1 TO 12:PRINT CHR$ (7);:NEXT N
410  PRINT "YOU FOUND IT IN ";K;" GUESSES"
420  GOTO 340
430  PRINT "GO";
440  IF Y = B THEN 490
450  IF Y < B THEN 480
460  PRINT "SOUTH";
470  GOTO 490
480  PRINT "NORTH";
490  IF X = A GOTO 540
500  IF X < A GOTO 530
510  PRINT "WEST";
```

J. DODRIDGE

```
520  GOTO 540
530  PRINT "EAST";
540  PRINT
550  RETURN
560  END
```

Example 8.1.

Beginner's Guitar

```
10   CLEAR
20   HOME
30   PRINT:PRINT:PRINT
40   PRINT "A GUITAR FINGERING"
50   PRINT "PROGRAM BY G. PALMER"
60   PRINT "& J. DODRIDGE FOR"
70   PRINT "THE ITT & APPLE II"
80   PRINT "COPYRIGHT-JANUARY 81"
90   PRINT:PRINT:PRINT
100  PRINT "SEQUENCE FOR A MAJOR"
110  PRINT:PRINT
120  PRINT "ARE YOU 1.  A BEGINNER"
130  PRINT "         2.  GOOD"
140  PRINT "         3.  VERY GOOD"
150  PRINT "         4.  EXCELLENT"
160  PRINT "         5.  VIRTUOSO"
170  PRINT "PUT IN A NUMBER 1-5"
180  INPUT Q
190  Q = 1200/Q
200  REM:-BACKGROUND
210  GR:COLOR = 15:FOR T = 3 TO 39:VLIN 3, 37 AT T:NEXT T
220  REM:-FRETS
230  COLOR = 2:FOR K = 3 TO 35 STEP 8:VLIN 3, 37 AT K:NEXT K
240  REM:-STRINGS
250  COLOR = 0:FOR S = 5 TO 35 STEP 6:HLIN 0, 39 AT S:NEXT
260  DIM A$(20)
270  FOR I = 1 TO 5
280  READ A$(I)
290  DATA "222324"    (A)
300  DATA "233221"    (D)
310  DATA "2513"      (E7)      Tune
315  DATA "32"        (Single D) Sequence
320  DATA "222324"    (A)
```

```
330   NEXT I
340   FOR 1 = 1 TO 5
350   REM:-PLAYING A CHORD
360   K = 4
370   A = 0
380   B = − 1:C = 0
390   B = B + 2:C = C + 2
400   D = LEN (A$(I) )
410   D = D + 2
420   X$ = MID$ (A$(I), B, 1)
430   Y$ = MID$ (A$(I), C, 1)
440   X = VAL (X$)
450   Y = VAL (Y$)
460   IF C = D GOTO 560
470   GOSUB 490
480   GOTO 390
490   V = 8*X:H = 6*Y − 2
500   COLOR = K
510   HLIN V, V + 2 AT H − 1
520   HLIN V, V + 2 AT H
530   HLIN V, V + 2 AT H + 2
540   HLIN V, V + 2 AT H + 3
550   RETURN
560   FOR S = 1 TO Q:NEXT S
570   A = A + 1
580   K = 15
590   IF A = 2 GOTO 610
600   GOTO 380
610   NEXT I
```

Example 10.1

```
10000   PP = 10
10005   ::::: REM ROB BEYNON
10006   ::::: REM PRACTICAL COMPUTING AUG81
10010   PRINT:PRINT    "THERE    ARE"   ;PP;   "PAGES   OF
        INSTRUCTIONS"
10020   PRINT "STEP THROUGH THEM USING THE"
10025   PRINT "AND RIGHT'ARROW' KEYS, AND"
10030   PRINT "PRESS'RETURN' WHEN YOU ARE"
10040   PRINT "READY TO BEGIN"
10050   IP = 0
10060   GET A$:IF A$ = " " THEN 10060
10070   IF ASC (A$) = 8 THEN 10120
```

```
10080   IF ASC (A$) = 21 THEN 10150
10090   IF ASC (A$) = 27 THEN POP:GOTO 51000
10100   IF ASC (A$) = 13 THEN RETURN
10110   GOTO 10060
10120   IP = IP - 1
10130   IF IP = 0 THEN IP = 1
10140   GOTO 10180
10150   IP = IP + 1
10160   IF IP = PP + 1 THEN IP = PP
10170   GOTO 10180
10180   HOME:HTAB 30:INVERSE:PRINT "PAGE #"; IP: NORMAL
10190   ON IP GOSUB 10200, 10250, 10300, 10350, 10400, 10450,
        10500, 10550, 10600, 10650
10195   GOTO 10060
```

←RUN
THERE ARE 10 PAGES OF INSTRUCTIONS STEP THROUGH THEM USING THE LEFT AND RIGHT'ARROW' KEYS, AND PRESS'RETURN' WHEN YOU ARE READY TO BEGIN

References

ARTWICK, B. (1980) 'British Ace-Flight Simulator' United States Sublogic.

BEAL, G. (1973) *Codes, Cyphers and Secret Writing* Hamlyn.

BEYNON, R. (1981) *Practical Computing* London, IPC Press.

CAREY, D. (1979) *How it Works – The Computer* London, Ladybird.

CHESHIRE EDUCATION AUTHORITY (1980) *Primary Mathematics Guidelines* Cheshire, Cheshire Education Authority.

CROOKALL, P. (1980) *The Census of 1851 – Welsh Row Nantwich* Mice & Cheese 1 – Cheshire LEA.

DUNCAN, T. (1979) *Adventures with Electronics* London, Murray.

ESCHER, M.C. (1961) *The Graphic Work of M.C. Escher*, Oldbourne.

MCWHIRTER, N. and GREENBERG, S. (1978) *The Guinness Book of Records* London, Guinness.

ROBINSON, R.E. (1979) 'Problem-solving Situations using Structured Logic Material' Keele University (unpublished thesis).

SEABORNE, P.L. (1975) *An Introduction to the Dienes Mathematics Programme* London, Unibooks.

TAYLOR, A. (1971) *Rules for Wargaming* London, Shire Publications.

VAN DELFT, P. and BOTERMANS, J. (1978) *Creative Puzzles of the World* London, Cassell.

WILDER, R.L. (1978) *Evolution of Mathematical Concepts* Milton Keynes, Open University.

YOUNG, B. (1972) *Computers and Young Children* London, Nuffield/Chambers/Murray.

Shall We Have a Microcomputer in Our Primary School?
Donald Walton

This question has become a major discussion point at all levels of the educational hierarchy from the probationer to the Secretary of State for Education. You will have noticed that this hierarchy is a horizontal rather than a vertical movement because, like most educational innovation, the attitudes of the class teacher are just as important as those of the administrators and politicians who try and influence the course of education. Having taught for over twenty years and have seen many educational innovations come and go, it has been fascinating to see the pressures brought to bear on all sections of the educational system by the media and public opinion, and how different innovation has flourished in the hands of enthusiasts and failed in the hands of the 'unbelievers' who have either refused to be involved or are apathetic towards it. This time the pressures are even more finely balanced and just as interesting, with the government taking a very positive step in the arena in the form of the Microelectronics in Education Programme (MEP). This time innovation is not going away. Of course there will be times of progress and times when other problems will be dominant before the computer is accepted as an every day piece of furniture in every classroom. As the technology is unlikely to stop developing, it is seldom likely to be out of the news as the potential is grasped and realized by education at all levels.

In this paper I have tried to point out possible pitfalls and suggestions for skirting round them or overcoming them, as well as indicating the potential of these machines in primary schools.

It is possible that you feel a microcomputer would be a good idea without having any idea what it can be used for in a school situation. It is not a good idea to talk to a computer dealer, enthusiast, or anyone outside the educational system. You know that duplicators always work like magic with the manufacturers' representative in charge. With the computer it is somewhat different. Typically there will be very slick demonstrations of non-educational programs or a disaster where nothing works. It is better to find a teacher who is using a computer day in and day out in the classroom situation. There are a few scattered about the country and MAPE, which stands for Micros and Primary Education, may be able to help you.

The next step is to find out whether you or a colleague are prepared to spend quite a considerable amount of time becoming familiar with the machine and introducing it properly into the school. It is possible to obtain quite a useful number of educational programs ready written for the machine if you choose a really well-known manufacturer. If you choose a machine which does not have a large number of educational users, you will find the whole problem immense and somewhat dispiriting as you will have to write all the programs yourself. If you think you will be interested in writing programs, then be prepared to spend many many hours at the key board learning the language and all the tricks as well as discovering that the computer will search out every tiny bit of illogical thought. Unfortunately the machine will not be explicit about this kind of mistake and leaves it to you to search it out into the early hours of the morning. You may find that the intellectual challenge of the machine is fascinating, but beware – remember that it was really introduced for the children.

It is hoped that this last paragraph will damp the enthusiasm of any headmaster who is thinking of buying a micro and thrusting it at a member of staff whom he last saw reading an article on microcomputers. A better plan for such a head would be to encourage that member of staff and a few others to attend a course on computer familiarization with a minimum of programming content and, if any of them are really interested, you will find them starting to search for courses leading into programming on their own. You will soon find out if you are fortunate enough to have an enthusiast on your staff: in that case be prepared to spend several hundred pounds to buy a good basic machine that does not have a limited potential, as well as a good insurance that covers the machine in school, in staff cars and in staff houses. May I repeat that programming is only learned from experience; it involves many hours at the keyboard and learning from others, but even then the problem is not resolved. I have met many excellent programmers without ideas and many people with ideas who do not wish to program. In an ideal world the two should be brought together and work together. This is how MEP are trying to get micros off to a good start in schools.

Having identified yourself or a member of staff as an enthusiast and bought a microcomputer, do not be in a hurry to thrust it into a classroom. Spend a little time getting some of the older children trained to act as trouble shooters who can deal with any problems which occur in classrooms where the teacher is tentative about the whole idea. Teachers, however enthusiastic, do not take kindly to systems which keep needing attention and taking them away from the job they are trying to do. Under these circumstances you soon find the computer is not being used. I would suggest that one or two useful crash-proofed programs which reinforce the teacher's existing style and curriculum should be used to begin with so that the teacher becomes familiar with the whole idea and is not continually badgered to try new software and perhaps new ideas at the same time. The teacher will see the children's enthusiasm and interest and this is very persuasive if they are at all doubtful about the value of the machine.

At Houghton School I have been fortunate that every member of staff is interested in the microcomputer and welcomes it in their classroom. Our policy was that it should be timetabled into all classrooms during the week and that staff familiarization was just as important as children's activities in the early stages. I think this has paid off. Ideas from the staff for fresh programs outstrip our ability to produce them. It may be of interest to know that we have tried two methods of timetabling the microcomputers. We have two Commodore PET 16K machines. One machine moves daily around the third and fourth year classes. I try to avoid moving the machine about between lessons as it can easily be forgotten or be difficult as I am, after all, a full-time teacher. The other machine is timetabled for half a term with our two first year classes and half a term with the second year classes as a sort of block booking. Our one infant class has a computer for a whole day and the remedial reading class has the other for half a day. All these different ideas were staff suggestions and they should be involved in all decision making relating to the computer, and its use. Out of school time, third and fourth year children are allowed access to the machines and programs but they are booked in in pairs. It is interesting to note that one or two children who seem to be attaining skills over and above that which you might expect from them are the cleaners' and caretaker's children – it is interesting to ask whether time on the keyboard is the crucial variable.

There is no doubt that you will be questioned closely about your aims and objectives by parents and advisers and other teachers. You could, possibly, have visits from the local press, radio, TV and HMIs. I, personally, find it easier to talk with a real example in front of me rather than trying to dredge up all the points I am trying to make. Houghton staff no longer feel threatened by visitors but it is often better to remove the computer with a few children to demonstrate; discussion is then not limited and the class organization is not disrupted too much. I also welcome criticism from the sceptics because it enables me to re-shape and re-define my ideas and reminds me of our main reasons for having the machines in school – that is, the education of the children.

It is easy to make statements in the present climate, such as 'We must bring children face to face with this new technology – after all this is going to be their future'. But this can hardly be a justification for using the machine as tables testers or an addition practice machine. This is not bringing the children into contact with the new technology any better than calculators, digital watches and space invaders. The microcomputer has the potential to be a valuable teaching aid in a whole range of teaching situations and roles. It was fascinating to read *Microscope* (a very useful magazine for those just starting out) in the aftermath of the Exeter Conference. In one contribution there was a plea for programs which were not 'behaviourist' but enabled the children to make reasoned responses and choices and, in another, there was a description of the kind of 'behaviourist' programs found useful in special schools. Another contributor talked about the computer not being used as a 'dog's body'. Without getting involved in any arguments about behaviourist and cognitive psychology and educational theories, may I suggest that the computer can and should be used to assist in any way which will make the teacher's job, whatever their persuasion, easier, more effective, and enriching.

Computer-Assisted-Learning programs, if they are chosen carefully, will certainly provide the variety and fascination to show some of the potential of the technology, but we must not forget that these machines or their derivatives are making a large impact in offices, factories, scientific laboratories, libraries, doctors' surgeries, etc., and it is possible to illustrate these uses with applications at Junior School level. I have, for example, a very simple program which simulates the results of dropping a stone out of a balloon at different heights. This illustrates its use as a scientific simulator – all big car manufacturers, ship builders, etc. use these now and it is possible for children to get a feel for all kinds of situations without knowing about the equations which solve them. Another program tests and collects DATA on short term memory abilities in the class, by presenting a sequence of numbers increasing in length until it reaches a sequence of ten numbers by which time their short term memory has broken down. The results can be examined and implications discussed as a simple psychological experiment. The children also use programs for a back up accounting system for School Bank and a word processor, as we have a printer. Again, primary applications in these kinds of areas are limited by one's imagination and enthusiasms. A useful application would be for marking, administering and testing the school mathematics scheme. If you can show children using the computer in these kinds of applications, then you are indeed bringing them into contact with the potential of the new technology.

Finally it is possible to teach children of primary age to program. If you have children who are really interested and have ability, then you will find the experience of observing how fast they learn very sobering. I know of no other school activity, other than sport, which captures the imagination and intellectual curiosity of some small boys and girls as much as computer programming, with all its vicissitudes and frustrations.

If by teaching them simple programming you can show them that however sophisticated the computer is it is limited by and reflects the attitudes and skills of those who instruct it, you will have taught them a valuable lesson.

You and the children in your school are about to embark on an exciting voyage. No one knows what the end will be but there is no doubt that man's future for good or ill is linked with microelectronics and there is no turning back.

References

Microscope: A journal devoted to primary school computing published by Ginn/Heinemann.

Microcomputers, Schools and the Initial Training of Teachers: A Case Study
Roy Garland and Bernard Lane

The advent of the microcomputer raises complex, difficult and largely uncharted problems for our schools. There is perhaps a feeling amongst many teachers that something of consequence, possibly of fundamental importance is happening that has implications for them and their pupils yet it is difficult to articulate the problem, to conceive of a response or indeed simply know how to start. This article is an account of one response to the intuitive feelings of the two authors – one a lecturer in a School of Education, the other the deputy head of a large eight to twelve Middle School – that microcomputers pose questions of importance both to schools and to institutions that train teachers. Initially the thinking was independent yet it was parallel: the way forward was not conceived as inaction born of despair or indeed of grandiose schemes doomed to be stillborn. A start could be made by a small innovative and exploratory project that used existing resources and did not rely for its implementation on special considerations or favours.

In life there are elements of coincidence, of good fortune that suggest the inevitability of the unexpected! We had worked together professionally in the past and had formed good professional and personal relationships. During this particular endeavour we also had joint interests. We wished to examine the concept of computer literacy. What should children of primary school age learn about microcomputers? How might this task be tackled? There were interests, however, that did not necessarily coincide and these were openly and freely acknowledged from the beginning, giving both variety and strength to the work. These differing emphases arose from the particular institutions in which we worked. One cluster of questions queried the ways in which the staff of a particular school might be sensitized to issues raised by micros, with the eventual possibility of purchasing one: what management approach might be appropriate? The other set of questions concerned the problems of introducing student teachers to the classroom implications, opportunities and limitations of micros: the creation of the inexperienced pioneer!

Our early, yet independent, thinking had unwittingly prepared the ground for the work that was to follow: perhaps unexpected good fortune is more likely to come to those who are prepared for it! In the School of Education an elective had already been advertised for third-year students lasting throughout the Spring and Summer terms. The elective was aimed at a group of students who would have successfully completed possibly the major personal challenge in an initial teacher training course – the final teaching practice. They would have been in school throughout the Autumn term and would be very aware of the demands and stresses that teaching imposes. On their return from the practice they would resume their academic studies with a major commitment to their main subject and to the theory of education. The planning of the microcomputer elective had to recognize that, with best will in the world and with impeccable motivation, the students would not be able to give it their highest priority.

The elective was advertised as an exploration of the classroom implications of microcomputers and it was made quite clear that the work would be primary school orientated. Interestingly and significantly, of the seven students who eventually signed up for the course six were training for secondary school teaching and only one of the group did not have a strong background in mathematics – and she was a scientist! Perhaps one should not be surprised by this but it does seem to suggest that the association of microcomputers with mathematics is deep-rooted and that this will have to be recognized as a real barrier to the creative and imaginative use of the machines within our schools. The way that the course is advertised in future years will have to be changed to stress this point and to emphasize that a prior ability to program is not a requisite. There is an enormous amount of work necessary, not only amongst children but with intending and practising teachers, to provide an informed and knowledgeable view of computers that moves away from the mathematical stereotyping which appears to be prevalent.

The initial approach to the staff of the Middle School to be involved, regarding the possible uses of the microcomputer in the curriculum, was preceded by personal research by one of us and correspondence with teachers in other parts of the country who had already started to use the machines. From this work it became evident that here was a new and significant technological development that had wide potential application across the curriculum. Much discussion followed in the school with colleagues focused on issues of a general nature but with a definite anti-mathematical stereotyping. This was done on an informal basis, often over a cup of coffee. The staff responded most favourably towards the idea that microcomputers might have a contribution to make to the work of the primary school – and this was without a single machine in the school! When, eventually, it was suggested that a small existing group of able second-year (that is, nine and ten-year-olds) should embark on microcomputer work, the idea was met by all the staff with unreserved enthusiasm. The stage was set for the first foray into the new technology but without doubt the preliminary and informal discussions that raised the awareness of the teachers to the issues had been most important.

Earlier mention was made of the intention to use existing resources – a 48K Apple II Computer with two disk drives was available at the School of Education but, unfortunately, because of problems of insurance, could not be removed from the campus: the children would have to visit the micro. The planning was developed with the possibilities and the potentials of the existing hardware very much in mind. In particular, the use of the disks to store a great deal of information that could be rapidly accessed and retrieved was considered to be significant. The limits of my language are the limits of my thinking and the boundaries to the ways in which micros are to be used will inevitably be drawn by the knowledge of those who conceive the programs. Planning sessions were held and a set of aims were agreed for the work of the Spring term. For the first part of the term the students were to become familiar with the machine and its operation and, if possible, develop their own programming skills. The actual work with children would begin once the students felt that they had a degree of confidence in handling the hardware. The time that this period of familiarization takes should not be underestimated. In the case of the students, even given the fact that the majority were already familiar with the concept of a computer language and had some programming skills, the process was slow. There does seem to be a strong case here for the production of self-help material that the learner can actually use with the computer in his or her own time, as 'hands-on' experience appears to be a key element in appreciation and understanding of the computer's potential. Such material does already exist but not with the particular needs of teachers in mind.

In planning courses, good and honourable intentions are not necessarily sufficient. Much of what happens in educational institutions is not new: it fits into existing and sometimes traditional ways of doing things and is conducted by professionals who have been through the process many times before. In these circumstances, extensive use of formal planning and preparation may not be needed. When, however, the enterprise strikes out in fresh directions and when a number of parties with differing expectations, degrees of knowledge and levels of motivations is involved, then careful and meticulous planning seems essential. Yet the planning must not stifle enterprise or prevent the exploitation of the unexpected. The early discussions of our work produced a number of intentions. The business of computer literacy was raised: what should the children know?; what sort of activities and educational experiences should be organized for them?. The activities that we organize for our children are the interface between our thinking and beliefs about education and their manifestation in practice, yet so often little thought is given to them in planning. What should the children learn about programming? Was there commercial software available or would we have to write our own? How would the work of the children be linked to their work in school? What would be the reactions of teachers in the school to the project?

The debate and the discussion resulted in a statement of intent by the School of Education. In it, the right of the school to be satisfied that the work was educationally worthwhile was publically acknowledged: schools are accountable for the learning situations they devise for their pupils. They have to be satisfied that ideas developed by 'outsiders', however well motivated, are likely in practice to lead to worthwhile and justifiable learning. The statement of intent was followed by a list of the actual aims for the remainder of the term's work:

1 to introduce the children to a microcomputer;
2 to teach the children how to operate the machine;
3 to demonstrate its capabilities for the storage and retrieval of information;
4 to explore how information may be displayed;
5 to present the concept of a program;
6 to enable the children to write simple programs.

At the time, the aims seemed appropriate: with the benefit of experience and of evaluation they seem to be over-ambitious. However, the children we were to work with were bright and keen and in planning, whether at the level of a particular lesson or for an extended programme of work, optimistic expectations will shelter one from a blight of teaching — not knowing what to do next! Arrangements were made so that a particular pair of students would take responsibility for the preparation for each of the one-hour lessons and also assumed responsibility for informing the rest of the group of their approach and their plans.

Three main themes were covered during the subsequent working sessions: the operation of the machine; the concept of a program; writing a program. The introduction to programming was through the idea of sequence: getting a task done by placing the necessary instructions in the correct order. The obvious examples were used: making a cup of tea; dressing in the morning; washing up; etc.. The children were then encouraged to place their thoughts in the form of a flow-chart. As one of us has argued elsewhere (Garland, 1981), there are doubts regarding the necessity for this type of symbolism at this particular stage. In this instance, the children coped because they were intelligent and because associated programming concepts such as choice and repetition were not introduced to further complicate the issue. The point still remains, however, that there is great value in allowing children to develop their own ideas on recording the sequencing of instructions to give them an intuitive feeling for the nature of the task that they are about. The early use of standardized methods is in danger of narrowing thinking in implying that there are single solutions to problems.

Probably the most successful lessons of the whole term were those where the children were taught how to write a program using BASIC. As an introduction, time was spent on writing programs to operate on numbers – addition, subtraction, multiplication and division. Again the children enjoyed it but it does tend to confirm stereotyped thinking regarding the mathematical associations of the machines. The approach used later would seem to be more appropriate: drawing pictures using the low resolution facility of the Apple. This allows one to plot a point or a series of points in a variety of pre-specified colours on a screen sized forty by forty. It seems a more appropriate introduction because it is easy to obtain results – the number of instructions required to program the computer is very few and the children are able to obtain a swift answer to the question: 'Will my program work?'. It also allows the children to engage in all sorts of imaginative fantasies when planning their pictures. Because of the pressures of time the majority of the children did not get much further than writing their initials, although one produced an image of a television screen, an indoor aerial and his initials as the program! Children in Chester have produced exotic tropical fish and animals using this technique. The approach also generated its own questions in a way that the programs to perform mathematical operations did not. The children were soon asking how to change colours and this led in a natural manner to the concept of iteration: of repetition. It is not much fun seeing your name display briefly in one colour. How could we systematically change them? Here the idea of a LOOP was introduced and names appeared in a dozen or more colours!

With so much going on it was not possible to examine the concepts of the storage and retrieval of data but the term's work raises many questions of importance to those wishing to engage in such an approach. A dominating point is that of the amount of time involved in preparation. All those concerned spent far more time in preparing work than is normally necessary or indeed possible. The work itself for all of us was breaking new ground and was of considerable interest: this meant that there were no text books or worksheets or other similar materials commercially available. Everything had to be home-produced. Given that a comparatively large number of adults was involved, it was possible to spread the load but the time involved in this type of work as well as the specialized knowledge that has to be acquired eventually should not be underestimated. Another issue of importance concerns the planning of the lessons: the aim should be to maximize the amount of time children have with the microcomputer. The laws of arithmetic will ensure that if one child at a time visits the machine then the time available is negligible. In this work only a third of a normal sized class was involved but the approach adopted could be applied in a whole class situation. The children were divided into groups and two types of activities were prepared for them: 'on' the computer activities and 'off' the computer tasks. Again this means extra planning, preparation and organizing skills. It is important, for example, but not always easy to ensure that the 'on' and 'off' activities allow for the particular point when the children have access to the computer. Those whose turn is first will not have time to prepare for their visit in the way that the later arrivals will. It has been noted by other commentators that children derive benefit from working in a small group at the computer; probably four is an optimum number. Here the problem of arranging for as many children as possible to have a reasonable period of time at the computer can be turned to advantage, as an enormous amount of exploratory type language occurs between children when they are deciding what is to be done. Not once during the whole of the two terms that the project was in existence did we witness children idly chattering while at the machine: time was too precious to waste and there were so many intrinsically interesting questions and hypotheses to explore. When the children were engaged with the microcomputer we tended to hover on the edges of what was happening with our professional eyes and ears atune but basically adopting a non-interventionist role. We were interested to note that the students were far more willing and anxious to move in and tell the children what to do next. There is a balance to be struck here and we do not wish children to spend long periods finding by trial and error how to get a program to run but, when ideas as opposed to routines are at stake, apparent disinterest on the part of the teacher is appropriate.

It is a salutary experience for any teacher to list the actual ideas that he or she has presented to a class during one lesson: in evaluating the work of the first term we were struck by the enormous amount of material that had been introduced to the children during a comparatively short period of time. We also became aware of a number of tacit assumptions that had been made regarding the children's understanding of the various experiences and concepts to which they had been exposed. In subjects that are well established in the curriculum, such as mathematics, there is a recognition of sequence and gradient of difficulty with well-established methods available for assessing the children's understanding. In the case of the new, this is not yet the case and there is still a need to discover what has been understood and what has been missed or mistaken. As yet there is little evidence of the actual effectiveness of computers in assisting learning in our primary schools: there is the assumption that enthusiasm is a sufficient outcome. The work that is required in this field is enormous. Individual teachers are not going to be able to mount large research projects yet it is worth raising the question of how we might discover or compare the learnings associated with the microcomputer.

In the work that has been described, fresh ground had been broken: conventional areas of the curriculum were not directly involved. The question still remained however: 'What had the children learnt?'. The answer would affect the planning for the next term's work. Various ideas were mooted, including conventional tests. Because of the range of ideas covered, and because we were interested in discovering what had impressed the children, these possibilities were discarded and the decision was made to ask the children to make their own computer manual with the audience in mind of a friend who knew nothing of operating the Apple computer but who was anxious to learn.

The children were given the briefest of briefs on the production of their own computer manuals, yet the finished products that impressed all who saw them contained a great deal in common. All for example included:

1 a diagram of the Apple II containing the children's ideas on the main parts: the central processing unit; disk drives; a screen for displaying things, etc;
2 a section on operating the machine: how do we know if it is turned on? is the disk inserted correctly? how to CATALOG; running a program; halting a program, etc..

It was evident from this section of the children's booklet that they had grasped the idea of order and sequence when operating a microcomputer and these ideas recurred when all the children attempted to illustrate a flow-chart. Other sections explained such BASIC terms as INPUT, GOTO, PRINT. It was also apparent from these manuals that the group had consolidated the basic operating procedures for APPLE II, had gained initial insights into the concepts associated with programming and had come to terms with the new technology: motivation was also high judging from the voluminous end-products. An excellent way of testing one's own understanding, that every teacher will appreciate, is to explain the idea to someone else.

There was general satisfaction with the children's attainments during the first term, although doubt was expressed regarding the possibilities of reaching such standards with the ubiquitous mixed-ability class. The plans for the coming term had to be considered and it was decided to explore the theme that appeared in the original aims but which had, to date, not been tackled – a demonstration of the computer's ability to store and to retrieve data. This might not seem a particularly exciting subject, with a picture of the analysis of columns and rows of dead figures, but it is possible to make the whole approach come alive to younger children. The way to do it is to use a principle close to the ways of working in primary education – start from the children's interests and experiences. This suggested that the data that were to be used should originate from the children themselves. As the result of a meeting of the students and ourselves, it was also decided that a focus to the work would be a search for the 'average' child. Does he or she exist?

The decisions made at this meeting had a number of implications: software would have to be written, as nothing appropriate to the tasks that we had set ourselves was readily available; data regarding children would be required that would be related to the software; individual responsibilities would have to be allocated for the organization and teaching of particular lessons. A substantial piece of software had already been written in anticipation of the term's work. It used the APPLE's disk facility and was capable of storing information regarding the names, addresses, birthdays and hobbies of a hundred or so children and it could also recall information regarding an individual or produce the names of those with one particular hobby who lived in the same road or shared the same birthday, etc.. Data were collected for this program and entered at the keyboard to be stored by the computer as a data file. This whole process was exceedingly time consuming – writing and debugging software is a lengthy process.

The decision had been made to collect information from all of the year group of ninety-two to which our computer group belonged. The task was a large one as information was compiled regarding no fewer than twelve variables, including such facts as names, ages, hobbies and heights. Both the children and the staff of the school were kept fully informed about the survey and gave their willing co-operation. Microcomputers with disk storage are admirable for storing and retrieving data. The data that are collected could form the basis of archives for individual schools on information of particular interest to the children concerning the local environment: the weather over a period of years; facts about the natural history; the industries and occupations. The work that we were engaged in pointed to the possibilities of this approach but, in view of the time spent in collecting information, the material should be of relevance in future years. Our material does not strictly meet this criterion.

The whole period of preparation was further lengthened when it was decided by ourselves that additional data would be necessary for the project that could not be stored using the existing software! It is fair to say that better planning would have avoided this position and the time-consuming partial duplication of work that it was to lead to. However, in planning, one cannot completely allow for the unexpected and certainly our own ideas regarding possibilities were developing. The actual result, however, was two programs containing information where one could have performed the task: it would have been possible at this stage to have scrapped the first program and started again from the beginning but we could not face losing so much hard endeavour! Because one of us had programming skills the position was not lost and, eventually, software was written that enabled the children to move from one program and its data to the other with ease. This does, perhaps, emphasize the point that it is extraordinarily helpful to have a teacher on the staff who knows something of programming to allow the modification of programs to meet particular needs. Programs in their documentation should indicate ways in which they can be modified. The ability to be adapted in this manner should be one of the criteria for determining a good program.

The preparation for the second term's work was now ready in both broad intent and in detail for the first series of lessons. Underpinning the idea of searching for the 'average' child was a number of aims regarding computer literacy. We wish the children to:

1 retrieve and interpret the data that they had collected;
2 generate their own ideas regarding ways in which data files might be searched to test hypotheses; and
3 discuss the wider social implications of the computer's storage and retrieval capability.

Although responsibilities for the first cluster of lessons in the term had been allocated, the plans for the final sessions were deliberately left less definitive at this stage. There was a feeling that we ought to do something a little bit different, even slightly spectacular, but we were not sure what might meet these vague aspirations.

The first lesson of the term was taken by one of ourselves. It aimed to prepare the children for the subsequent tasks by demonstrating how the software could be used. By a discussion and demonstration, the power and the limitation of the program was established: it could store the information that the children had collected; it could recall information that had been stored on the disk in various ways; but it could only handle the data that had been entered. Facts regarding all the ninety-two children in a year group had been stored on disk: at the touch of a few keys all the names could be listed; all those with the same birthday could be revealed along with those with allegiance to particular hobbies – including the boy who claimed with pride that he was an ecologist! The introduction to the lesson was supported by program documentation supplied to each child to act as a reference point when, later in the lesson, they would be working at the machine. When operating the microcomputer individuals were asked to type in their own names and within a split second a display of information regarding themselves would appear on the screen: the children found this quite fascinating and it gave opportunities for valuable discussion.

We aimed to raise questions regarding the social implications of computers within our society but not as a formal lesson: we used the opportunities that the teaching situations presented. When children typed in the name of an absent friend we asked: 'Have you a right to this information?'. Mistakes were present in the data: a name spelt incorrectly; an address that was wrong. Whose duty is it to correct these mistakes? Why did they occur? Are there occasions when mistaken information might harm the rights of individuals? This is opportunistic teaching. It can, in a sense, be planned, in that we can be reasonably certain of our intentions and alert to the potentials they offer: we cannot necessarily anticipate the moment when an opportunity will arise. One of the most interesting points that emerged from the work over the two terms was the manner in which an apparent 'mistake' could be used to build a teaching point: the incorrect data; the hitch in the program; the unexpected facts produced by the machine. Fixing things, getting things to work properly is an extraordinarily powerful learning tool and far removed from the traditional correction with all its overtones of censure.

Subsequent lessons built on this start. The children were given puzzles to solve and were introduced to the second program that contained data regarding heights, weights and the physical appearance of children, as well as more personal information regarding position in family and the number of schools attended. The computer was used for an activity that became very popular and was to lead to what proved to be the grand finale of the work: the identification of an individual given certain facts about him or her – for example, the person's weight, height and number of schools attended. To solve this problem, not only is logical thinking required but skills have to be developed in computer use and the children swiftly mastered both demands. The work was used to investigate the concept of 'average' child by asking what might be meant by this phrase in terms of the available data. Not surprisingly, at the end of the day, the limits of the idea of 'average' became apparent. The group had also been asked to suggest ways in which the data might be searched that were not available and would aid the search for individuals and a number of worthwhile ideas emerged – for example, 'could we obtain the names of all those with the same height, weight, etc?'. The original programs had been written in a modular form with possible later expansion in mind and it was easy, but nevertheless time-consuming, to incorporate the suggestions. This again demonstrated the advantages of having access to someone who can program so that software can be amended to match the particular teaching needs of the moment.

From the outset of the work the idea had grown that there should be a novel ending to the work that would involve all the children who had been involved in the survey and their teachers. The result was an idea that started with the secret creation of a video film of three of the children. They came to the School of Education without their friends or teachers realizing what was happening and a short colour film was made that gave clues to information about them that was already stored on the computer – their height, weight, eye colour, hobbies, etc.. Great care was taken during the filming to prevent easy identification: there were, for example, no full face or side shots but only tantalizing clues as to the person's identity. The three 'mystery personalities' accepted their anonymity fully – and thoroughly enjoyed the responsibility of keeping a secret.

The opening of the finale commenced at 9.30 a.m. when all three second-year classes arrived in the main school hall. At this stage no child had any prior knowledge of what was to follow. A degree of uncertain anticipation and a break from the expected routine are good motivational factors! The children were asked to watch the three short films to be shown on the television: the majority thought that a schools broadcast was to follow! What was happening soon became clear, however, amongst every indication of growing excitement. The children returned to their classrooms accompanied in each case by the members of the elective and pupils who had been working with the students on the microcomputers.

Each class was asked to comment on one specific video film and, led by the student member, a discussion followed that resulted in a list of observed attributes. The question that was obviously in the children's mind was: 'Who is the mystery person?'. Each class eventually came to an agreement on this point and returned to the hall where they were introduced to the Apple computer by fellow pupils who were members of the microgroup. The attributes identified by the class were typed into the computer by these children and after a rapid search of the data file names of children within the second-year were displayed upon the screen. The names were compared with those arrived at by the class as the result of the discussion and eventually each class produced a definitive choice. Amidst considerable excitement the children again watched the video but this time the ending was shown: each of the mystery personalities slowly turned to face the audience and gave a triumphant wave!

A lively and fascinating discussion followed to which teachers, students, children and ourselves contributed. One class, for example, had reached full agreement based on an identification of attributes and the computer had agreed with them – yet they were wrong! This provoked further discussion indicating that computers are only aids, rely on the accuracy of the information that is fed to them and do not remove the need for judgement or indeed vigilance. The session finished at morning break on a high note of success: all had enjoyed themselves; appetites had been whetted for more; and many people had met the micro for the first time in a context that was far removed from drill programs in arithmetic but, in contrast, contained strong elements of problem solving.

It would not be sensible to draw too many conclusions of wider domain from such a short and small scale experiment. Yet it does, perhaps, suggest that ways forward can be found at local level, to meet the difficult problems created by the swift development of a technology that has implications for education, by the identification and the utilization of existing resources: if we wait for central and distant solutions to our problems, then we are likely to have to wait for a very long time. What has emerged from this work is a hint of the necessary conditions for the imaginative use of the microcomputer. A pre-requisite is the goodwill of those involved but this is not in itself sufficient. Goodwill will not run a micro: what is also needed is hard factual knowledge. To be more than an uninformed operator, teachers and students need to have grasped the concept of a program and they need an appreciation of the potential of the machine for storing and processing both numerical and textual information. They need to examine examples of software that illustrate a range of uses across the width of the curriculum. Above all, they need that most precious and scarce resource of time to experiment with the machines at a personal level. It is utopian and unnecessary to expect every primary school teacher to become an expert in a technology that has only hinted at its potential and not yet established its usefulness. A possible solution is to follow that what is often used in a subject such as science where primary school teachers may lack knowledge: have one person on the staff who has expertise and who can act as an adviser and consultant to colleagues.

Schools are unlikely to solve the problems that face society and it is doubtful if initial training institutions can instantly provide their students with detailed knowledge of the new technology – the trainers need training! What should be possible for an institution is to give all of its primary oriented students an introduction to the microcomputer so that they can load and run programs and be aware of the classroom implications. For the minority who wish to progress further there should be opportunities to study the subject in greater depth but in a manner that does not move the focus too far from the curriculum. For our students, as well as ourselves, the pupils that we will be teaching are indeed the micro-children!

References

GARLAND, R.G. (1981) 'Primary Schools Microcomputers and the Curriculum' Unpublished paper, School of Education, University of Exeter.

Some Observations on Children's Attitudes to, and the Role of, Microcomputers in Primary Schools
Tony Mullan

Throughout the history of education, aids to learning and teaching have been used in the classroom. These have varied from text books to various technological aids such as film, filmstrips, tape recorders and, in more recent years, television. However, in the last few years, a new piece of technology is becoming available to teachers – the microcomputer. Initially this was only to be found in the secondary school, where it was used almost exclusively within the framework of Computer Studies, but more and more its impact is being felt across the curriculum and it is now being developed as an aid to learning/teaching in the primary school. The Primary Education Conference at Exeter University in April 1981 is a strong indication of the concern teachers are feeling with regard to the microcomputer in primary education. Since the micro itself is going to become a part of the world our children will inherit and, in the very near future, will become part of the household furniture, it would seem necessary to enquire into its role in teaching and also to look at some of the effects it may be having on the children. This chapter will attempt to identify areas that may need eventual investigating. It is particularly concerned, however, with the attitudes children may have towards the microcomputer. Since, as has already been stated, the micro will become more and more ubiquitous, it would seem important that children's attitudes should be positive. Within this context I would hypothesize that a positive attitude would be shown by the children if they found the microcomputer in some way an aid to their learning – if, for instance, it could be shown that microcomputers had a large motivational role. If children meet the microcomputer in an exciting and pleasurable role in school then one could argue that there is a greater likelihood of them accepting it as an aid in the world of work which they must experience in the future.

The microcomputer will bring a new dimension to the classroom and the learning situation. As is right and proper, its applications are coming under detailed scrutiny by the teaching profession. Important questions can be asked regarding it: 'How are teaching styles going to be affected?'; 'What effect will it have on the curriculum?' and more. The centre of the educational process is the child: it is the children who are going to inherit the world of the microcomputer not ourselves. It would seem vital that the child has a positive attitude to the microcomputers which already are in our society. Business and industry are being changed by the application of microprocessor techniques; employment patterns are altering and we have a responsibility as teachers to prepare the children in our care for this new world they must enter. A recent Department of Industry report stated that if we are to survive as a trading nation we must embrace the new technology. They have backed up their report by investing money in microcomputing in education and this has been enhanced by the Government in the creation of MEP (Microcomputers in Education Project).

What then are attitudes? There are many definitions but the one that has stood the test of time would seem to be Allport's:

> An attitude is a mental and neural state of readiness organized through experience, exerting a direct and dynamic influence upon the individual's response to all objects and situations with which it is related.
> (in Jahoda and Warren, 1966)

Attitudes would therefore seem to be internal states that affect an individual's choice of action within any situation. Thus a person may have a particular attitude, for example, towards coloured people or cars and this attitude would affect his response to that object. Allport (1937) suggests that attitudes are dependent upon experience and this in its turn suggests that attitudes are learned. If this is the case, then we could ask from where are attitudes learned. Is it from the home, or school or from peer group pressure; could one not argue that a particular attitude is held to please the person one is interacting with at a particular time? One could legitimately ask if a child could have an attitude to microcomputers if they have never seen one before, as one could ask what formulated an attitude to the microcomputer in those children that have come in contact with it?

Allport also suggests that the attitudes held by an individual determine what they will see and hear, what they will think and do. This is, I suppose, another way of saying that there are none so blind as those who do not want to see. A person will form an attitude to a particular object and if that attitude is fully internalized then no argument will sway him.

Attitudes themselves are tied into beliefs and values, and all three of these share common attributes. They are all psychological constructs – that is, they are introspective in their operation. This creates a problem since one of the few ways of investigating attitudes is by the use of introspection. However, it is not the sort of introspection that was abandoned very early in psychological investigations, since it is not the investigator who is being introspective but rather his techniques, such as interviewing. Beliefs are based on assumptions that do not necessarily have any basis in fact. For example, I may believe that the microcomputer is going to be a very potent force in education but, at present, I have little evidence of an objective kind to substantiate my belief. My belief serves as a basis for action. Values are basically a desire for the truth of a belief. My belief in microcomputers makes me give them a high value and means that I strive to find out more about them and how I can use them within particular contexts.

Throughout this chapter one must bear in mind that the microcomputer is a very new and relatively untried aid to teaching/learning. However, as has already been pointed out, it is going to become a potent force in the world of employment and, in order for the future citizens of the country to react in a positive way, their attitudes must be positive. The use of computers and other microelectronics-based devices is of growing importance not only in computer studies but also in mathematics, science and other areas of the curriculum. Many aspects of adult life and work are likely to be transformed by developments in computer science and in information and control technology (DES, 1981).

This study does not claim to be rigorous. Seven children were interviewed using a twenty point questionnaire and their replies recorded on a tape recorder. These replies were subsequently transcribed for the purpose of this article. The children were all between the ages of eight and eleven and had had a small amount of experience in using the microcomputer in school. They were of mixed ability and both girls and boys were represented. The smallness of the sample is a disadvantage but, from observation of children using the machine, I would maintain that the attitudes shown are widespread.

Generally the reaction of the children to the microcomputer was favourable. We seem to find a very high motivation level when children are using the microcomputer. For instance, Kevin's answer to the question 'Do you think the computer would be a bad thing or a good thing to help people learn?' was, 'children get bored just sitting in the classroom and if you've got a computer you can work on that and have a lot of fun'. The educational process for this child would not seem to be the exciting experience we fondly imagine education to be. This was the predominant attitude to the micro. Continuing with the motivational aspects, Samantha says, 'it starts off easy and when it gets longer, and you want to get your answer in because you want to play with it afterwards'. Danny shows a different level of motivation, 'better than doing it, (work) with cards or in a book, you don't have to write things down'. Lisa's reply, 'people get more fun at learning on the computer', is again indicative of the motivational aspects of the machine.

Since the microcomputer tends at present to be a small group tool the first question asked was 'Do you prefer working: by yourself, with another child, with your teacher, with other children and your teacher?', to see if there was any connection between the child's working preferences and manifested attitudes. Of the seven children interviewed four preferred to work with other children and their teacher and two preferred to work by themselves, one child varying his preference dependent on the task presented. All the children indicated that they thought the microcomputer a good thing to help children learn, with the exception of Caroline's qualification. (She is my daughter and has heard me when a program will not work!) She said 'Well it's bad when it doesn't work properly and you get angry and it's good when you can play something like "Lemonade" which you can't at school'. There does not seem to be any particular pattern apparent here. One may have hoped for a correlation between 'independent' children and a preference for the microcomputer, but this is not apparent. This may be an indication of the widespread acceptance of the micro amongst children.

The second question asked 'What other things do you use besides your teacher to help you learn?' and was used to give an indication of the way the children viewed aids to teaching/learning. It is interesting that most children had to be prompted regarding these aids. Their responses show differing views. Four children responded that they used books, two had responses of peer support and one thought the computer was the only aid to learning they used. This in its turn may be a reflection of the role the teachers see themselves in. Has the instructional aspect of the teacher's role become predominant to the exclusion of the perhaps more important aspects regarding problem solving? I would say I am as guilty as the next man in this respect.

Several questions were included to give an indication of the children's knowledge and responses to learning through games. These questions asked generally about games and then focused on games on the microcomputer. Responses to the game situation indicate a strong reaction towards the computer. Four children preferred the computer alone, two preferred another child and the computer and one preferred the teacher and the computer. It is perhaps indicative of the positive attitudes to the computer that it figures in the preference of all the children in the sample. I would like to make one observation here regarding the response of using the computer alone. All the game situations used were set up in a pseudo-competitive manner among several children. From these responses little cooperative interaction would seem to appear. However, observations of children using the microcomputer indicate a high level of cooperation between the groups. With younger children there is a great deal of cooperation in looking for the correct keys on the keyboard, and with the older children cooperation existed in the solution to a problem. The first case suggests that there would seem to be a need to introduce keyboard skills into the primary curriculum, even though such aids as microwriter are becoming available; there would be a lot of opposition to the abandonment of the QWERTY keyboard. However Papert (1980) has some observations regarding what he calls the QWERTY syndrome in its relationship to the 'sabre toothed curriculum'.

One problem however would seem apparent. For a child to have a meaningful attitude towards an object-class, they should have the required concepts associated with it. In this case it is the computer that is the object-class in question. What then are the child's concepts regarding the computer?

Several of the children saw the machine as a game player – *viz* Kevin, Lisa, Samantha. The main reason for this, I suggest, is that the programs the children have come in contact with to date have had a game format. This indicates that it may be necessary to expand their knowledge of the potential of the machine. I have suggested that there are indications that children have a positive attitude to the computer, but I feel that it may be necessary to do some more work in order to isolate the concepts that could contribute towards a meaningful attitude in its fullest sense. At present there is ambiguity regarding their concepts.

We can, however, look at the children's replies regarding their knowledge of the computer, in order to form a tentative indication regarding that knowledge. To this end several questions were inserted to enquire about the children's knowledge of the computer and what it can do.

15   What other ways do you think the computer can be used to help you learn?
16   What things do you think your teacher can give you that the computer cannot?
17   What things do you think the computer can give you that your teacher cannot?
18   Can you think of other things the computer may be able to do?

We see, I suggest, a grouping towards the concepts needed. Thus David says, 'it can help you learn how to do things and how to know things'. Samantha says, 'could help you with different languages'. Richard's response to questions 15/16 is interesting since it would seem to indicate a greater grasp of the concepts involved, 'could be used when you are reading because when you learn your spellings you are learning to read as well', and 'the teacher has to program the computer first', an indication maybe that this child is beginning to form the concept that the machine cannot operate independently. In the main there was a negative response to question 15, though I suggest Samantha's response to question 16 is another proto-concept when she says, 'I like the teacher talking to me'. Perhaps the greatest indication that the children did not have an internalized concept of the computer is the universally negative response to question 18.

Although, as has already been indicated, it would be dangerous to generalize from these results there is an indication of a positive attitude to the microcomputer. Gagné (1965) suggests that of major importance in the formation of attitudes is the fact that learner identification with the human model should have been internalized. Since one cannot suggest that the computer can be modelled by a human, one could suggest that the attitudes shown could possibly be a reflection of the attitudes of the teacher who provided the microcomputer. The children see his positive attitude to it and model their own attitude on his. Another suggestion is that there is learner recall of a pleasant learning situation when the special attributes of the computer are used.

The attitudes manifested in this small study seem to be predominantly within the affective domain. All of them would seem to be on the like/dislike continuum and the cognitive aspects of these attitudes would not seem to be so well represented.

The children were all aged between eight and eleven. It is perhaps a salutary observation to those of us that are slightly 'longer in the tooth' that they were not born when Neil Armstrong landed on the moon. The children, however, have grown up in a technological society. They all probably have a television, radio, hi-fi in the house. I am aware that few of the children have a computer in the house, but most will have access to a calculator. Kevin's reference to the Little Professor is, I suggest, a response to an accepted technology. The children do not hold technology in awe as many adults tend to do. Some adults blame many of the ills of the world on technology, and therefore tend to be antipathetic regarding new technology. To children the world of the microcomputer and the new technology is an exciting one; they do, I suggest, feel in control of a situation when using a machine. On the other hand, adults, I feel, are slightly frightened of computer technology. All they tend to see are the mistakes that the programmer has initiated, such as the £1000 gas bill, and this has coloured their attitudes. Papert (*op. cit.*) has suggested that, using the computer, children are encouraged to think about thinking. He uses the argument within the framework of the child as a programmer, since he argues that in the main the computer has been used to program children and become a surrogate instructor. This may be true in the United States but, within the confines of primary education in this country, I would suggest that this is not so. Programs may still be written that are drill orientated, but I suggest that the thinking program is becoming more widespread. However I have noticed that teachers who give a high value to the micro as an aid put emphasis on the drill programs but the children prefer the programs where they have to think. An excellent example of this new type of thinking program is in Barry Holmes' (1981) 'Spanish Main'.

If the attitudes manifested by the children in this sample are in any way typical then it will be instructive to enquire into the possible uses of the microcomputer and suggest what aspects of these uses may contribute to the formation of attitudes.

There appear to be three main areas where the microcomputer could be effective in the formation of attitudes. Since attitudes are learned, the mere use of the computer will contribute to their formation. However, the computer has certain attributes that may have influenced the children's attitudes, although there will be a considerable contribution from the teacher himself, the structure of the classroom and, in turn, the teacher's view of education, knowledge and children. These are very broad areas which can be subdivided.

The three areas I wish to explore are: the role of the computer functioning alone; the role of the teacher functioning without the computer; the role of the teacher functioning with the computer as an aid. Within the confines of this article I shall only be able to give each area a simplistic description.

In examining the roles of microcomputer functioning alone, one is assuming a child/microcomputer interface where the child is using the microcomputer for some task designated by the teacher. Regardless of the task set, it is assumed that teacher intervention is minimal. I will not go into detail regarding the construction of programs for this role save to say that they must be very user friendly. However it is necessary to explain why I should consider the micro interacting with the child without teacher intervention.

I would maintain that in the limited time available for teaching in the usual school day there is a possibility of delegating some of the duties of the teacher to the micro. This does not mean that the teacher is delegating his responsibilities, only some aspects of his task. Things that spring to mind immediately are the practice situations that of necessity arise in the course of the teaching day. Consider tables tests and spelling tests. One could ask, 'are these activities necessary for all children?'. What if the child knows his tables and can recall them at random easily? Under these circumstances giving a weekly tables test is a waste of that child's time. If the retort to this is that we must continue to give tables tests to ensure that the children remember them, could it not be argued that we should perhaps be providing experiences where the child has to use his knowledge of tables? There are children who are going to need this experience and a delegation of this purely mechanical aspect of teaching is a possibility. Regardless of the task, some of the attributes of the micro can be utilized in this situation where there is a direct child/computer interaction.

The first of these that I would like to investigate is the speed of response made possible by the microcomputer. This acts at two levels. Firstly, the microcomputer is an extremely patient animal. It will wait forever for a particular response. All too often the teacher will ask a child a question, and the child is immediately put under pressure to supply an answer. The pressure may not be overt but it is there, since both the teacher and the rest of the class are waiting for the answer. It is the publicity of the pressure that 'addles the child's brains' and makes the answer, that was there before, vanish. There automatically follows the sense of ridicule if the answer is wrong. With the microcomputer there is no feeling of pressure and the child knows that the machine will wait for him. This is shown from the reply one child gave to the question asking for children's working preferences. He replied he would prefer to work with the computer because 'you get more time with it'. The incorrect response is ignored and if the program is arranged properly then a second go is allowable or the program branches to present problems at a different level. It is a private failure between the child and the machine; children soon come to realize that the machine does not tell tales. Secondly, the microcomputer can respond very quickly if the occasion demands. The answer to a question is there straight away; the child knows if he is right or wrong immediately and does not need to wait until the teacher is free to mark his book to become aware of his result. Thus correct responses are reinforced immediately, and incorrect responses are detected. How often do we see the queue of children waiting at the teacher's desk? When the child gets his turn he then finds the work is wrong. How much better to get the immediate feedback the micro can give.

The second aspect I would like to consider in this section is the use of animation and graphics as part of a computer presentation to the children. Perhaps the most ubiquitous aid to teaching/learning is the blackboard. This aid, however, has its limitations. Unless the teacher is a good artist then the blackboard presentation can conceal more information than it supplies. The teacher must import film to give movement to his presentation but, with the microcomputer, animation and exciting graphics can be included in the complete learning package. This increases the motivation factor since, if the movement is arranged to be user controlled, then the child can feel in control of the situation. For instance, consider children working on geometric ideas. Although they will have been working with concrete material, many of the ideas that they could conceivably investigate would need a considerable range of equipment. One could suggest that, after initial work using concrete material, the children could transfer to a computer to investigate further – for example, if they were working on investigations of triangles. Children could determine the apices of any triangle. The program could then shade in the angles and then rearrange these angles to show the angle sum is always constant regardless of the triangle. The rules of similar triangles can easily be demonstrated using the graphics potential of the computer. The advantages over the more traditional methods of presentation are obvious, perhaps the main one being that the child is more able to learn independently. Consider a problem solving situation where the child has to interpret text and pictures. If traditional sources are used then, unless a great deal of work is done, the problem becomes a 'one off'. However, using the computer, random events are possible, and are possible in such a way that the teacher does not have to control them. If these events can be associated with pictures, movement and sound, then they are going to become a great deal more motivating.

Papert (*op. cit.*) gives a further description of the way graphics can be used in education. In talking of the turtles he mentions 'floor turtles' and 'screen turtles'. The screen turtles are interactive graphics that respond to a child initiated program. Thus the child controls the turtle to design various shapes, to produce art in colour and movement. Papert argues that in a situation such as this the child can think about thinking, can internalize the powerful ideas involved in Euclidian and Cartesian geometry and can come to a greater understanding of the world through this interaction. This sort of activity would not be available to the child in the traditional educational environment since a great deal of symbol manipulation would become necessary, and the symbol manipulation would become an aim in itself to the exclusion of the concepts under consideration.

Many would see the whole of primary education as a question and answer situation. Within this situation there would be a place for the computer to pose questions and provide answers. Primary education is concerned with basic skills and in this the microcomputer can be used. It can pose questions of a simple skill building nature and can be used as an information retrieval system. The computer, however, is capable of posing more powerful questions and providing deeper and more easily accessible answers to children's questions. Programs like the ITMA program 'Seek' are already breaking this ground of using the computer as an answer providing medium.

I would like to suggest that perhaps the education system does not ask the right questions, or asks questions for the wrong purpose. Why are questions asked of children? I would agree with the suggestion that in the main they are asked to test the children's knowledge of facts or skills previously taught (Pate and Bremer, 1967).

Are questions asked where the teacher genuinely does not know the answer? It has been suggested that children know inwardly that when teachers say they do not know the answer to a question they do really and the children, loyal creatures that they are, enter into the spirit of the situation and play the game. We have all of us at one time played the game of 'guess what teacher is thinking about' when we ask questions of children. We want a particular response to pursue our own aims, and a valid answer that does not fit into our scheme is praised but ignored. One could also ask who poses most of the questions in the classroom, and it is found that it is the teacher. Barnes et. al. (1968) concluded that most questions were closed questions and children were seldom asked to think aloud or to explore implications. It could be argued that since the computer is capable of generating random situations in which nobody could possibly know the answers previously, the child and teacher are together in the land of 'don't know – lets work it out together'. The questions that could be generated from this sort of situation are no longer the 'what is 3×4?' type of question, but of the sort, 'what would have happened if ...?' type. In this case the micro could simulate a possible answer for real discussion, either amongst a group of children working as a group, or the children and the teacher.

It is within game situations that the computer comes into its own. Games have a high motivational factor, and children learn by playing them. However, children often need a referee to overlook their work in a game playing situation and this is a drain on the teacher's time. Using the microcomputer, the teacher can set up a game situation to develop some aspects of learning and know that the microcomputer will act as the referee. It has been my experience that, when children are playing games within a learning environment, the game board gets upset at the crucial time. Using the computer, the game is viewable at all stages, and the teacher can intervene at all stages. One of the most important aspects of using games is the thinking aspects associated with the strategies children employ. With the micro there is perhaps a greater opportunity to investigate these strategies and develop a heuristic. Games of many different sorts can be used, in fact I can see a place for games such as chess in the curriculum. Any game that demands a strategy to win is worthy of inclusion. My reason for saying this is that strategy demands thought, and thought and thinking is one of the neglected areas of the curriculum. I was working recently with a group of third year juniors using a computer game called 'Blackbox'. This game randomly puts a number of 'atoms' into an eight by eight box and, by shining light into the box and observing its behaviour, one has to deduce the position of the atoms. It is not an easy game. At the end of the session one girl went 'phew' and made a great show of wiping her brow. I asked what was the matter and she replied she would rather do long division. Well this piqued me rather so I enquired why. She replied that she had to think when playing Blackbox, and had to do little thinking when doing long division. I felt vindicated! The games can be competitive or not as the teacher desires, there could be competition between the child and other children or competition against the computer. The child can also compete against himself.

Perhaps the most potent argument for using the computer in the primary school classroom is the possibility for individualization. Programs can be tailored to a particular child or group of children. There are obvious advantages here for remedial education. The program can also be made self adjusting dependent on the child's performance. Skinnerian psychology would suggest that each step in the learning process should be short and that it should grow from previously learned behaviour. It is also suggested that, at the early stages, learning should be continuously reinforced and that continuous and intermittent reinforcement should continue throughout the learning process. The reward of reinforcement should follow quickly on the heels of the stimulus for behavioural modification to take place (Child, 1973). If one adheres to this model of learning then the microcomputer would seem to be an ideal instrument to use within this context. Outside of the Skinnerian view of the learning process, the computer has a great deal to offer. The child as an instrument of its own learning is a philosophy embedded in most primary school idealogy and, with the computer at their disposal, the possibilities of this occurring are increased. Children learn at different rates and to take this into account the teacher usually groups his class out into fairly autonomous groups. These can never be completely autonomous, but with the computer at his disposal it becomes more possible.

The microcomputer can, at times, demand cooperation among the children to formulate an answer, thus propagating the true group situation. The true group situation demands an interaction among the children with group discussion and decision making. If we consider children in a group situation there is often not a group in existence; the children are working individually and the interaction needed for a group situation is missing. Invariably, in what is ostensibly a group situation, the children are working individually, merely being in a group for the convenience of the teacher who perhaps has put children of similar abilities together. The interaction is not apparent. That is not to condemn such a practice. It is often very useful since the teacher's instruction can be directed at a reasonably homogeneous group. However, one can envisage a situation where a group of children interact to come to a decision based on the information they have available and then act on that decision. One could also consider children cooperating in a problem solving situation – perhaps a 'Junior Egg Race'. Without the computer the teacher would have to act as a referee and perhaps an arbiter but, using the computer, this role can be delegated. For instance, in any problem solving situation there is an inherent logic; could not the computer be programmed to hold a heuristic of problem solving so the children can refer to it – if they need to? Children learn their own language by using it and forming generalizations from experience. With problem solving, children also need valid problems to solve in order for them to become problem solvers. I am, myself, working on a program the aim of which is to allow children to interact within a group to discuss information at their own level and then to allow the computer to change the situation dependent upon the instructions given by the children. This is only the start, the problem the children will have to solve in this program is artificial but it should allow a genuine interaction in a group situation to take place. It will not be welcome in a classroom where the traditional educational role of the teacher as a giver and the child as a receiver are prevalent – but is this the teacher's prime role?

I have been considering the role of the computer working without teacher intervention. However, if we examine this idea in greater detail, there has been teacher intervention at the initial stages. The teacher has made the decision to introduce the computer into his classroom, he has selected the programs to be used and may in some cases have written the original program. Thus a great deal of the responsibility has still devolved onto the teacher's shoulders. I have suggested that there are times when the teacher can profitably delegate some of his tasks to the machine, and that there are some times when any teacher intervention may be counterproductive to the learning situation. This does not mean that the teacher is redundant in the learning situation – on the contrary, it means he will be able to fulfil his prime role, for there are some aspects of the art of teaching that cannot be duplicated by the machine, at least within the present state of the art, and I would maintain that there will never be a time when the teacher will be redundant. His role may change over the years, schools may be completely different by the time this century is out, but there will still be the need for the human guide who can bring his greater knowledge and experience to the learning situation. I would like to consider some of these roles.

Perhaps the first of these roles we must consider is that the teacher can teach. This attribute is used in a particular way. I personally do not think marking exercises is teaching, nor to some extent the inculcation of basic skills. These are necessary but can be done by a microcomputer. It is within the realm of understanding that the teacher should function, understanding being used in terms of Skemp's (1962) dichotomy of relational and instrumental understanding. Relational understanding is to understand why a thing happens and instrumental understanding means the child gets the 'right' anwer but does not understand why. Obviously the first is embedded in concept formation and the second in skills. We can conceive of a situation where there is no 'right' answer and it is here that the skill of the teacher should be used. Papert (*op. cit.*) has pointed out that there tends to be an automatic rejection of 'incorrect' answers, and continues to argue that if people learn from mistakes then the mistake is as important as the corect response. He cites the powerful idea of debugging, as is done in a computer program, to introduce children to the problems of self-analysis. If I might introduce a parable. I asked a class of children how many had ever got a sum 'wrong', the whole class put their hands up. I then asked them to keep their hands up if they had found the mistake themselves – all but a handful put their hand down. Have we not all the right to be wrong at times?

The teacher in his teaching role is the guide to the child as he reaches out to encompass a new reality into his present. It is the full realization of the meaning of the word 'education' with an appreciation of its root, 'educare' – to lead out, not to mainly put in! If I seem to malign teachers in this I apologize. I am as guilty as the next man, but more and more I have been taking to heart and thinking about the way children learn. If a child comes to school with a considerable command of the English language in its oral form then we can surmise that even the least able of the children in our classes is capable of learning. Yet we seem to spend an inordinate amount of our time battling with rules of grammar that the children already intuitively know. Children when they come to school have a great facility with everyday language but, I would maintain, we as teachers are still groping for ways of translating this spoken language into the written form. Children, however, do not come to school in the main with a great deal of language that encompasses areas of mathematics and science and the skill of problem solving. The new technology will enable us to delegate parts of the instructional side of the curriculum, releasing time to explore problem solving and relationships and suggest deeper understandings of the world. Teaching is aiding accommodation and assimilation; it is a direct interaction between the child and the teacher, each contributing in his or her own way to the problem area under consideration. The teacher's role is that of the human interpreter of the world the child sees, extending that world, not in the restrictive sense of setting such and such page of exercises but being the person who poses pertinent questions to direct the child to a deeper understanding of the matter in hand. This is the aspect of the teacher's task that cannot be taken over by the microcomputer, and is the role that I feel will become more and more important in the years to come.

The teacher is not just a person who passes on the knowledge of the society – he can respond on a personal level towards an individual child. The teacher has an intimate knowledge of the child. He is aware of the home background, the child's attitudes, and his developmental level. In the interactive situation that is called teaching, the teacher can react with all this knowledge towards an individual child. Even if we could define beauty to encompass all its aspects, and thus program a computer to recognize beauty, many would say (and I would agree with them) that we would be dehumanizing life. It is the teacher who brings to the children's attention the beauty of the leaves in the autumn, the intricacies and the marvel of a flower, who encourages the child in many subtle ways to look at other sides of a question. As a child said to Roy Garland, 'computers cannot pick flowers'.

The teacher can change direction depending upon the situation. He can do this easily by modifying strategies and exercising greater discrimination in encouraging children's response to a situation. Consider the classroom where children bring different things into it. One day a child will bring in an object that demands discussion and investigation. The teacher can abandon what he intended to do in order to capitalize on the motivation often shown by young children to an *objet trouvé*. The computer could not make this adjustment to class needs.

The teacher can respond at an emotional level towards a child's problems. He can bandage the cut knee and wipe away the tears. He has the sensitivity to understand and appeciate a child's individual problems. To the teacher the child is not just an object of instruction but a living breathing organism with its strengths and its weaknesses. Consider the child who has had a bereavement; no computer in the world can take that child to one side and maybe find the words that will comfort and still the sadness. No, this situation demands a thinking adult. Children form relationships with their teacher that are far deeper than any they may form with the microcomputer. The child cannot talk to the microcomputer or ask it individual questions.

There are many ramifications in the teacher's armory to respond to a child's needs. The teacher can operate at more than one level at a time, subtly adjusting the situation to achieve some particular aim. He can stimulate and explore with the child many situations, develop language and encourage a creative response. The teacher can adjust to the individual child in a more flexible way. He can detect non-verbal communication, and use non-verbal cues as prompts to the child. The teacher can take reasoned decisions with regard to the learning environment. He determines the task to be completed, the materials to be used and the presentation of the task.

The teacher is continuously diagnosing problems and responding to these problems. He can do this by reason of his knowledge of the child, the learning process and the subject matter under consideration. Although the computer can be programmed to adjust itself to individual differences in the teaching situation, it would be difficult for it to take a completely different approach. If a child has a problem in his learning it is of little use to give it more of the same, the problem will be compounded. The teacher can then introduce new material to overcome an individual difficulty, and approach a problem from many different directions using all his knowledge and experience.

It can be seen that there are many roles within the learning environment that could not be delegated to a machine. The teacher is a central part of the educational process, but one might consider that a more Platonic teacher and a more Platonic teaching role could evolve in a computer rich world. The teacher is also an influencer of attitudes, and his attitude to an object-class will have a considerable effect on the attitudes formed by children. We have seen there are certain attributes of the computer that are important in considering what influences children's attitudes towards it. We have considered the role of the teacher within the classroom and suggested that there are certain roles that belong exclusively to the teacher. We can now consider the combination of the two and consider the teacher using the computer as an aid.

It has been accepted that part of the role of the primary school lies within inculcating basic skills. However it may be instructive to enquire what is meant by a basic skill. Generally accepted in this category are the skills of numeracy and literacy, but it could be maintained that a new basic skill is now necessary in the society that is developing. That is the skill of information processing. There is more information available than has been available at any time in the history of mankind. The microcomputer and the teacher working together can access this data and make it available to the child. There is all the information on the national databases such as CEEFAX, ORACLE and PRESTEL that needs to be taken into consideration. Books used to be our main avenue of information but these avenues are increasing. The skills of sifting information, representing it, and interpreting it are becoming extremely important. To take an example, one could consider advertisements and discuss how they are influencing the society we live in, in order to introduce discrimination to the children. We could look at various pages of the database and explore the information included in them. The databases are becoming more used; the computer to be sold by the British Broadcasting Corporation in connection with its computer literacy programmes will have a facility to load programs direct from the database, with its obvious implications.

All the attributes of the computer already mentioned can be turned to good use to aid the teacher in the presentation of a lesson. Within the secondary school, programs are becoming available to support different aspects of the curriculum. The same thing could happen in the primary school but, with the philosophy of child-centered education, they will be different. Mention was made in *Primary Education in England* (DES, 1980) that many topics lacked depth. Using a computer the teacher could explore with his children the 'why?' of a situation and a 'what happens if?' situation. Although aimed primarily at secondary schools, the ITMA program 'Transpots' is looking at these sorts of questions. Consider a local history study in the primary school. The depth possible using the computer far exceeds anything possible without and can be easily accessed. Perhaps all the census information could be put into in database and search routines could print out any information the child wants. Perhaps they are looking at the number of dressmakers in an area in 1850 and then look at the same catagory of occupation in 1950. There will surely be a difference, and the question could be asked why is there a difference? This would necessitate more research into the locality using archive material, with history becoming more real as information access becomes easier.

One aspect of learning that has not been extensively developed in the classroom is that of problem solving. This is probably due to the logistics of the situation. Using the microcomputer the teacher could explore situations in greater depth, allow greater discussion to take place and then use the microcomputer to analyze the decisions taken by the children and present the likely outcomes. These decisions can then be modified in the light of further information. Consider a program that we shall say simulates a situation. The child can get some information and, working on this information, come to certain decisions. These decisions can be fed into the computer which will calculate the possible results. This may mean that the decision has to be modified. We are thus into a hypothesis formation situation, a prediction exercise with the important implication that children will realize that the first answer is not necessarily the best one for the situation and that ideas can be modified in the light of further information.

Papert (*op. cit.*) has suggested that the child as a programmer is a very real possibility in the future. This is an aspect of cognitive development that has to be considered in considerable detail. I would tend to agree with his analysis and would perhaps advance it a little further. Thinking and thinking about thinking should perhaps be the central pivot on which the curriculum is built. De Bono (1969) has been advocating teaching thinking skills for a number of years, but it is only with the advent of the computer that the means has become available to explore thinking in any real depth. I am sure many will disagree with me on this score, but the paper and pencil aspects that have been developed to date do not have the same impact upon the child as writing a program would have. They would also seem to suffer from one other drawback in that they omit the concept of debugging; this is an integral part of thinking and problem solving that has not been appreciated in the past.

All the roles mentioned above could contribute to the formation of children's attitudes to the computer. That children have these positive attitudes I would contend is self-evident. I would go so far as to say that the motivation shown by children when interacting with the computer surpasses that in the traditional educational situation. In my own experience, I have had four and a half-year-olds work for an hour at a stretch, I have had remedial children work through their playtime to finish a spelling program. If this motivation is apparent then it would seem incumbent on the education profession to reexamine the whole curriculum now that the computer is becoming increasingly available. I suggest that the positive attitudes shown to the computer are a force to be reckoned with in education. The attitudes seem to have been formed because working with the computer is fun. Whether this is an aspect of the computer or an aspect of the programs the children have met would have to be investigated, but I would suggest that it is a combination of the two.

The programs used in this study were all predominantly in a game format and, consequently, one cannot overlook the motivational aspects of games in learning, but several of them deal with spelling and arithmetic practice, even tables. The children work at them though, and work hard; as one little girl said to me, 'you don't mind learning if it's fun'. This seems to be the reaction of all the children – using the computer is fun. Papert (*op. cit.*) has indicated that using the computer allows childrens to be agents of their own learning. This raises a fundamental question. If, as we have seen, children have positive attitudes to the computer, can use it easily, gain pleasure from learning with it, and develop greater independence, then what will the role of the teacher be in the future? I would contend that much of the instructional aspects of schooling will be redundant as far as the teacher is concerned and that we need to see the development of the teacher as a teacher, not as an instructor or as a provider of information. The situation could conceivably occur in which these aspects of learning need not be done in school, that the school could become a centre for professional advice, a repository of advanced thinking, and a resource bank for learning. The role of the teacher could become that of the guide and a true 'leader-outer', not a 'putter-inner'.

My final conclusion is that the study has raised more questions than it has answered. Given the apparent positive attitudes to the computer, much more investigation is needed regarding the genesis of these attitudes. Questions regarding the children's concepts of the computer need answering. What aspects of the role of the computer contribute to the positive attitudes also needs investigating and, finally, how should the computer be used in the classroom in order to capitalize on the positive attitudes and motivational aspects indicated in this study?

Once books were the new technology. Can we conceive of a time when the computer has an all embracing effect on society as books have now? Will there in the future be an entry on a child's report, 'could do better at programming'? The computer is no panacea for any educational ills; it is a tool, albeit a very powerful tool. Much work has yet to be done, but this new technology is going to lead us into avenues as yet unthought of. It is an exciting time!

References

ALLPORT, G.W. (1937) *Personality* New York, Holt.
BARNES, D., BRITTON, J. and ROSEN, H. (1969) *Language the Learner and the School* Harmondsworth, Penguin.
CHILD, D. (1973) *Psychology and the Teacher* (2nd ed.) New York, Holt, Rinehart and Winston.

COLLEGE OF ST MARK AND ST JOHN (1980) *ITMA Newsletter* College of St Mark and St John, Plymouth.
DE BONO, E. (1969) *The Thinking Class* London, Ward Lock.
DEPARTMENT OF EDUCATION AND SCIENCE (1980) *Primary Education in England* London, HMSO.
DEPARTMENT OF EDUCATION AND SCIENCE (1981) *The School Curriculum* London, HMSO.
GAGNÉ, R.M. (1965) *The Conditions of Learning* New York, Holt, Rinehart and Winston. Inc..
HOLMES, B. (1981) *Spanish Main* Cambridgeshire Software House.
JAHODA, M. and WARREN, J.M. (1966) *Attitudes* Harmondsworth, Penguin.
OPEN UNIVERSITY (1976) *Attitudes* Milton Keynes, Open University Press.
PAPERT, S. (1980) *Mindstorms Children Computers and Powerful Ideas* Sussex, Harvester Press.
PATE, R.T. and BREMER, N.H. (1967) 'Guiding learning through skilful questioning' *The Elementary School Journal* 6, pp. 417–422.
SKEMP, R.R. (1962) 'The need for a schematic learning theory' *British Journal of Educational Psychology* 32, pp. 133–142.

The Spanish Main: An Exploration of an Educational Role for Computer Simulation
Barry Holmes

The advent of the 'micro-chip' is currently transforming society as we know it today. The introduction of computerized control, information processing, etc., in both the industrial and commercial worlds, is making a definite impact. Although it is not yet certain where this transformation will eventually lead, it is observable and therefore we must attempt to both understand and control it. In education, particularly the primary sector, there is a growing awareness of some of the possible consequences of the introduction of these machines. Many important ethical and moral issues are raised when we consider the use of microprocessors as instruments of education, in addition to the problems of relating the applications of Computer Assisted Learning (CAL) to our understanding of the current theories of learning.

Too often the central theme of any discussion of CAL tends to revolve around facilities which the machine can offer or techniques of programming; for example, speed of response, animation techniques, screen formats, motivation, etc.. The emphasis appears over-whelmingly placed upon the technical skills of programming. An educational analysis of the programs, how they relate to a theory of learning or philosophy of education, is rarely conducted to the same depth. What we can do with the machine seems to be more important than the question of what we should be aiming to achieve. This is, possibly, understandable in the circumstances. Any new innovation needs time to become established and for the techniques which it offers to be fully explored. However, now is the time to appraise the potential of these machines, not just from a technical viewpoint but rather an attempt must be made to establish a dialogue as to their possible uses within education.

I believe it is essential first to develop a clear philosophy of education in order to provide a frame-work within which the use of the computer can be explored, and to which that work can be related. Although we cannot look to philosophy to provide high-level directives for education, it will help to make explicit those conceptual schemes which our beliefs and standards presuppose. These presuppositions can then be tested, criticized and revised; the grounds for beliefs can be challenged and alternatives suggested.

I would argue that understanding is the key; it is of paramount importance in the educational process. There is little or no point in having knowledge without understanding. Understanding implies the ability to apply knowledge whereas knowledge does not necessarily imply that there will be understanding. I may know that three times four is twelve as a rote response, thus I have a piece of knowledge, but it does not imply that I understand the concept of multiplication. Further, understanding implies the ability to reason about an area of knowledge and reason suggests the ability explicitly to employ generalizations and rules in the forming of beliefs and in the planning of actions.

Inextricably interwoven with this desire for understanding is the need for a respect of the learner and a concern for his personal dignity and sense of worth. It is this respect for persons which is central in education, for without this the value judgements made, on how education shall be transmitted, can have no true moral basis. For instance, if we are only concerned with the acquisition of a set of facts, without concern for the learner, then we may consider that the use of brain-washing techniques is an acceptable and efficient form of transfer. Certainly this is an extreme example and is only defensible if the value judgements made regarding transfer procedures neglect the morality implicit in the situation.

Adopting any philosophical stance will, if it is based on rationality, shape the ways in which it is morally defensible for us to influence the minds of children. It will define our pedagogy of education, eliminating those theories which our rationality defines as unacceptable to that philosophy and causing us to examine critically those which we have adopted. The rigours of this examination will apply to both the old and the new, for it must be a constant reappraisal of what we are doing against what we should be doing. Therefore we must apply to any new feature of education, be it technological or theoretical, an examination of its values based upon the criteria of acceptability in terms of our philosophy.

Using these constraints, I suggest that, only if the situation is meaningful to the learner, can there be conscious awareness, voluntary participation and an intelligent, educational doing. Therefore when considering CAL the following become essential features of its pedagogy.

1 Respect for the learner and his personal development.
2 Respect for reason.
3 Respect for understanding.
4 To allow decision-making within the limits of experience.

AN EDUCATIONAL ROLE FOR COMPUTER SIMULATION

The vast majority of the programs, which constitute the current CAL package, are little more than electronic worksheets. Their pedagogy is based firmly on the behaviourist theories of learning, which implies a routine of operant conditioning. The types of program which fall into this catagory can be illustrated by those whose aim is to practise basic mathematical skills of the four rules of number. The sum appears on the screen, the child types in an answer and, if correct, receives an immediate positive response. This may take several forms, most common being a smiling face or a 'well done'. In some programs there is a difficulty level which changes after the child answers correctly a set number of sums. Many programs attempt to explain to the child where he has made a mistake when this occurs, but all too often the explanation is in the form of words and the language level is not consistent with the mathematical level of the program. Although the programmer may be striving for the learner to understand the processes involved, by using a variety of means, there appears little evidence that this type of program has a meaningful educational purpose. It certainly presupposes a certain degree of competence and conceptual understanding on the part of the user. It serves only to give practice to that competence. This is not meant to imply that there should not be occasions when skills are practised, rather, that if the practice assumes a major proportion of the activities of the learner then it becomes at variance with an educational philosophy concerned with understanding.

After using a computer for some time in school it was realized that in order to make full use of its potential and be consistent with such a philosophy, the area of computer simulation needed to be explored. The most difficult area of CAL is that of computer simulation and modelling, a field which relates closely to the theories of concept formation. Here the program attempts to model closely real situations and allow the user to control events by his inputs. The only programs of this nature available at this time are commercially produced and not aimed at the primary child – 'Lunar Lander' and 'Star Trek' are examples. Both these games give an insight into the power, complexity and possibilities of computer simulation.

Initially, before attempting a full simulation, it was decided to try to use the computer in a slightly more open way from the stimulus-response programs we had designed. Therefore the 'Hall Area' program was initiated. The school hall has two alcoves – one in the middle, used for the storage of P.E. apparatus, the other, used for the storage of the dining-room furniture – and is only entered by some of the children when returning their plates at lunch time. The program was designed to check the children's measurements of the length and width of the main body of the hall and, if measured, those of either or both alcoves. The program uses the children's measurements, so long as they are within predetermined limits, to calculate the area of the hall. This is then checked against the area the children input as their answer to question five. If the two do not agree the children are asked to check their calculations and question five is repeated. If the two do not tally a second time the children are told to check their work with the teacher (see figure 1).

The children worked in pairs for this program and it was interesting to see how the boundaries of the hall were defined, especially as there was no prior discussion on the problem. There were, in fact, two categories of answers which emerged. The first, a minority, did not include either of the alcoves in their calculation. The second only included the area of the middle alcove in their area, presumably as it was frequently used by the children. No one included the area of the alcove where the tables were stacked in their initial calculations. The program initiated a great deal of discussion amongst the children about the definition of the boundaries of the hall, without participation of the teacher. Groups requested that they be allowed to repeat the exercise in order to include both alcoves. The program had stimulated interest and had certainly promoted discussion which was spontaneous. Obviously the children participating in this program had already gained the necessary skills to complete the task with reasonable success. It is interesting that they were stimulated sufficiently, without any encouragement, to calculate a re-defined area and were not prepared to accept what they had come to see as a partial solution, even though this was accepted as correct by the computer. There are probably many individual reasons why the children adopted this attitude, varying from those who merely wished to have another turn on the computer to those who are perfectionists and will always wish to include all the possibilities and look for an absolute answer. Whatever the reason for the attitude they adopted, the interest stimulated by the computer in a fairly mundane task was most encouraging. We are now looking at the possibility of producing a set of programs on area which will include others with similar problems of definition of boundaries.

As I have already stated the 'Hall Area' program was our first real attempt to use the computer in a more open-ended situation in preparation for our first venture into the area of simulation. I decided that the next step was to develop a true simulation exercise for primary children which would be closely related to the theories of concept formation. The task, I found, is not that simple. This is borne out by the virtue of the fact that I could not discover an educational program of this nature for primary children. The researches into CAL which related to simulation exercises were based on higher

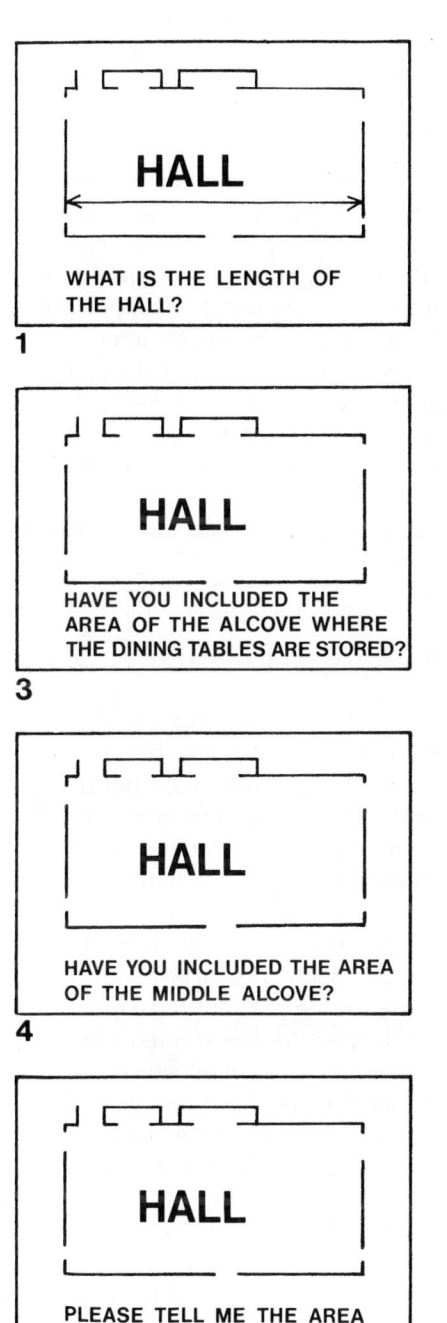

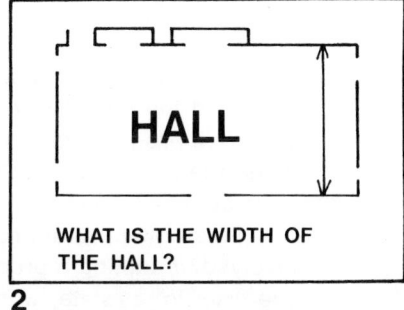

AN EDUCATIONAL ROLE FOR COMPUTER SIMULATION 173

1. WHAT IS THE LENGTH OF THE HALL?

2. WHAT IS THE WIDTH OF THE HALL?

If YES then the program checks these measurements. If NO then it runs to question 4.

3. HAVE YOU INCLUDED THE AREA OF THE ALCOVE WHERE THE DINING TABLES ARE STORED?

If YES then these measurements are checked. If NO it runs to question 5.

4. HAVE YOU INCLUDED THE AREA OF THE MIDDLE ALCOVE?

5. PLEASE TELL ME THE AREA YOU HAVE CALCULATED?

Figure 1   A Run of the Hall Area Program

education. For example, Computer Assisted Learning in Chemistry (CALCHEM) developed by Leeds University in co-operation with others, is aimed at simulations in chemical theories at university level and the others already mentioned previously. Commercially produced programs are aimed, as I have already mentioned, at an older age range. The problem became a question of (a) should we try to adapt a commercial program or (b) should we try to develop a complete new program based on our knowledge of the age range involved? Adapting a program would, I felt, (a) possibly reduce the exercise to a state where it may be too trivial, limiting the parameters of choice would possibly remove the validity of the simulation, (b) the programs examined did not develop the factors relevant to primary education. So with the limitation of available simulations it was decided to develop our own simulation for third and fourth year juniors.

First, the areas of skills to be practised or introduced were chosen and were as follows:

a Practice with co-ordinates
b Practice in the use of degrees
c Introduction to vectors

Secondly the program was required to involve the children in logical thinking related to planning, strategy and group co-operation.

Thirdly the program must be able to run with the minimum of teacher involvement – for example, it must be able to stand alone so that teacher guidance did not influence the decisions made by the children.

The skill areas were chosen as they most certainly dictated the use of a map – a benefit in relation to our second set of requirements as this would provide a concrete base for the abstract strategies we hoped for to be developed. Having defined the requirements of the program it was now necessary to design a simulation which would make those features explicit. The map, the idea of co-ordinates and movement (vectors), quickly suggested the idea of treasure maps and pirates, a topic, I felt, which would most certainly interest this age range of children.

The initial concept became crystallized fairly quickly. One group of children would hide treasure on an island, possibly one of four, and try to defend it. The second group would attempt to discover the whereabouts of the treasure and try to capture it. The program would allow for various factors of movement and the fight when the two sides met. It certainly seemed the basis for a good program but critical examination soon found several flaws. Not least was the possible lack of activity of the group who were hiding the treasure,

AN EDUCATIONAL ROLE FOR COMPUTER SIMULATION 175

whilst the group who were seeking it carried out their search. This appeared as a definite imbalance between the required strategies of the two groups. Also, planning the battle was going to require the children to make decisions which were purely of an intuitive nature and would have little real value in terms of the requirements that had been predetermined. The problem with simulation programs was becoming very apparent. A simple stimulus-response program takes a relatively short time to define the parameters and about twenty-four hours to write and program into the computer. Here, approximately thirty hours had already been worked defining the program's aims and deciding upon a scenario. Yet it was clear that this particular simulation was not going to fulfil our requirements adequately.

The basic idea of the pirates, search for treasure seemed to be a promising one, so this theme was kept. The question of how to balance the decision-making requirements for both groups was the real problem. This was overcome by defining separate and different tasks for both groups, so that each had specific aims independent of but still related to the actions of their opponents.

The first crew – the Spaniards – were given the task of collecting treasure from each of four islands on the map and then sailing out of the area with a full load. The order in which they visited the islands and the routes taken between the ports were left entirely for them to plan. The second crew – the Pirates – were simply to search for and capture the treasure ship by finishing on the same co-ordinate. This seemed to balance the tasks of each group, requiring both to plan ahead and become involved with the movement of their ships. The moves were simulated periods of four hours and the distance sailed was based on the direction sailed relative to the direction of the wind. The wind speed and direction are constant in this particular simulation so that the strategy is not dependent upon variables for which they cannot plan, although it is intended later to randomize the wind speed and direction so as to introduce variables which may alter and thus make the simulation more realistic. The ports were positioned within the internal (invisible) boundaries created by the four islands and safe zones just outside these were planned. This meant that within these safe areas and in the port the treasure ship could not be captured. The pirates were encouraged to visit ports by the provision of information gained if they did so. For instance, if the treasure ship had visited that particular port the pirates would be given the following information:

a the amount of treasure on board the treasure ship
b the direction it set sail in.

If the Spaniards had not visited this port then they would be told this and given no further information. The importance of the amount of treasure on board was significant. The amounts of treasure were defined in chests of gold and chests of jewels. The proportions always remained the same (that is, 5:3, 4:2, 2:2, 3:4), though the placement on the islands was randomized and stated at the beginning of the program. Thus, if the amount loaded was known, then a relatively simple calculation would enable the pirates to decide those which had already been visited and those which the treasure ship had still to go to. Needless to say the treasure on each island could only be collected once.

In order to further encourage movement of the pirates, their ship was moved further in each sequence and the treasure ship slowed as it gained a greater load of treasure. Sighting distances (two co-ordinate points), and penalties for the pirates being in port or a safe zone at the same time as the Spaniards, were introduced to give the slower ship a chance to escape.

This period of planning had already taken about sixty hours and writing the program had not yet commenced. The computer was going to be used to:

a set up the starting positions
b to calculate the new position from the decisions of children
c check the position
  i remained within the boundaries of the map
  ii was not on an island
  iii if in port
  iv if in safe zone
d if in port
  i treasure ship
    1 load with treasure
    2 total the amount of treasure currently on board
    3 give information on the pirates (if they had visited that port)
  ii pirate ship (if treasure ship had visited that port)
    1 give information as to the total load of treasure
    2 give direction the treasure ship left
e give information on the sighting of another ship and its position
f decide if capture made or treasure ship escaped
g decide if both in safe zone or port and penalize the pirates if necessary.

Thus the computer was to be used for information storage, retrieval and processing and act as overall judge of the situation. The two groups of children interacting *via* the computer rather than with the predetermined logic of a program This, therefore, made the simulation different from the commercial and higher education packages in which the student interacted solely with the machine. It also aimed at promoting an element of competition between the groups and cooperation within the group.

Although aimed at practice and introduction to the skills already listed, the simulation required that those children involved had reached Piaget's 'concrete operational' stage, in terms of his classification of concept formation, at least. The children were expected to consider several factors, such as the direction of the wind, the direction of travel, wind speed, the time when making any single move, regardless of holding in their mind the general strategy which they had decided to adopt. Therefore, whilst the game may be played by taking each move as a separate event, the need for a forecast or plan three or four moves ahead is essential. Initially, at the concrete level, the plan may be in terms of visiting the nearest port and the strategy develops in a sequence of decisions as to which port next, on the successful completion of each visit. This level of planning, although not precluded, is not consistent with Piaget's description of the formal operations level. It is not hypothetical reasoning based on the logic of all possible combinations, it does not view the model as a limited whole. At the formal level an overall strategy may place in a secondary category what first appears as a possible immediate goal – for example, sailing to the nearest port – it may be because of other factors that a particular port should be visited last.

The children are expected to consider several factors at once during their planning and it is anticipated that with practice they will begin to formulate strategies which will take into consideration the whole situation. The aim is that the children will define a strategy which is intended to last throughout the game. It is also hoped that there would be evidence of an increasing use of hypothetical reasoning, being based on inferences drawn from the logic of the information obtained. Thus, the level of the children's thinking and reasoning was, I felt, going to be fully tested.

Therefore we knew what we required from the computer and the children – the writing of the program and programming the computer was the next task. This took in excess of a hundred hours for the initial version to be ready to run. The program itself had to be restructured on several occasions before the first trial with the children. Maps and models had to be made in order that the simulation could be physically represented in a concrete and stimulating manner.

A group of third year children was chosen for the trial run. At first they were extremely hesitant, as the amount of information they were given was limited to the skills they required and the aims of their group. A prescription for fulfilling the task was deliberately not forthcoming and this certainly affected their confidence initially, as to how to proceed. A partial transcript of the pirates first game was made and this indecisiveness during the opening moves is evident. Shaun wants to go to Red Rock Island first before he even knows the starting position. Neil, who emerges as the group leader, constantly reiterates their aim. The general idea of a strategy or plan is lost whilst the children gain confidence in handling the more immediate problems of navigation and where to move next. Slowly as the problems of coping with the skills are successfully handled the group begins to make a more definite plan. They visit the port on Palm Tree Island first then, although they gain no information, continue to Treasure Island and in fact sight the other ship. The subsequent chase produces an immediate change of plan and the discussion evolves around what they should do if:

N If they go into port we'll go three hours there, so they'll probably be there and we'll be there.
S We'll be attacking them, we're not allowed to attack in port.
L Or in a safety zone.
N We'll go two hours then.
S Yes.
N We'll go two hours in that direction . . . if they move down to there then.
S They'll only go like that if they have . . .

(Here is an example of Shaun using his knowledge of how far his ship has been travelling in the simulation and applying it to the other ship, knowing that it does not move as far. A case of formal reasoning?)

By the end of the first game the children have overcome their apprehension of the game's complexity and the feeling that the pirates didn't stand a chance. Their reactions were positive, especially the pirates who had succeeded in capturing the treasure. The Spaniards requested that they have a turn at being pirates.

Conclusions

The area of computer simulation for higher education, business and the armed forces is already becoming well established. It is yet an area to be really explored at the primary school level. The most obvious problem affecting the development of such programs is that of time. To date, this particular simulation has grossed over two hundred hours from its inception to its present form, but I am certain that time spent in the development of such programs will be worthwhile. Not only is the problem related to programming the computer but, further, the time required to analyze a situation. It requires an analysis of both the potential and the actual learning that is expected of the children. It makes demands on teachers, in terms of analyzing the kinds of thinking that they wish their children to partake in. These are the types of problems that teachers may well be facing in the future as the computer is introduced into more schools.

Already we have developed a similar game for infants, 'Hunt the Thimble', and are in the process of writing further programs which will explore this area of computer work in the primary school. I am convinced that it is in this area that the computer has most to offer education. Not only is this type of program consistent with our philosophy of education but also increases the number of children gainfully using the computer at any one time.

It is this role of the computer, as a stimulus, a tool which can simulate events and situations, which will ensure its future in education. It can be used to generate motivation in a very positive sense aimed at developing the children's thinking and understanding, rather than abusing the natural curiosity and interest which it evokes in the limited way in which many are using it at present. The potential is there. It is the educationalists who must decide how best to use these machines so that the potential continues to evolve.

Teachers and the New Technology – Servant or Master?
John Lane

Prospects

> ... and so do we live under shadow, with acts of faith in functioning of inventions, as up in the stratosphere, down in the subway, crossing bridges, going through tunnels, rising and falling in elevators where our safety is given in keeping. Things done by man which overshadow us .... Well, then what makes your existence necessary, as it should be? These technical achievements which try to make you exist in their way?
>
> Saul Bellow, *The Adventures of Angie March*

You can't stop progress. It is difficult enough even to begin to count its cost. We might ask: 'progress for whom?'. Technological change brings social change, economic change, new relationships. Some gain: always, too, some lose. What, for instance, were the costs of the first Industrial Revolution? It is too early to tell. But certainly they extend beyond the immediate threats to livelihood perceived and resisted by the Luddites.

Inventions have given us dramatic extensions of the senses: lenses, amplifiers, receivers. Yet, our senses are dull – cavemen were surely more sharply attuned. Cars carry us far and fast, but pollute and kill. Tranquillizers worry me. The city itself cuts us off from nature.

Extensions of the power of the arm, the speed of the foot, may be easy enough to assimilate. Mere muscles seem comparatively external and machine-like. It is when the evidence of our very eyes and ears is called in question, superseded by technology, that a greater sense of unease attends. How, then, shall we cope with the computer, the super-brain, the most intimate usurper of our humanity?

For teachers, it is not just a question of taking sides, of welcoming or resisting the advent of computers. What matters is to come to terms with the new phenomenon. It is neither panacea nor poison. In some areas it will fit smoothly to augment established practice, but in others it will be totally out of place. Also, entirely new opportunities will be opened up, new courses and methods created to exploit the machine's vast potential. Successfully identifying these distinct cases is a vital task for the balance of new development.

How well is the profession prepared to achieve such a balanced view? It would be only too easy for further polarization to develop. Teachers of science and maths are often seen as natural allies of technocrats and robots. Against them, arts teachers guard the pass, in the name of human values: 'I know something about history. I know when I'm being threatened'. We still teach two cultures.

True, the division is less sharp in primary schools. This could be a cause for optimism. Here, if anywhere, is an integrated approach to the curriculum, with education of the whole child firmly established as the priority, ahead of any subject bias. Involvement of primary teachers with computer enthusiasts should lead to a particularly fruitful dialogue, serving to humanize the field.

This is a genuine hope, and a crucial one for further development. However, it must be admitted that the absence of an arts/science schism in primary schools is not due to a positive balance already achieved. It is more a matter of default. Science is not represented adequately. The vast majority of primary school teachers have their backgrounds in the humanities. Furthermore, most of them are women, and the stereotype of female antipathy to science and maths is based partly on an uncomfortable and self-perpetuating reality.

The central purpose of the school system, preparation for life, has traditionally been interpreted through the transmission of established values, skills and knowledge. Increasingly, an alternative and radically opposed call is being made. Such is the pace of change, that we know that the lives of children now entering school will be unlike the lives of their teachers and parents. They will do jobs not yet invented with the help of technology we can only guess at.

Much of education till now has been characterized by the struggle to master knowledge and to acquire associated skills. The imminent information explosion seems a threat to sanity. Yet, paradoxically, the next technology promises a release from much of the drudgery of memorizing and handling facts. New skills appear, of storing, organizing and retrieving information. The language skills needed by children will be radically different from those in the age of the book.

There are disturbing social and political problems yet to be faced which will have serious implications for schools. Currently, high levels of unemployment are being explained in terms of a world-wide recession. This may be masking the beginning of a permanent effect of increasing automation, bringing with it increasing leisure opportunities.

The new technology has vast potential for revitalizing democratic processes. Instant referenda and simulations to predict the consequences of complex choices are examples of the possibilities. The alarming alternative is the shadow of 'Big Brother'. Universal familiarity with computers, including confidence in their beneficial uses and healthy scepticism about their limitations, seems the only way to forestall the development of a technocratic élite of controllers. This may prove the most important argument of all for introducing computers at primary school level.

Revolutionary changes are imminent. How and where will people learn to adapt accordingly? Could the schools become the leading agency of adaptation? Their inbuilt conservatism, their limited resources and the usual time-lag of educational change all seem against it. But teachers have remarkable abilities to accept challenges. Unless the humanist values in the school system become a significant part of technological development, the field is likely to be dominated by commercial interests and narrow technical purposes.

In the following pages an attempt is made to predict some of the likely consequences and issues for teachers, as microcomputers become part of the primary school scene. Any such attempt is foolhardy: hindsight will no doubt show many of the predictions to be wildly inaccurate. They are offered, even so, as a contribution to a debate which has already begun. The demands on the teaching profession for a far-reaching re-orientation are already strong. There are more awkward questions here than easy answers.

Most primary schools will shortly acquire and begin to use microcomputers as a resource. There is powerful encouragement and material support from government, industry and the manufacturers. The machines are intrinsically attractive to most children. They can very easily become compulsive for many teachers! Their versatility promises many uses and advantages. Computer Aided Learning (CAL) is likely to be far more significant and wide-ranging than the limited concept of teaching machines. Word processing techniques will quickly dispel any illusion that this is just a superior calculator, with applications mainly to mathematics. Graphics facilities provide almost limitless scope for imaginative approaches in any area of school work. Information processing and data searching are powerful tools which will transform many aspects of the curriculum.

The rapid spread of highly adaptable computers must create many problems. There will be much duplication and fragmentation of effort, many hours wasted on trivial developments. We are a long way yet from establishing even tentative principles of good practice, and farther from the thorough research needed to provide a sound foundation.

The development of the necessary professional awareness and competence presents a massive task of retraining. Is this development likely to match the pace of the spread of hardware and of a bewildering proliferation of software? Prospects are not good. In-service training has never yet received the priority and resources it deserves.

Yet there is now a golden opportunity. Falling rolls in schools and colleges have left space and resources sufficient to adopt a serious programme of retraining, including a substantial element of secondment. The need for this level of commitment is a measure of the tasks facing the profession. They amount to nothing less than planning the new roles of educational institutions for life in the twenty-first century.

Retraining

A rational programme of retraining will have to operate at many levels.

Elementary technical instruction, to the point of switching on and running a prepared program, seems straightforward in principle. The logistical problems – availability of machines, instructors, centres – will be overcome, often in the teacher's own school. Psychological problems may prove stickier. A fear of machines in general and computers in particular is widespread amongst primary school teachers. These fears will inevitably combine with legitimate doubts about the investment of time and money and the long-term educational results of these developments. Such resistance deserves respect and understanding: it will not be easily brushed aside by helter-skelter enthusiasm.

An alternative introduction for some teachers could be through courses in computer awareness. Preparation for life in a computerized society has many implications for primary schools. The sociology, psychology and philosophy of education will all be radically affected. The exchange of information on any aspect of teaching will be facilitated. The computer is news: this will be increasingly reflected in the availability of television programmes, newspaper articles and journals. The BBC project in Computer Literacy to be broadcast in 1982 has provided a major resource.

Even at this level of general awareness, there is a danger that the profession could adopt too passive a role, observing and keeping abreast of developments coming from outside, merely responding to the initiatives taken by computer specialists. It is important that some teachers, at least, become capable of anticipating and guiding events according to sound educational principles. Some of the courses to be planned will have to operate at this level of professional involvement.

Many teachers will first be drawn in through the activity and enthusiasm of colleagues. Observing children at work with computers leads directly to the main centre of interest for primary teachers – the impact on the curriculum and on learning patterns.

Two initial responses to this experience seem to be typical. One is amazement, tinged perhaps with relief or envy, at how readily the children accept the equipment and make themselves at home with it. The other is speedy recognition of the attractiveness of the computer to children, and of the high levels of motivation and concentration achieved.

Beyond these commonplaces, any claim to a comprehensive evaluation would clearly be premature. We are in an early experimental phase, and current practice is extraordinarily diverse in styles, objectives, ambitions and achievements. Some software developed in an apparently amateurish way is remarkably ingenious or satisfying in use. Some commercially available software is trivial or unreliable. There is no agreement yet on what makes a good program. Technical standards for documentation and presentation should be easy enough to establish: but educational criteria will remain a matter for investigation and controversy for a long time yet. Teachers will need to develop their judgement of what is effective and valid from observation. An exchange of views can then follow with the purpose of creating guidelines for selection of software and for further sound development.

A separate but related task is the organization of catalogues and systems for the distribution and exchange of software. The sheer volume of information to be processed is less daunting when we recall the potential appetite of the new technology for just such a task. To develop and operate such systems calls on new roles for teacher-leaders in schools in consultation with advisers and analysts.

Evaluation will be a feature of a teacher's response at any level of involvement. As soon as children begin to work with a computer, searching comparisons become necessary. Could similar results be achieved with conventional resources? What is the quality of learning? Will facts be retained in long-term memory? Are skills acquired superficially or at a deeper operational level? Is any gain in motivation due to novelty, and does it outweigh the distracting 'noise' generated by the medium? Is there an overall loss in pupil-teacher interaction and classroom communication?

Careful research, including longitudinal studies, will be necessary for an authoritative treatment of these issues. Meanwhile, teachers will cooperate to establish some common ground, to promote the most promising approaches and to discard the trivial or potentially damaging ones. It will be a function of in-service training to contribute to raising these issues and to encourage the exercise of professional judgement.

Innovation

Evaluation skills of a new kind arise in the detailed examination of the program itself. Many inadequate programs contain valuable ideas which can be salvaged. Even a successful program can be amended, modified or improved. It is crucial for several reasons that teachers should adopt this attitude of constructive criticism. It will be a rich source of sound and relevant software. It will bring classroom teachers into a mutually fruitful dialogue with program planners and writers. And it will lead to a positive sense of identification in the teacher with the objectives and outcome of the program: without this, he could feel by-passed by the entire process and unable to contribute effectively.

The process of evaluating existing programs will help to identify principles for good programming in primary schools. Many features have already appeared useful and are likely to become more familiar. In interactive programs, 'friendly' properties seem particularly appropriate with young children. A variety of levels allows precise application to individual needs, and encourages progression. Diagnostic testing and recording of individual results are valuable additions. Control options in the hands of the user create a sense of purposeful involvement. Graphics facilities provide an almost limitless variety of screen output, controlled in some cases by the user. Internal documentation on the screen may provide a convenient alternative or supplement to written support. A program designed in distinct stages or units, plentifully labelled with descriptive REM statements, is easy to read and to amend. In practice, some of these desirable features may be mutually exclusive: each program must select priorities to achieve specific objectives.

Other elements of current practice may prove to be more controversial, or more difficult to reconcile with general educational aims. The prevalence of flashing lights as extrinsic reward for correct answers reflects an influence from television commercials. More generally, the relative merits of those programs based on an 'operant conditioning' model of learning and those designed to encourage the adoption of logical strategies call for deeper study and debate.

If progress is to be made on a broad front, teachers who are not specialists (and who are certainly not programmers) must be able to contribute positively to new developments. Their professional experience of the curriculum and of how children learn provide the soundest basis for advance. If they are to achieve the confidence to propose new applications and suggestions for new programs, they need an initial introduction to the potentialities of the microcomputer. An urgent task for in-service training is to identify the minimum components of such an introductory course, and then to provide opportunities on a large enough scale. The computer will no doubt continue to be, for most users, a mysterious 'black box'. It is a question of what a teacher needs to know about it in order to make it serve his purposes.

Every aspect of the curriculum can be considered as a candidate for likely new applications of the microcomputer. Participation by primary school teachers at an elementary level, but on a massive scale, is needed if all the areas of expertise and enthusiasm are to be explored.

From the teacher's viewpoint, the challenge is to learn to develop an idea from its starting-point in the traditional curriculum to the point where a specialist can see what is intended and write a program. The farther the initiator can see along the path, the more likely it is that his original conception will reach fruition and not become distorted.

Although much of this is new territory, it is closely related to precisely those qualities and judgements which are recognized as the hallmark of good teaching. Clear articulation of objectives is the first essential. There follows a systematic analysis of the way the program is to develop. An algorithmic approach is required. Correct sequencing is emphasized, along with branching, repetitions and jumps, and selection of levels. Modes of input, output and control options are similarly educational decisions related to objectives, and should be specified from the start. It may be desirable to allocate an intervening role for the teacher-user, in providing local or topical data, or determining the time allowed for responses by the pupil.

This first stage of program specification can be as ambitious and demanding as imagination permits. But the program writer is not a fairy godmother, capable of granting every wish. The micros involved may have limited capacity. The characteristics of the programming language selected may have an influence. The availability of high-resolution graphics, or colour, affects the design fundamentally. The writer may be able to utilize existing subroutines or entire programs with similiar objectives, without losing anything essential from the new idea. Equally, he may be able to suggest additional features which will be welcome.

Within these constraints of what is practicable, some of the original objectives and intended effects may prove to be mutually incompatible. Modifications are undertaken according to educational priorities. In this stage, a dialogue is proposed between the teacher initiating the idea and the experienced program writer. In practice this will often prove to be more of a collective process, with working groups of teachers producing ideas for specifications, and some of them may also have programming experience.

These levels of participation, in evaluation and planning, are essential to ensure a broad base for advance. Some teachers will wish to go farther and get involved with the actual writing of the programs. This may prove less of a hurdle than is commonly imagined. It is one of the more clear-cut tasks for in-service training to provide courses on the scale and levels required. Many primary school teachers show remarkable aptitude for the necessary skills but, for a few, the patterns of logic and the structure of the language seem totally alien.

Writing a workable program for use in the teacher's own school is particularly satisfying. Advanced principles of good programming can follow later, taking up such issues as efficiency and transferability as well as sophistications in graphics and string handling. As his skill develops, the teacher is likely to seek consultations with other writers, inside education and outside, and to find support in specialist journals and user groups.

Consultation

The principle of consultation is a vital one with many applications. The worlds of primary education and of professional computing are very different. Events have thrown them together, in the tempo of a whirlwind romance rather than a long dignified courtship. But the couple do not share the same backgrounds, purposes, outlooks or even languages! There will be misunderstandings, tension, perhaps conflict. But the over-riding strength of mutual interest holds promise for the relationship.

For the teacher, working for greater understanding has two aspects. One is to learn to elucidate his own educational attitudes and aims clearly and convincingly. The other is to begin to explore the potentialities and constraints of the unfamiliar world of technology.

Any primary school taking an early step towards acquiring some hardware comes quickly to this new interface: manufacturers, salesmen, technicians, programmers, technical manuals, specialist journals; enough jargon to choke on. It may be comforting, or chastening, to remember that the specialized workings of the primary school can seem just as mysterious and ritualized to the outsider.

It would be naïve to play down the implications of the commercial interests involved. For manufacturers of hardware, high investment and potentially rapid obsolescence call for considerable returns. The production and commercial distribution of software for education bids to become a substantial industry. Problems of plagiarism, copyright and royalties could prove extremely thorny. All this may seem a far cry from the familiar spirit of easy co-operation in other areas of curriculum development.

Consultation of a different calibre may become relevant as national and regional programmes develop. To the professional systems analyst, educational organization often seems amateurish and inefficient. In industry, a tight control structure allows a determined pursuit of new objectives, once set: phasing out, retraining and the concentration of new resources can all be rapid. This model is not evidently appropriate for change in education, at least in the Western tradition, where goodwill and consensus are closely related to professional integrity. Once again a dialogue between the two professional worlds, based on mutual respect, could prove particularly valuable.

Colleagues and Children

A favoured administrative model for curriculum development proposes a teacher-leader who, through training, ability and enthusiasm, can act as a focus for associated work throughout the school. He initiates activity, encourages interest and stands by to give support. In practice, progress is often more patchy, and some staff-rooms seem full of enthusiasts while others cannot sustain an interest.

There are several possible roles for teacher-leaders in computing, which need not be combined in a single person. He might write programs, but that is not essential. He might be creative in imagining new applications, or logical in setting out program specifications. He could be an enthusiastic member of a user's group, or keep colleagues informed of events outside through reading journals. Skills of communication could help colleagues to formulate evaluations and plans. Most valuable of all is the rare ability to give fellow teachers confidence in their own increasing involvement.

A possible negative outcome must be recognized before it can be overcome. Some teachers will inevitably fear the advent of the computer as divisive, as separating enthusiastic experts from the rest of the staff. This may be intensified if the role of teacher-leader is institutionalized, giving rise (at best) to the feeling: 'Let him get on with it, then'. Such fears can only be overcome by the exercise of caution, tact and genuine consultation.

The importance of positive attitudes cannot be exaggerated. Teachers cannot operate effectively if they feel as if they are passively transmitting somebody else's program. This is not a new conclusion and it applies just as well to the use of textbooks, commercial apparatus or traditional schemes in any subject. The many levels and modes of participation sketched above have one common purpose: they encourage the teacher to take the initiative with the machine. It must be our tool, our servant, not a hydra-headed monster which threatens us anew with fresh demands each time we struggle to cope with its challenge.

Such an approach stands a good chance of increasing goodwill and drawing on the expertise of enthusiasts in all aspects of the curriculum. Without this broad basis, progress must be uneven and incomplete.

This standpoint also gives an overall perspective to the relationship of the children to the computer. Limited and passive sequences of responses seem to have purpose, and could probably be achieved as easily by traditional means. A stronger aim is for the pupil to achieve mastery of the program and, through it, of the machine and of the subject matter.

The heart of the educational progress is in the interaction of child and teacher. It might appear that reliance on computers could reduce, or by-pass completely, this interaction. At a programming level it has been emphasized that it is the ideas of teachers which are presented. The class teacher also selects a program closely geared to individual needs. The strongest safeguard lies in the next stage of the process. The pupil learns directly from the material presented – a very traditional insight! The teacher is freed to concentrate on a vital tutorial follow-up, to check and help to fix the learning achieved. Used flexibly as a support for achieving specific objectives, the computer could enhance the quality of relationships in the classroom.

Standing back a little from the detail of stimulation, instruction and recording, the teacher can take a longer view of the work in progress. More attention can be given to the child's developmental needs and to the balance of the curriculum.

Theory and Practice

Only experience can help us to determine which applications of the microcomputer prove most worthwhile. Some subjects may, in the end, be better served than others, even after the fullest exploration of possibilities. Well-ordered material is easily programmed. Is it possible, for instance, to conceive of sound programs in maths and science which will help to raise standards in these areas? The question is uncomfortable, raising again the spectre of machines replacing teachers, but it has positive implications too.

Some children may take to the microcomputer more readily than others. It may also favour some learning styles. Some aspects of programming rely on analytical modes, and it may be much easier to use the computer to encourage logical and convergent thinking. Intuitive and divergent thoughts are necessarily more difficult to anticipate and follow up successfully. Yet strategy games and simulations could be valuable in prompting just this kind of creativity.

Directions for advance may not all arise from conversions of the existing syllabus. Technical innovations will themselves suggest new possibilities. There could be a matching response from the psychology of learning itself, as teachers and psychologists evaluate the new processes.

Current practice in primary schools already owes more to empiricism than to respect for theory. This would be compounded if the technology of education continued to advance more rapidly and persuasively then any corresponding development in the theory of instruction. Fashionable bandwagons, blind prejudices and commercial preserves would create an intolerable muddle. Academic research in distant ivory towers offers little hope of a solution.

The massive task of re-training facing the profession must go far beyond the acquisition of new technical skills. Teachers will need a deeper understanding than ever of the learning process. Theory and practice can develop together in professional courses used to initiate and monitor new applications for the microcomputer.

The potential rewards are incalculable. The difficulties to be overcome are daunting. If teachers are given the opportunity, they can take the initiative and control the microcomputer for educational purposes. Then it could provide a genuine extension of human capacities.

Thoughts for the Future
Derrick Daines

The microcomputer was born roughly at the same time as the children who are now about to move from the primary to the secondary sectors, and there can be no doubt that, just as they have their entire careers before them, so too, the microcomputer will undergo considerable development in the years ahead. The fact that we now have small computers that perform very well and are available at an astonishingly low price does not mean that we have reached the end of that particular line of development. On the contrary, all the indicators are that the 1980s are going to bring us even greater and more far-reaching innovation than did the 1970s.

If this is true of computing generally, then how much more so is it true of educational computing and especially in the primary sector! My own school was arguably the first in the field, but even our fourth-year juniors were already attending infant school before we bought our first computer.

This fact is well worth stressing because it enables us to draw out two or three points. First, no-one can justifiably claim that one method of using a computer in the primary school is better than another, because the time-scale is too short and the experimental evidence is too scanty for anything more than first impressions.

Secondly, the point is made that we are all pioneering. The field of experimentation is wide open, with countless discoveries waiting to be made, and you don't have to be the first in the field to make the most important discoveries. Nor do you have to be particularly expert. There has been more than one diamond or nugget of gold picked up by an innocent.

Thirdly, because primary computing is so young, we must resist with all our might any attempts to apply restraints and restrictions on the way it should grow. There is about primary computing at the moment an air of youthful enthusiasm and joyous adventure – precious commodities – and it would be a monumental tragedy if this was stifled because of administrative convenience or professional pedantry. The time for the formal presentation of conclusions will come, but not for some considerable time yet.

Finally, it must be said that there is no such thing as an educational computing expert – some person who has all the answers. There are only those with a little more experience than others, who know one or two of the answers – and a few more of the questions.

When a computer is installed in school, it is not only the children who learn. The teachers learn too, even those not immediately involved. The head learns, the parents and governors learn, as do the advisers, inspectors and members of the LEA. Perhaps some of the resistance to computers has come about through the subconscious recognition of this fact and the reluctance to enter as a child into a new learning situation. The advent of the computer into schools has meant that we must be prepared to rethink and restructure just about everything that we do, as well as learn about the new technology.

For example, a teacher responsible for mathematics faces a very real moral dilemma posed by calculators and especially the computer. Does he ignore them, insisting upon computational methods rarely used outside the classroom, or would his time be better spent in showing how to get the best out of the machines? If he believes in the necessity for pupils to at least know how to multiply, for example, what level of attainment is satisfactory? Is it truly to be as high as when all calculation was done by hand, or would it be better to spend time stretching the mathematical – as distinct from arithmetical – ability of pupils, to explore concepts that hitherto have been closed to us because of the sheer magnitude and drudgery of the arithmetic involved? This, at least, is one of the points that the late Christopher Evans must have had in mind when he wrote, 'Future generations will seek out and find the answers to questions that we have not even thought of yet' (Evans, 1979).

A similar dilemma is soon to be posed to all teachers, and not just teachers of mathematics. Without a great fanfare, computers capable of correcting a secretary's spelling are already arriving in the office. Some 25,000 of the most common words are held in store and the input is checked against them. The inference is obvious: as such machines become widespread, how important is it that we should spend time teaching correct spelling? Would it be better to release the literary wings of our pupils and let the computer take care of the rest?

Even at a mundane day-to-day level, the computer poses problems of reorganization. It is natural that the school should wish to use the machine efficiently, but how is this to be done? Does the teacher use it for drill and practice, reinforcing what has been taught, or for 'higher', more exciting things? How can it be ensured that anyone using the computer does not lose an important lesson on something else? With one machine and a class of forty children, more than half of the week is taken up if you allow each child to have fifteen minutes on the computer. Is there a better arrangement? What about the other classes? Should slow learners have more time? What do you do with all those children who clamour to use the machine during play-times or lunch breaks? (An eye-opener in itself!)

Some firmly-held and long-cherished beliefs are under scrutiny too. For instance, teachers commonly view the arcade type of computer game with distaste and would disgustedly walk out of a classroom that harboured one. Why? No doubt the answer would be that such games are not educational, but can we be so sure of that? Why are children so addicted to such games – and not a few adults? Can we turn the attraction to our own purposes? Do such games throw any sidelights on the way in which children learn? They must get something out of the games, otherwise they would not shovel coins into them. What are they getting? If nothing else, could the teacher use such games as reward? To these and a multitude of similar questions you will find no answers – only a million different impressions and viewpoints loudly expressed. Our motto should be, '*Let's find out!*'

A much more fundamental change is under way; the scrutiny of what exactly we mean by an education, and the role of the Primary School in supplying it. As one educationist put it, 'By the time the child born today graduates from college, the amount of knowledge will be four times as great. By the time the same child is fifty years old, it will be thirty-three times as great, and ninety-seven percent of everything known in the world will have been learned since he was born' (Robert Hilliard, US Federal Communications Commission). With this scale of increased knowledge, the mere acquisition of a few facts is not enough, and our examination system may became inadequate and inappropriate.

The learning process for the teacher then, can be divided into the following parts:

1 Familiarization with the characteristics of microcomputers in general.
2 Intimate knowledge of the capabilities of one particular machine, in all probability the one installed in school.
3 Finding ways to utilize the machine efficiently within the classroom situation.
4 Observing the educational, psychological and social effects and attempting to influence them where possible.
5 Being alert to new technology, especially in the electronics communications field, and being prepared to take it 'on board' as devices become available at a reasonable price.
6 Last but not least, attempting to extrapolate into the future, especially where it impinges upon the future of our charges and education generally.

Only when we have undergone these learning processes do we have the right to expect our voice to be heard. In short, we must do our homework.

It should be obvious that efficient use of a computer is totally dependent upon the teacher's understanding of what the machine is capable of doing. This does not necessarily imply that the teacher must understand the machine at an electronics level or be able to write programs, although clearly it is better if he or she is capable of doing so. Understanding can come about through reading, attending courses or obtaining ready-made programs, but if the teacher is blinkered into believing, for example, that the computer is limited to number-crunching, then number-crunching is all that his computer will do. One is reminded of the classic review that read, 'If you like this kind of play, then this is the kind of play that you will like'.

An open mind is necessary and an imagination alert to all possibilities, which in turn implies that having completed our own re-education, we must then be ready to do it all over again. As one graduate teacher wrote, '... I am reading your letter in sections .... The truth is, I have just never been taught to think in this way'.

A typical learning pattern for teachers starts with the computer being utilized exclusively for games and other programs bought from the supplier. Bearing in mind my comments above, I have no desire to sit in judgement upon any of these programs. I will simply observe that sooner or later the teacher – or one of his colleagues or pupils – will feel the desire to alter them or write his/her own.

It happens that writing programs for number manipulation is extremely easy, and so it comes about that we have so many maths drill programs – everybody learning to write programs produces them. My earlier comments may now be seen in a new context – it ill becomes us to scorn such programs. Not only have they a use within the classroom, but they are also a necessary step along the way for the teacher himself.

Many teachers at this learning stage hurry precipitously to applications they consider to be 'better' or somehow more worthy of their new-found skills. In no time they are writing programs with string (alphanumeric) manipulation, arrays, matrices and graphics. This is a pity because there are many good ideas waiting to be followed up that utilize simple number manipulation. Number-guessing (or number-deducing) games are legion, for example. They are highly educational and great fun both to play and to write. Then there are games involving the use of money; easily written with the computer limited to two decimal places – isn't that why we turned over to decimal currency?

Fundamentally, you see, the computer may be programmed in several different ways; it may be programmed to give you the answer to any equation that you care to type in, or it may be programmed to ask the user the solution to the equation and to check his answer. Better still, it may be programmed so as to take the user step by step through the stages necessary to arrive at the correct solution, setting questions to check for understanding, providing additional tuition where necessary and looping back until the user shows the correct level of attainment. Even better is the type of program that makes a game of a teaching point, so that pupils *want* to play and, in playing, learn.

I have talked about typing-in equations and there immediately springs to mind the type of equation produced that omits the operational symbol, for example, 3 ? 4 = 12 or 5 ? 4 ? 2 = 18; this is easy to program, as are number series, in which the pupil is required to supply the next number. For the teacher in his learning role, such series can lead conveniently and easily to alphanumerics, for a series that can be devised with digits may just as easily be translated into alphabetic characters.

When the teacher gains facility in writing programs in BASIC — or has access to a large number of them — there opens up a truly enormous range of possibilities; so vast in fact, that so far no-one has even glimpsed the limits, and it seems that every day new ideas are put forward. Because of this, uses are difficult to categorize, although lines are becoming clearer.

At the current time, in terms of numbers of programs written, simulation games appear to be the majority use. It seems that virtually any situation can be modelled and used to advantage in a teaching situation, from sailing a ship around Cape Horn to landing on a distant planet; from ruling Ancient Sumeria to running an atomic power-station; from exploring dungeons inhabited by a multitude of mythical monsters to planning a new town in the face of conflicting interests — all are grist to the mill.

In educational terms, all such games aim to have the player come to rational decisions, usually involving some mathematical juggling and very often risk-taking. One game, for instance, presents the child-user with a choice of routes through a graveyard. There are short routes and longer routes, plus the ability to switch from one to another. At various nodal points the child must solve 'clues', which are obviously education—type questions, the harder questions being on the short routes.

In another game, the player — in the role of ruler — must balance his use of corn as a medium of exchange against his need to provide food and save enough for seed. The resulting balance is very fine indeed, with possible disaster on every side. He may run short of seed corn, suffer a population explosion, drive up the price of land, and so on. The learning potential is enormous.

There is, of course, no reason why there should be only one pupil at the keyboard. If two or three children are playing the same game, they pool their knowledge and enhance their communication skills at the same time. Then, too, it is quite easy to have competing children at the same keyboard, playing games such as Scramble (the computer derivative of Scrabble) or any one of a multitude of games.

One of the arguments advanced against the installation of a computer is its seeming lack of cost-effectiveness. The argument goes something like this, 'How can I justify spending hundreds of pounds on a machine when only one or two children can use it at once?'. I can sympathize with the dilemma, but do not consider the argument very weighty in an educational environment. For the price of one of my daughter's riding lessons (lasting one hour), I can buy two ounces of tobacco that lasts me for five days. Or, if you do not like that analogy, two of her riding lessons will buy a text-book that will serve dozens of children over a number of years. Is that an argument in favour of scrapping her riding lessons? Clearly not; partly because we are not in an either/or situation, and partly because no value can be put on knowledge and skill.

This is not the place to go into the argument very deeply, but it must be pointed out that the one-child/one-computer situation envisaged can in fact be very far off the mark. For many years now we have had computers that will easily handle a number of terminals at the same time, and the latest Unix system from Bell Laboratories will handle dozens of users, all connected to the same microcomputer. Other manufacturers will no doubt follow suit.

What is envisaged is a reasonably-priced mother computer, with extremely cheap (say £20) daughter keyboards. With such an easily-expanded system, each user may be transparent to the others – doing 'their own thing' – but equally easily two or more terminals might be utilized for the same activity in an inter-reactive way. The first thought that springs to my mind here is that children might be engaged in 'real-time' simulation games that do not require them to wait for turns.

Even before we get to the multi-user school installation however, one terminal can keep an entire class or indeed an entire school busy – business studies courses have been doing it for years. Two years ago we engaged ninety children in a project called 'Dungeons and Dragons', in which they explored a dungeon filled with monsters and treasures. The children were divided into exploration groups of six, each group being responsible for its own exploration decisions. The three teachers involved used a simple die now and then to determine if the group had met a monster. When this happened, tables were consulted to see what kind of monster had been met, then the children went off to do their research, art and craft, story-writing and so on. This was the real 'meat' of the project.

After the research had been completed, notebooks written up, etc., the children went to the computer to determine the outcome of the confrontation. The computer was fed with the monster's code-number and full details of the composition of the exploring party. It then went into an exciting blow-by-blow account of the battle. There was a random element but, principally, the outcome was mathematically controlled by some very sophisticated formulae. This was the 'number-crunching' part and the computer was ideally fitted for it. Because the machine was so fast, however, it could easily handle all ninety children, since the bulk of their time was taken up by research.

That is but one illustration among many. One wonders what the proponents of cost-effectiveness would make of it. One must reiterate: the computer will do only what is asked of it. We cannot be blinkered into utilizing it only for maths drill or allowing only one child to use it at once, although such applications do of course have their place.

When one looks beyond BASIC as a programming language, we find that software suppliers are ready with lots of fascinating packages for us, or we can write our own, for some software does tend to be expensive. For instance, at the Primary Schools Microcomputing Conference at the University of Exeter in 1981, two representatives from ILEA showed work done by children utilizing a Text Editor. The teacher had then used a word processor to turn the child's text into beautifully-formatted print.

The Editor allows the child to write his/her story and, in conjunction with the teacher, to correct it, insert paragraphing, titles and so on. However, apart from this obvious use, an Editor is fantastically useful for all computer work. I would estimate that some sixty per cent of my time is spent using the Editor – for writing programs, preparing texts of all kinds, inserting and/or correcting data on files – and there is no doubt that time spent by pupils will be well repaid.

Another fascinating package is a Speech Synthesizer, which must surely have a place in school. Pupils have great fun making the computer talk if you use the phoneme method. First, the desired speech must be broken down into phonemes and typed into the machine. This produces a flat 'Dalek' voice to which inflections may be added, bringing the sound output closer and closer to the tone desired.

Such speech synthesis has, to my mind, two clear and separate uses. First, there is study and thought by pupils for them to achieve the desired aim. It was notable how children's own speech improved when they were required to listen to and study the sound of their own speech. Secondly, there is the possibility of having the computer talk to pupils – perhaps non-readers or slow-learners – although obviously in the classroom situation an earphone output would be desirable. Time could be taught by a speaking clock, or spellings posed – the possibilities are endless. Yet other packages allow the computer to synthesize music or sound effects, to draw pictures or graphs, etc., etc..

Even more is available once one starts thinking about the world outside the confines of the computer housing, for here it is literally true to say that the sky is the limit. Using cheap or school-made interfaces, the computer can be connected to any electro-mechanical device whatsoever. Some of these devices can be attached to just about anything you like – growing plants, hive entrances, tide- or wind-measurers, rain gauges, cameras, ovens, doors, human muscles – the list is endless. To my mind this is the ultimate reason why computers are so exciting, so far-reaching in their effect, and why all schools should have them.

The keyword here is not 'computer', but 'microprocessor', that wonder-worker that is about to turn our world upside-down. The microprocessor stands in relation to the computer as the internal combustion engine does to the motor car; it is the driving force; the *raison d'être*. Only a tiny proportion of microprocessors are or will be installed in computers – by far the greater number will be installed in an enormous range of goods, from an automated coal mine to children's toys. It follows, therefore, that the microprocessor is more important than the computer, but how do you study it? It is an uninteresting piece of black plastic with a few bits of wire sticking out of it. The only way to study it is to attach a few switches and little lamps, and one has in effect a miniature computer.

It will be seen, therefore, that in education the computer has the supreme virtue of affording us a window into the world of the microprocessor. To put that another way, anything the computer can do, the microprocessor can do – and probably better.

That statement may seem a little staggering to some, so I shall qualify it by adding that the computer is a general–purpose tool, while the microprocessor is 'dedicated' – confined to one application, defined during manufacture.

Since the computer is a multi-purpose tool, it may, therefore, be utilized to mimic or 'write large' one small part of itself, the microprocessor. The uses of the microprocessor are quite literally staggering in range and number, the vast bulk of which are yet to be uncovered, but let us take just one as an example. The Road Research Laboratory is hard at work perfecting 'accident-proof' vehicles which *inter alia* would follow a metal strip in the road and also sense the distance to the vehicle in front. The speed of the vehicle is taken into account, the steepness of incline, angle of

THOUGHTS FOR THE FUTURE   201

curvature of the road, and so on; clearly a case for computerization or, in this case, the application of a dedicated microprocessor.

It would be beyond the resources of a primary school to mimic all of these functions, but it is easy to make or acquire a toy vehicle that can be steered by computer, thus imparting the basic principles.

Looked at objectively, the microprocessor provides the missing link between devices, and between man and his full understanding and control of his environment. That is the reason why our world is about to be turned upside-down. For us in the primary schools, preoccupied with instilling basic knowledge, it is important not to allow our view to be too narrow. We may not want to control a power-station with our little microcomputer, but the children will learn an awful lot if we control a model railway. The Bigtrak toy demonstrated at the University of Exeter Conference was an example of this principle, and much important work with children has been done using computer-controlled turtles (three-wheeled toy vehicles).

It might be said that so far I have fulfilled the promise of my title only very little. I would justify myself on the grounds that what is possible now for some of us is indeed the future for most. However, now is the point at which I must attempt to extrapolate into the future; to look at developments that lie ahead.

Only a few days after the Conference, I was able to try out Cy Endfield's Microwriter and am now finding out how swiftly children take to it. (My own daughter required just ten minutes of instruction.) Is this the writing instrument of the future? Cy certainly thinks so, and the ability to dump its contents into the computer or onto paper or cassette tape makes it very attractive. Time will tell. Full editing facilities are available and memory contents are not lost when the handy little machine is switched off. I can say that compared with ILEA's use of one computer per child for story-writing, it is highly cost-effective.

Lately the Japanese have been invading the market with pocket-size computers – and of course, Clive Sinclair's ZX80 and ZX81 have been highly successful. I expect more, and more powerful, pocket machines. For school use, however, I have my reservations. One would need to screw small machines to large pieces of wood, as one does with calculators.

Teletext, Viewdata, etc., have been rather slower at taking off (or being taken up) than was anticipated, but now they are fully launched and spreading rapidly. Their arrival opens up some very interesting possibilities, especially when one combines them with a simple home- or school-computer. A week or two before the Conference, for example, it was announced that *Practical Computing* magazine was to make a large number of computer programs available on Teletext. Just a few hours before writing this paper, I saw another report which said that difficulties had been encountered and that so far, users were copying by pencil and paper! Critics will gloat, but there is no doubt whatsoever that these teething troubles will be overcome.

As long as two years ago I was invited to try out the prototype model of a computer housed within a domestic television set. This machine by-passed the Teletext system by taking its program direct from the air – the method is now known as Videotext. It remains to be seen whether it will ever be installed in every domestic television, as its inventor hoped, adding a mere £30 to the cost. Whether it is or not, before long most schools will have computers as well as Videotext and Prestel.

The point here is that with thousands of pages available, Prestel can be easily accessed. Before long, enthusiasts will program their computers to do the accessing of dozens of pages in seconds, thus keeping down line charges. The computer will then display the stored text page by page or dump it onto paper copy or disk for retrieval later. The trend should be obvious. The cost of text books and other printed matter is ever upwards, as is the enormous cost of distribution. At the time of writing, Oundle School students are hard at work putting a number of standard reference books into their computer system – no more dog-eared copies for them. This is an indicator for the future. I would guess that standard works will in a few years be available on disk, thus slashing their price, while Teletext might find their market in more transient up-to-date works or in up-dates of standard texts such as dictionaries, gazetteers and so on. When that day comes, there will certainly be an upheaval in school purchasing policies!

An even greater upheaval may come about through social pressures – and here I am treading on dangerous ground. Mixing my metaphors, I am peering to the limit of my vision, which is about fifteen to twenty years.

Last year I visited a firm of computer manufacturers who, even at that time, were actively considering whether or not it would be cheaper for them to tell most of their employees to stay at home and log in daily on their home computers. No more hassle getting to work; no more wear and tear on company-provided motor-cars; no more heating of large premises; no rates, etc.. It was sufficiently interesting for them to carry out a full-blown investigation. I don't know the outcome, but I do know that since that time petrol and other transport costs have climbed, as have taxes; the proposition is even more attractive now than it was. It is highly likely – if not absolutely inevitable – that in the next decade many people will find themselves doing their office work at home, shuffling bits of paper about (for that is what most office work is) through the medium of a computer and attached printer. Most mail will come to them through a telephone link (modem) attached to the computer, which will provide almost instant communication with cheaper running charges than surface mail.

Consider these people for a moment. They will know that something approaching a half of their rates and taxes goes towards paying the salaries of teachers and maintaining expensive buildings. They will also see that an increasing percentage of all knowledge will be available right in their homes through Teletext and the like. They will ask themselves the very serious question, 'can they make a significant cut in their tax burden by keeping their children at home, educating them through the TV and the computer?'. The idea is not so very far-fetched; they've been doing something like it for fifty years in the Outback of Australia.

I don't know what the answer will be. We will have an enormous inter-reaction between powerful forces – economic, technological and social – but one thing is certain; the teacher's voice will be a small one. What will be important is not how he views his role, but how it is viewed by others who pay his wages.

Of course, much education cannot be conducted in the home (*pace* Professor Stonier). Much of education requires expensive or not very common equipment, but this is not so true of Primaries as it is of Secondaries so, if it comes about, a School of the Air will in all probability be a primary one. What then will be the role of the primary teacher fifteen to twenty years from now?

I have little doubt that it will be much as it is, but with a shift of emphasis; a restructuring rather than a dismantling. It is probable that we shall begin to see an expansion of the 'Social Teacher' service – teachers who (already in the Secondaries) go out to society rather than waiting for society to come to them. At least one vital role for the social teacher would be to probe for and fill educational gaps left by the Computer/TV combination or by lack of home discipline or application. One eventual outcome of this is that we might see a blurring of the distinction between social workers and teachers – and perhaps even an amalgamation of the two.

With the explosion of knowledge previously mentioned, one can confidently predict that there will be a renewed interest in – and eventual settlement of – a core curriculum. With so much knowledge available, it will be vital that (a) basic skills are learned early, (b) that some disciplined study is maintained and (c) that all acquire the accession skills – the ability to find necessary information. The interesting point here is that (a) and (c) are self-evident, but that (b) will (in my view) be retained not so much for its immediate value as its character-forming potential.

That, then, is my view of the future — the immediate and not-so-immediate. Should we be frightened of it? Not at all. For one thing; it is not going to happen tomorrow. Anyone who has seen a film shot in the immediate post-war years will recognize that the world today is vastly different from what it was, and that the change has come about gradually, almost imperceptibly. We don't take giant steps into the future; we shuffle into it, inextricably linked together.

Another reason why we should not be afraid of the future is that nowhere is the demise of the teaching profession postulated. What *is* in prospect is simply a subtle and gradual shift of emphasis; the recognition and acceptance of some highly-sophisticated and vitally important technology.

There is a final thought. It may well be that the role of the teacher will become more important than ever before. With an explosion of knowledge and methods of retrieving it, guides will become more and more necessary. Infinity and infinite knowledge are frightening, humbling concepts and the young or uneducated may turn even more to those who can chart a path. Hence it may well be that the teacher will be valued not for what he or she knows or is able to do, but for the ability to ask the right questions and access the right information. But isn't that true already?

References

EVANS, C. (1979) *The Mighty Micro* London, Gollancz.

Microcomputers and the Primary Curriculum
Michael Golby

I take it as an assumption held by readers of this book that the impact of microcomputers on the primary curriculum is entirely problematical. We know neither the potential power of the machines themselves, as generation by generation they develop, nor the possibilities for development inherent in the primary curriculum itself. Thus, we are dealing with two very large imponderables, the nature of the machines themselves and the nature of the primary curriculum. I therefore wish to sound a cautionary note against both the utopianism of those who may hope for and expect instant revolution and the Luddite mentality of those who reject technological progress in any form. My intention is to attempt to make a balanced view of the prospects for development bearing in mind what we already know about educational change. I do not wish to go into what the *Hitchhiker's Guide* calls improbability drive (Adams, 1979) where literally anything is possible.

I further take it as fundamental that we should be concerned with qualitative change in the educational process rather than with the simple addition of new means to old ends or old wine in new bottles. Further to this, I take it that the essence of education is that it should be a transforming experience for individuals and not merely a personal accumulation of facts. Education should be concerned with wisdom rather than data, personal perspectives rather than encyclopaedic knowledge. This view of education, which has been well established since R.S. Peters' (1966) *Ethics and Education*, emphasizes the personal integrative function of education. It rejects the idea that education cannot be distinguished from training, indoctrinating, conditioning and other social processes whose ends can be pre-specified. Education is nothing if not open-ended and is guided by procedural principles concerning the authenticity of experience for the individual pupil. This much is, as I have said, orthodox but it is nevertheless an important back-drop to the consideration of advance in the primary curriculum.

I wish to approach the difficult questions before us not as an expert in microcomputers but rather as one who has considered the capacity of primary schools to accept, adopt and consolidate innovation in general. I acknowledge that each and every possible innovation is unique. Some, like *Science 5-13*, seem to succeed while others such as *Primary French* founder. While there may not be a single formula for success it seems to me that we need to consider the deeper structure of the host curriculum if we are to make a sensible appraisal of the prospects for any particular change. This deeper structure I take to be composed of the long-standing and often conflicting traditions in primary schools. These traditions are in my view not mere historical encumbrances but the very stuff of the attitudes and opinions of both teachers and parents (and of course children). We can have no opinions or attitudes and formulate no policies without drawing upon the values and forms of thought handed down to us in the institutions in which we work. By institutions here I refer not just to particular schools but rather to the 'schools of thought' of which we are all in one way or another part. We all participate in the progress of education, whether we are classroom teachers or work in the training institutions, by drawing upon the values, forms of thought and assumptions handed down to us. These traditions transcend individuals and particular institutions, though of course they could not exist without the concrete social life embodied in all our practices.

I therefore think it may be of value to distinguish three broadly separate 'traditions' in the above sense which are still discernible in the primary field. They are discernible, as I have said, both in the practice and in the discourse about primary education. Two of the traditions represent the familiar antithesis of the elementary and progressive ideologies while the third, which I shall call the technological tradition, is a relatively new arrival; and one of particular relevance to the questions before us in considering the microcomputer.

We could perhaps deal with the first two traditions summarily. The elementary tradition takes as its guiding metaphor the inculcation of essential knowledge into passive pupils. Most of us learned to reject or at least become highly sceptical of this utilitarian tradition in our early training but many of us returned to it in various modified forms later in our careers. I suggest that this tradition is by no means dead and the modern primary curriculum is still heavily underlain by a 'drills and frills' approach. The nineteenth century elementary curriculum lives in many schools' division of the curriculum into the 'basics', consisting of the three 'R's and the 'extras', consisting in an uncertain melange of literary, aesthetic, humanistic and now scientific ingredients. I shall defend the inclusion of the last of these ingredients later. The elementary tradition expressed a political will to 'gentle the masses' through the controlling power of a curriculum which would be limited in scope. This curriculum is an education (though today's philosophy might deny it the title of education at all, and substitute socialization or training as the appropriate concepts) for subservience. The elementary curriculum survives, despite the abolition of the 'eleven plus', in the deeper structure of many schools by emphasizing certain conforming performances rather than the expansive qualities of questioning and imagination.

The progressive tradition has very largely gained its identity not through the coherent expression of new rationales but through its romantic opposition to the elementary tradition. Thus, instead of stressing control, subservience and conformity, it celebrates self-expression, individual autonomy and personal growth. None of these formulae have, in my opinion, been adequately defended in philosophical terms. The tone of progressive teaching has always been enthusiastic and evangelical. The contents of the curriculum have always been poorly defined and this for the simple reason that content is not to the fore in this line of thinking. Indeed, it is the weakness of the progressive tradition that it has no adequate theory of knowledge to help it define the curriculum above the rhetorical level. Accusations of incoherence in *practice*, however, seem to me to be less well substantiated than those against the theory of progressive education. In practice, progressive educators know very well how to bring to bear all manner of subject matter in the interests of individual children as they individually grow and develop. There is, I believe, a practical logic composed of a blend of fundamental opposition to the values of elementary education with a perception of children not as empty vessels but, rather, as centres of consciousness and potentialities beyond what we can preconceive. It is also possible, I believe, to assert that progressive ideas have a romantic and rural texture much in contrast with the practical and urban fabric of the elementary tradition.

These contrasts are vastly over-simplified. This should go without saying but needs repetition here as I am about to offer a third, also over-simplified, opinion. There exists, I believe, a more recent tradition which may be broadly labelled technological. This tradition has emerged most noticeably in the years since 1976 when education has come under a closer political scrutiny. What I have in mind here is the recent emphasis since the Great Debate on the utilitarian values associated particularly with the pursuit of science. The association of science with social progress has a very long history and in recent years we have seen the reassertion of an age-old belief in the power of science to improve the efficiency of society. This most recent variant of a long-standing idea has taken curricular form in the emphasis on the production of 'personnel' skilled in technological areas. The link between an efficient technological education and, in particular, economic recovery seems to have been taken for granted. Yet, of course, it is, to say the least, questionable whether, without accompanying capital investment and the appropriate economic climate, the regeneration hoped for can be expected to take place at all. One need only look back as far as Harold Wilson's 'white heat of technology' and the development of the Colleges of Advanced Technology into would-be technological universities to see that magical changes are not available through educational action alone. The technological tradition I perceive has its most tangible emphasis in the continuing and developing concern of HMIs, for example in their Primary and Secondary working papers and surveys. In both of these endeavours the place of science and in the secondary field of Craft, Design and Technology is taken for granted as an aspect of the 'core curriculum'. The debate about the core curriculum has not as yet penetrated beyond the level of such atavistic assumptions as the above concerning science and we have to look into still relatively unknown theoretical literature for a clear defence of the position of Science, Craft, Design and Technology in the 'protected core' of the curriculum. Perhaps most obviously this new technological tradition comes into view in the Primary survey where the conclusion is drawn that improvements in science teaching in primary schools are greatly to be desired. Yet no rationale for the inclusion of science, a subject of very low visibility historically in the primary curriculum, is to be found in the survey itself. While we should not expect of the kind of research which the survey was an accompanying philosophical statement on the rationale for the 'whole curriculum', we could hope to see the issues raised somewhere. And the literature, both from official quarters and from the research community seems to me deficient in this major respect. I assert then, that I perceive a new tradition, building on old assumptions, making inroads into the primary curriculum. 'Hard science' – and, perhaps, especially, 'science that works' or technology – is making a claim; a claim I do not reject or concede here but merely hold up for inspection. It is no part of my task here to take up a side in this as yet unformed debate but rather to point out that the primary curriculum, though it has seen the rather successful innovation of *Science 5–13*, has traditionally not found space for the sort of utilitarian emphasis on technical skills that may be implied in the crudest form of this new technological imperialism over our curricular thinking.

My question is, rather, how will the new microelectronics fit within and between the three broad traditions I have characterized above, the elementary, the progressive and the technological? At our most optimistic we could hope that the advent of an entirely new technology might challenge the assumptions held in all three traditions and produce some higher synthesis of our understanding of what we are offering young children.

Putting to one side, then, the use of microelectronics for

administrative purposes (for example in the timetable) we may identify a number of possible uses of the new microelectronics within the curriculum and consider their impact. We may, first, consider that microelectronics will vastly alter the society in which we live and the culture within which our children will obtain their maturity. For this reason we may go on to prescribe an expanded and transformed social studies curriculum which offers to children a glimpse of possible futures, futures changed by the chip. Here our aim will be to help children understand the importance of the new technology and to expand their awareness of its potential. This departure would be essentially a change in the cultural map we are offering in the curriculum, and the curriculum development it represents would best be described as social or cultural studies. That is not to say, however, that mere futurology is all that is demanded here. To understand microcomputers and their social impact will, in all probability, demand a first hand acquaintance with the machines themselves. This curricular emphasis could not be achieved without the presence of the machines themselves in classrooms, or at least their ready availability. However, skill in the use of the machines is not the prime curricular aim here. Although computing skill may be necessary to what is fundamental in this conception – namely, a new vision of the changed social life, means of communication, access to information, etc. the new technology will make possible – skill is not sufficient to this educational end. That this is so is apparent when one considers the necessity to introduce children to the moral dilemmas hinging, for example, on the storage of information about the private citizen in medical, educational and other data banks. In this country we have as yet no Freedom of Information Act and as the computers develop and as the possibility of the inter-linking among the powerful computers of various governmental and non-governmental agencies, develops so too will the urgency to consider and decide upon the desirability of such an Act. Again, I do not take it as unquestionable that the kind of legislation at present on the statute book in the United States is what is required. What I do consider is that the development of the new technology is bound to pose serious questions for our concept of the privacy of the individual; the privacy of the individual is not a question that can be resolved by further application of microelectronics but one that demands reasoning at a high level of moral and practical sophistication. Our children will need to develop the intellectual qualities and the moral perception to handle these questions and it is part of the task of a redefined social studies to address these questions with our children. It is important to see here that such a redefined social studies can never be neutral, in my view, as to the desirability of one form or another of social change. In addition to an indissoluble element of fundamental values, for example a certain concept of privacy for the individual over against a concept of the rights of the State in the above example, a transformed social studies must put children in a position to make informed judgements on the likelihood of particular developments influencing social change in specific ways. For example, what might be the impact on family life of CEEFAX, PRESTEL or the like in every home. We know that television has changed the fabric of family life; will the new technology make no difference, exaggerate an existing trend or produce a qualitative change? If so, how do we view that change and how do we make a judgement as to its desirability?

Finally, in this first version of a curricular implication of the advent of the new electronics, I must stress that I do not see a once and for all answer either to the sort of social and moral questions I have suggested or to the curriculum problems in the social and cultural studies area they suggest. Rather I wish to indicate the kind of question that will face all educators in the face of technological change and indeed has always faced educators. We have traditionally responded in an *ad hoc* and often unsatisfactory way and this I consider to have a certain inevitability about it since curriculum change is itself a form of social change which simply cannot be totally engineered. I am pointing here only to the desirability of a cooler look at the curriculum throughout compulsory schooling and beyond lest we are carried away by our enthusiasm for new machinery into a still less considered future than we might otherwise enjoy.

My first curriculum implication for the advent of the microcomputer is in the area of social studies and I have discussed some possible forms of revision that will be required in an expanded curriculum making a sensitive response to a new cultural situation. My second curriculum implication is perhaps more readily understood. I have in mind here the use of microcomputers as highly sophisticated teaching machines. There are already many examples of programs which will admirably serve as technological aids to well established goals within our primary schools. There are many problems available in the areas of basic arithmetic, spelling and for the accessing of abundant information – for example in history. My personal disquiet about such technological aids˙ is that those which have come to my attention seem to me often to address only very small, although not always insignificant, aspects of school work. In the wrong hands they could become substitutes for the close relationships with pupils necessary for effective learning. They could depersonalize the teaching process. On the other hand, in the right hands they could, at a stroke, eliminate the still widespread phenomenon of queuing at teacher's desk for spellings or to be heard to read. What is important here is that new devices should be viewed within a framework of understanding of our aims for children and we should guard against being carried away by the enchantment of machinery. Clive James, in his recent book of television criticism identifies this enchantment in the context of television production:

> One of the reasons people want to spend their lives in television is the beauty of the technology, the thrill of walking into the production gallery and seeing all the heaped jewellery of big and little lights, with the sound and vision engineers sitting in a row like the crew of an airliner a mile long.
> Just the colours are enchanting: there is one kind of waveform display, expressing the picture information as a curve of light, which is the delicious green of emerald juice. The whole deal is a treat for the eyes: Science Fiction City! And before long you are armed with all kinds of jargon ('Give me a buzz when you're up to speed') and have persuaded yourself that you know what's going on. *But you don't know what's going on*. Only about two people in the entire building can really understand how the toys are put together.
>
> James, 1981

It will be a great pity, in particular, if teachers should become seduced into taking more effective means to unconsidered ends. It is not that I am rejecting spelling or basic arithmetic or the acquiring of historical information but that I wish to re-emphasize the importance of seeing such activities only as building blocks in the whole experience of the child. I hope I am not being pessimistic, nor doing an injustice to other contributors to this volume in saying that I have yet to see the prospect of a *qualitative* departure in the nature of children's learning in the very few examples I have seen. I would deplore the situation where the sort of teacher who, decades ago, was constructing models of the Tower of London out of match sticks now took up his government-provided microcomputer and set about it with no re-consideration of its possibilities. [I am grateful to Andrew Dean of Torbay Teachers' Centre for this telling example.] For this reason, teacher training is essential and a thoroughgoing review of what such teacher training should consist in is urgent. Again, there is the danger that such a review would be limited to providing teachers at both the initial training and in-service levels with computing skill only.

My third curricular implication is less tangible. I would hope that the qualitatively different learning which we must all hope for, given the paucity of much of the experience of children in all our schools, might be assisted by a sensitive application of the new technology. The other contributors to this volume offer glimpses of such possibilities. Perhaps, at the risk of further over-simplification, it is possible to suggest that the first departure might be that all primary children in the foreseeable future will have a knowledge of the functioning of the machines themselves. Microcomputers might be considered as technological phenomena in their own right. Even in their present state of development, which we all consider to be embryonic, the microprocessor is a huge achievement of the human mind. How they work and how they have come to be as they are is a subject of immense interest and importance to anyone today. Young children should not be denied this knowledge, neither should they be denied the sense of potential development in the technology. Most especially, I would want children to understand (and I would want to understand myself) the basic logic, which I believe is mathematical, upon which the machines depend. I would like children to understand, and I would like to understand myself, the nature of the electronics which utilizes the mathematical logic concerned. This is a major departure for understanding machinery has not been to the fore in primary schools historically. I myself survived thirteen years of compulsory education without a knowledge of how the internal combustion engine works. Yet my daily travel to school and the whole fabric and well being of the society in which my schooling was conducted depended on the efficiency of the internal combustion engine. My schooling was thus parasitic upon a whole range of achievements which it did not acknowledge and indeed implicity rejected. I feel much the poorer for this deficiency in my schooling and I would hope that all children in the future will be permitted a proper understanding of the dependency of their lives upon practical achievements in many areas, among which microelectronics will certainly be prominent.

The sort of learning I refer to is characterized not only by knowledge but also by feeling. The interdependency I refer to is not a mere obeisance to technologists, medical scientists, architects and engineers but it is also a sharing in the world they create and we contribute to. Sir Karl Popper refers to three 'worlds': the raw world of nature; the inner world of experience; and the 'third world' (not in the political sense) of human achievement and culture. While there are intimate connections between these worlds, our interest as educators must be in the third world of human achievement and culture. The examples I have given here have been technological but, of course, this third world comprises also all those areas of human achievement of which we are the inheritors. I only attempt to redress an imbalance in our curriculum by referring to the practical achievements which have gone unacknowledged in our schools. I do not wish to suggest that those other achievements in poetry, literature, philosophy and history should suffer from any new emphasis we may wish to develop in the curriculum. This again only highlights the need for a clearer theory of knowledge within which we can locate our curriculum development.

I will move towards the conclusion now by recording four of my hopes for the near future and two reservations. My hopes are that in the era of the knowledge explosion sufficient educators will be forthcoming who can produce conceptually-based learning programs rather than mere access to information. In this hope I draw upon Bruner's concept of 'structure' in knowledge. The structure of knowledge in Bruner's view consists in those fundamental concepts and procedures which make possible advances in any given area of inquiry. It has always been the aim of thinking primary teachers to teach pupils how to learn. The sort of learning a conceptually-based program might make possible is learning that in Bruner's words 'goes beyond the information given'. Indeed the aim of such structured learning is quite unlike the aim of most, if not all, of the early programmed-learning schemes. It seeks to make possible the pupils' transcending the teacher's own understanding. These indeed would be teaching machines worthy of the name.

My second hope is less ambitious. It is what I have referred to earlier as an increased efficiency in teaching those areas of the curriculum where pre-defined skills are possible. There are models already available of this kind of program. I hope they will become more prevalent and sensitively used.

My third hope is somewhat ambiguous. I hope for the demystification of print. Books will, it seems to me, for a very long while remain our principal means of access to knowledge and the chief resource of the educator. Books, however, have been very badly used as tools for learning in schools and, indeed, in universities. Too many schools fail to teach the skills of handling books, using indexes, skim reading, note taking, etc.. The printed word has too often been presented in indigestible packages and few children have been able to make the best use of them or, indeed, enjoy them. If key books could be re-processed into programs which will answer a developing line of inquiry in a child's mind and provide for idiosyncratic styles of learning in individual children, then we would have gone a long way towards rendering the inaccessible book a manageable educational tool. Again, this hope is a rather long-range one. There are few enough teachers who can teach the skills of using books. We would need to find such teachers and also persuade them to make their skills available so that print may be made systematically available in various forms on the microelectronic screen. This is an ambiguous point, of course, since I have no wish to see the end of books. Books are, in fact, highly tractable devices for the storage of information and the skills I mentioned relatively easily acquired. I fear that the dense and distilled experience available in books may be trivialized in the process of translation into computer programs. Most seriously of all, I fear the growth of two curriculums, the one for the illiterate depending upon the simplification of the computer program, the other for the literate child who will retain a traditional curriculum based on books.

My fourth hope is that the application of the new instruments in our classrooms will not be confined to specific or narrow curriculum areas but that we shall seriously consider the use and the application of the new microelectronics in, for example, the aesthetic area. Certainly, micro-technology is heavily used in the industrial world for design purposes and it is to be hoped that the educational dimensions of aesthetic expression will not be forgotten as we plumb the possibilities of microelectronics in our classrooms. I connect this point, perhaps fancifully, with the observation that the Exeter Conference was attended overwhelmingly by men rather than women. Yet the primary school is staffed predominantly by women. Without setting up too crude a distinction between feminine and masculine interests and propensities in education, I do feel that the aesthetic and expressive texture of many good primary schools is associated with the feminine influence. Computers seem to be a man's world at present. My fourth hope is, then, that we shall exercise that creativity with the new opportunities before us that has always been apparent in the expressive dimension of the primary curriculum.

My two reservations consist in one smaller point and one very much larger one. The smaller point is that there is a clear danger in the next few years we that may repeat the experience of programmed learning by failing to learn how schools respond to, adopt or reject innovation. Programmed learning never took root in either the primary or secondary curriculum to any significant degree and this was because it was framed by no clear idea of its appropriate place in the *whole* curriculum. There is a danger that microelectronics may go the same way if we fail to take careful account, first, of the nature of the host curriculum as it now is (including the fundamental traditions I have mentioned above) and, second, of the flexibility we should be looking for from innovation. By this, I mean that an innovation, if it is to be successful, must both adapt itself to the existing situation and go some way towards transforming it. I would hate to see an increasing uniformity of teaching and learning styles brought about by the arrival of microcomputers in the classroom. Instead, I would like to see a much wider range of educational experience being offered. Children will certainly be able to learn as individuals at the console but it will be important also that they learn alongside the teacher and in groups constituted in a multitude of different ways. Looking further forward, as connections develop, it is possible to envisage groups or consortia of schools sharing their expertise through a microelectronic network. This is a long-termed hope but one which may be hastened by the phenomenon of falling rolls and the need for neighbouring schools, particularly in country districts, to cooperate together. A computer link between schools may, one day, be a way of effecting liaison while preserving the social presence of a school in a community where it is badly needed.

My final note of reservation brings me round full circle to my first point. It is the essence of education that it should be transformative rather than merely accumulative. The point of education is not the acquisition of information alone but the provision of ways of interpreting information and going beyond it in making judgement possible for an individual developing to his conception of himself and the world in which he lives. Education consists not in the accumulation of data but rather in the gathering of perspective, intelligence and, to use an unfashionable word, wisdom. The shallowest response to the new situation would be merely to adopt new means to out-moded ends. The profoundest response would be to undertake a rethinking of the whole business of teaching. In considering what the new technology can do for us we should find ourselves reconsidering the very nature of the art of teaching itself. Were this to be so, we could confidently say today that education tomorrow will be a greatly more sensitive and exciting business and we should agree with T.S. Eliot that:

> What we call the beginning is often the end
> And to make an end is to make a beginning
> The end is where we start from ...

and

> We shall not cease from exploration
> And the end of all our exploring
> Will be to arrive where we started
> And know the place for the first time.
>
> Eliot, 1963

References

ADAMS, D. (1979) *The Hitch-hikers Guide to the Galaxy* London, Pan Books.

ELIOT, T.S. (1963) *Little Gidding* in *Collected Poems 1909-1962* London, Faber and Faber.
JAMES, C. (1981) *The Crystal Bucket* London, Jonathan Cape, p. 29.
PETERS, R.S. (1966) *Ethics and Education* London, George Allen and Unwin.

Contributors

Derrick Daines has taught in primary schools for eighteen years and throughout that time he has designed and built computers for use in his classroom. He was the writer of the 'Young Computer World' column in *Personal Computer World* and his book *Gateways to Logic* was serialized in 1980.

Peter Davies taught mostly in primary schools in and around London for nearly twenty years with a brief three year foray into the petrochemical industry. This experience helped in his development of a technological problem solving primary curriculum. He took his MA at the University of Sussex and from 1973 to 1981 was Warden of the Honiton Teachers' Centre. His interest in computers dates from 1979 when he bought his own system.

John Dodridge read mathematics, geography and botany at the University of Southampton. He taught in schools for eleven years before his appointment to the mathematics department of a College of Education. He is currently Senior Adviser for Mathematics in Cheshire where he has had a special responsibility for the county's microcomputer education programme.

David Ellingham is Headmaster of Marlcliffe Junior and Infant School. He first became interested in computers in education in 1977 and as a consequence was invited by the Sheffield Authority to run a small project within his school. This work has developed considerably and has resulted in his involvement in INSET courses in the city.

Roy Garland taught for fifteen years in primary schools before his appointment as a first generation teachers' centre warden in the mid-1960s. Since the early 1970s he has taught in higher education. He is a Lecturer in Education at the University of Exeter School of Education.

Michael Golby taught in primary schools, a College of Education and the Open University before taking up his present work at the University of Exeter where he is a Senior Lecturer in Curriculum Studies.

Marjorie Holloway is at present Headmistress of Beanfield Infant School, Corby. She has taught in the area of adult education and initial teacher training. Her academic study of Educational Technology led to innovations in the area of audio-visual aids and an increasing and developing interest in the use of a microcomputer in her own and a neighbouring junior school.

Barry Holmes is currently the Headmaster of St Helen County Primary School, Bluntisham. He has recently completed an Advanced Diploma course at the Cambridge Institute of Education and has become interested in computer applications across the curriculum. His school has a disk-based system and he has written a number of simulation programs for it.

Ronald Jones is the Headmaster of Upwood County Primary School in Cambridgeshire where he is responsible for developing the use of the microcomputer throughout his school. He conducted a national survey of primary schools using the microcomputer in 1980 and is author of *Microcomputers – Their Uses in Primary Schools*. He was joint organizer of the Homerton Conference on Microcomputers in 1981 and is a member of the Primary Schools group of the British Computer Society.

Bernard Lane has taught in further education and in middle schools. In the latter he had experience as the head of a mathematics and science department before his appointment as a deputy headmaster. He is now Headmaster of Topsham Middle School, Devon.

John Lane began teaching in Leicestershire primary schools in the mid-1960s where he found himself in the middle of a wave of educational innovation. Experiments in the integrated day, vertical streaming, the open-plan classroom and resources for learning were all around. They did not all fulfil their promise. For the last ten years he has been a lecturer at Newman College, Birmingham, developing his interest in the education of young children. This is the standpoint from which he examines, critically, the advent of the computer. He is editor of *Microscope*, a journal for teachers in primary schools interested in the use of microcomputers.

Tony Mullan has been working with children and computers since 1975. He is now the Headmaster of St Maurice Primary School in Devon where he is extending his interests in software development and applications of the microcomputer across the curriculum.

Michael Thorne lectures in the Department of Computing Mathematics, University College, Cardiff. He has published many papers on educational computing topics and writes the 'Breakpoint' column in *Computers in Schools*. Having taught various subjects from all levels – primary to tertiary – his current research includes various projects with local schools concerned with making computing easier.

Donald Walton is Deputy Headmaster at Houghton County Primary School, Huntingdon. He has been teaching in secondary and primary schools in the area since 1957 and has been involved with computers for almost three years.

Author Index

Adams, D., 205, 215
Ahl, D.H. 46, 88–90, 99–100, 109
Alcock, D., 78, 109
Alcuin of York, 116
Allport, G.W., 150, 166
Artwick, B., 119, 128
Atherton, R., 18, 31

Barnes, D., 80, 109
Barnes, D., et al., 158, 166
Beal, G., 117, 128
Bellow, S., 181
Beynon, R., 122, 128
Bird, J. and Diamond, D., 109
Botermans, J.
 see Van Delft and Botermans
Bremer, N.H.
 see Pate and Bremer
Britton, J.
 see Barnes et al.
Bruner, J.S., 213
Buxton, L., 20, 21–4, 26, 28, 31

Carey, D., 118, 128
Cherne, L., 33, 46
Cheshire Local Education Authority, 115, 128
Child, D., 159, 166
Coan, J., 73, 109
Cognitive Research Trust, 43
College of St Mark and St John, 167
Critchfield, M., 84–5, 109
 see also Dwyer and Critchfield
Crookall, P., 118, 128

Daines, D., 1, 8, 9, 193–204
Davies, P., 4–5, 71–110
Dean, A., 211
De Bono, E., 43, 46, 165, 167
Department of Education and Science (DES), 80, 108, 110, 151, 164, 167
Department of Industry, 150
Diamond, D.
 see Bird and Diamond
Dienes, Z.P., 114
Dodridge, J., 5, 111–28
Duncan, T., 118, 128
Dwyer, T. and Critchfield, M., 110

Eliot, T.S., 215, 216
Ellingham, D., 3, 33–46
Endfield, C., 201
Escher, M.C., 114, 128
Evans, C., 194, 204

Fiddy, P., 27, 31

Fraser, R., 20, 94

Gagné, R.M., 42–3, 45, 46, 70, 154, 167
Garland, R., 1–10, 98, 135–47
Gibbon, V.
 see Sealey and Gibbon
Golby, M., 8, 9–10, 205–16
Greenberg, S.
 see McWhirter and Greenberg

Havelock, R., 102, 110
Hilliard, R., 195
Hockey, S., 30, 31
Holloway, M., 4, 57–70
Holmes, B., 7, 155, 167, 169–79
Horton, R., 16, 31

Jahoda, G. and Warren, J.M., 150
James, C., 211, 216
James, E., 99
Jones, R., 1, 3, 47–56

Kuhn, T., 103, 110

Lane, B., 6, 98, 135–47
Lane, J., 8–9, 181–91

McWhirter, N. and Greenberg, S., 112
Morgan, 85, 86
Mullan, T., 7, 149–67

Open University, 167

Papert, S., 16, 20–1, 25–30, 31, 45, 46, 153, 155, 157, 161, 165, 166, 167
Pate, R.T. and Bremer, N.H., 158, 167
Pavlov, I.P., 28
Peters, R.S., 205, 216
Phillips, C., 75
Piaget, J., 177
Plowden, B.H., 102, 108
Popper, K., 212
Postman, N. and Weingartner, C., 101, 110
Press, L., 88, 90–1, 110

Richards, S., 94, 110
Robinson, R.E., 116, 128
Rogers, C., 81, 86, 110
Rosen, H.
 see Barnes et al.
Rushby, N.J., 84, 110

Schools Council, 83, 110
Seaborne, P.L., 114, 128
Sealey, V. and Gibbon, V., 64, 70

221

AUTHOR INDEX

Skemp, R.R., 161, 167
Skinner, B.F., 159
Sledge, D.K., 15, 18, 31, 47, 50, 56
Stenhouse, L., 102, 110
Stonier, T., 16, 203
Sweeten, C., 19, 31
Stout, J., 76

Taylor, A., 120, 128
Thorne, M.P., 2–3, 5, 11–31
Thorne, M.P. and Wharry, D., 31
Thorndyke, E.L., 58, 70
Toffler, A., 72, 110

Van Delft, P. and Botermans, J., 115

Walton, D., 6, 129–33
Warren, J.M.
  see Jahoda and Warren
Weingartner, C.
  see Postman and Weingartner
Wharry, D., 20
  see also Thorne and Wharry
Wilder, R.L., 113, 128
Wilson, H., 208
Worsley, P., 110

Young, B., 117, 128

Subject Index

analogue interface, 15
animation
  see graphics
Apple computer, 40, 137, 139, 141, 142, 146
art, 118–19
Association of Teachers of Educational Computing (ATEC), 104, 106
attitudes
  of children, 6–7, 27–8, 29, 51–2, 149–67
  of parents, 52
  of teachers, 50–2, 190
audio-visual aids, 60–3, 64–5
authority, 28–9
  see also attitudes

BASIC language, 11, 17, 38, 42, 45, 76, 139, 141, 197, 199
Bigtrack (electronic toy), 25–9, 201
British Broadcasting Corporation (BBC), 164, 184

cassette-based systems, 16–18, 40, 73–4, 108
  see also disks
CEEFAX, 164, 210
Chelsea College, London, 19
choice
  of computers, 2–3, 11–31
class teaching, 33–46, 198
classification
  see organization
College of St Mark and St John, 94
communication, 112–13
Computer-Assisted-Learning (CAL) programs, 23–30, 34, 35, 38, 49, 88, 132, 169, 170–9, 183
Computer Club, 38
computer languages, 75–6, 112–13, 187
  see also BASIC, Pascal
computer literacy, 6, 38, 45, 138, 164, 184, 212
computers, passim
concept keyboard, 16
conferences, 2
  see also Primary Schools Microcomputing Conference
consultation, 188–9
costs, 24, 49, 108, 198–9
  see also purchasing
curriculum, 4, 5, 21, 34, 57–60, 64–8, 70, 79–101, 102, 104, 111–28, 164, 165, 182, 187, 203, 205–16

debugging programs, 28–9, 104, 161
disks, 6, 16–18, 74, 79, 108, 137, 142–3
  see also cassette-based systems
drill and practice programs, 5, 21, 24, 27, 29–30, 84, 85–92, 194
Durham Microcomputer Project, 15, 18

educational computing, passim
educational philosophy
  and microcomputers, 35–7, 169, 195–6, 205–16
encoding programs, 34, 58, 96, 130
enhancements
  for basic computers, 13–14
environment
  school, and microcomputers, 49–50
evaluation, 63–6, 185–6, 188

Factoring whole numbers program, 24–5, 27, 29, 30
Fractions program, 24

gadgets, 15, 30, 118
games, 85, 94, 152–3, 158–9, 166, 191, 195, 196–7
  see also simulations
games paddles, 15, 30, 118
geography, 118
graphics, 14–15, 17–19, 93–4, 119, 156–7, 183, 186, 187
groups
  see numbers

Hamurabi program, 92–3
hardware, 3, 11–19, 30, 40–1, 52–3, 74–5, 107, 184, 189
History, 118
houghton School, 131
Humberside project, 44, 93–4

infant education, 4, 57–70
information retrieval, 85, 97, 142–7
initial teacher training
  see teacher training
Inner London Education Authority (ILEA), 201
in-service education, 71–110
in-service training, 36, 38, 44–5, 50, 54, 101–5, 130–1, 184–6, 187, 188, 191
interfacing microcomputers, 74, 200
ITMA project, 20, 94, 158, 164, 167

joysticks, 15

keyboards, 15–16, 62, 153

223

SUBJECT INDEX

language skills, 161–2, 199
light pens, 15, 30
Local Education Authorities (LEAs), 12–13, 52–3, 106–7, 194
literacy, 80, 88, 164
  see also computer literacy

maintenance, 12, 40, 52–3
management, 3–4, 47–56, 111–12
  see also school administration
Marlcliffe Primary School, 33–46
mathematics, 5, 21–30, 65–6, 73, 113–14, 136, 139, 171, 194
mathophobia, 20–30
memory size, 78–9
microchip, 1, 9, 73
Microcomputer Users in Education (MUSE), 19, 54, 108
microcomputers, passim
Microcomputers in Primary Schools (MIPS) project, 20, 27
Microelectronics in Education Programme (MEP), 54, 129, 130, 150
Micros and Primary Education (MAPE), 54, 108, 129
Microscope, 132, 133
Microwriter, 201
mobility, 41, 53
modelling, 84
motivation, 33, 39, 68–70, 141–2, 149, 151–2, 157, 158–9, 165–6, 185
multi-media packages, 70
music, 118–19, 126–7

Nonstallon Primary School, 27
number, 114–16
numbers
  of children using computer, 34–5, 39, 61, 130–1, 140, 152, 160, 172, 177–8, 194, 198–9
numeracy, 80, 86, 164

ORACLE, 164
organization
  of information, 5, 42–4, 121–2
Oundle School, 202

parent-teacher associations, 3, 11, 13, 44
Pascal language, 76
Pascal's triangle, 116, 122–3
patience, 33–4, 156
  see also attitudes
pedagogy
  of Computer Assisted Learning, 169–79
PET computer, 17, 24, 38, 40–1, 131
philosophy
  of computer use in schools, 20–1, 48
  see also educational philosophy
pre-computer skills, 4, 59
PRESTEL, 30, 164, 202, 210
primary schools, passim
Primary Schools Microcomputing Conference (University of Exeter), 132, 149, 199, 214
printers, 16, 53, 74, 132
  see also word processing
problem solving, 34, 114, 158–9, 163, 196–7
programming, 19–20, 64–7, 85, 94–6, 99–101, 117, 132–3, 138–47, 165, 187–8, 195–200
  see also software
programs
  see software
purchasing, 3, 12, 14, 40, 52–4, 75
  see also costs
puzzles, 116–17
  see also games, quizzes

quizzes, 67
  see also games, puzzles
QWERTY syndrome, 16, 153

recreation, 120
remedial education, 159
resource provision, 71–110
  see also purchasing

school administration, 85, 98–9
science, 117
Seaweed numbers, 116, 124–6
Sharp MZ-80K computer, 40
simulations, 7–8, 9, 84, 85, 92–4, 169–79, 191, 197
  see also games
Sinclair ZX80 and ZX81 computers, 30, 201
social implications
  of computers, 10, 37, 71–2, 144, 181–4, 195, 209
software, 3, 7, 11, 13, 18–30, 35, 38–46, 53–4, 55, 58, 64–70, 75–9, 85–99, 105, 108, 121, 122–8, 130, 138–47, 169–79, 184, 185, 195–200
Spanish Main simulation, 8, 169–79
speech synthesis, 199–200
  see also voice boxes

teacher training, 135–47, 211
  see also in-service training
teachers, passim
technology, passim
Teletext, 201–2
television, 2, 59, 73–4, 108, 145, 211
time pressure, 22, 26–8, 34, 156
traditions, 206–8

Turtles, 25-30, 157, 201

upgrading
  see enhancement
USPEC, 16, 52

Videotext, 202
Viewdata, 201

visual display unit (VDU), 61-70
voice boxes, 15
  see also speech synthesis

Walsall Educational Computing Centre, 16
word matching, 66
word processing, 9, 132, 183, 199

LB
1028.5
.M49
1982

Microcomputers and
  children in the primary
  school